THE LOST GOSPEL

THE LOST GOSPEL

The Book of Q
&
Christian Origins

BURTON L. MACK

 HarperSanFrancisco
A Division of HarperCollinsPublishers

DESIGN   Design Office / Bruce Kortebein

THE LOST GOSPEL. Copyright © 1993 by
Burton L. Mack. All rights reserved.
Printed in the United States of America.
No part of this book may be used or repro-
duced in any manner whatsoever without
written permission except in the case of
brief quotations embodied in critical arti-
cles and reviews. For information address
HarperCollins Publishers, 10 East 53rd
Street, New York, NY 10022.

FIRST EDITION

Library of Congress Cataloging-in-Publication Data

Mack , Burton L.
    The lost gospel : the book of Q & Christian origins / Burton L.
Mack. — 1st ed.
        p.   cm.
    Includes bibliographical references and index.
    ISBN 0–06–065374-4 (alk. paper)
    1. Q hypothesis (Synoptics criticism)   2. Christianity—Origin.
I. Title.
BS2555.2.M2535   1993
226'.066—dc20   92–53921
                                                   CIP

93 94 95 96 97 RRD(H) 10 9 8 7 6 5 4 3 2 1

This edition is printed on acid-free paper
that meets the American National
Standards Institute Z39.48 Standard.

CONTENTS

THE LOST GOSPEL

The Challenge

Once upon a time, before there were gospels of the kind familiar to readers of the New Testament, the first followers of Jesus wrote another kind of book. Instead of telling a dramatic story about Jesus' life, their book contained only his teachings. They lived with these teachings ringing in their ears and thought of Jesus as the founder of their movement. But their focus was not on the person of Jesus or his life and destiny. They were engrossed with the social program that was called for by his teachings. Thus their book was not a gospel of the Christian kind, namely a narrative of the life of Jesus as the Christ. Rather it was a gospel of Jesus' sayings, a "sayings gospel." His first followers arranged these sayings in a way that offered instruction for living creatively in the midst of a most confusing time, and their book served them well as a handbook and guide for most of the first Christian century.

Then the book was lost. Perhaps the circumstances changed, or the people changed, or their memories and imagination of Jesus changed. In any case, the book was lost to history somewhere in the course of the late first century when stories of Jesus' life began to be written and became the more popular form of charter document for early Christian circles.

It makes some difference whether the founder of a movement is remembered for his teachings, or for his deeds and destiny. For the first followers of Jesus, the importance of Jesus as the founder of their

1

2

movement was directly related to tue significance they attached to his teachings. What mattered most was the body of instructions that circulated in his name, what these teachings called for in terms of ideas, attitudes, and behavior, and the difference these instructions made in the lives of those who took them seriously. But as the Jesus movement spread, groups in different locations and changing circumstances began to think about the kind of life Jesus must have lived. Some began to think of him in the role of a sage, for instance, while others thought of him as a prophet, or even as an exorcist who had appeared to rid the world of its evils. This shift from interest in Jesus' teachings to questions about Jesus' person, authority, and social role eventually produced a host of different mythologies.

The mythology that is most familiar to Christians of today developed in groups that formed in northern Syria and Asia Minor. There Jesus' death was first interpreted as a martyrdom and then embellished as a miraculous event of crucifixion and resurrection. This myth drew on hellenistic mythologies that told about the destiny of a divine being (or son of God). Thus these congregations quickly turned into a cult of the resurrected or transformed Jesus whom they now referred to as the Christ, or the Lord, as well as the Son of God. The congregations of the Christ, documented most clearly in the letters of Paul from the 50s, experienced a striking shift in orientation, away from the teachings of Jesus and toward the spirit of the Christ who had died and was raised from the dead. It was this myth that eventually made the narrative gospels possible.

Narrative gospels began to appear during the later part of the first century. Mark's gospel was written during the 70s, Matthew's during the 80s, John's during the 90s, and Luke-Acts sometime early in the second century. These gospels combined features of the martyr myth from the Christ cult with traditions about Jesus as he had been remembered in the Jesus movements, thereby locating the significance of Jesus in the story of his deeds and destiny. Naturally, these gospels came to a climax in an account of his trial, crucifixion, and resurrection from the dead. They followed a plot that was first worked out by Mark during the 70s in the wake of the Roman-Jewish war. The plot collapsed the time between the events of Jesus' life and the destruction of the Jerusalem temple which took place during the war. Mark achieved this plot by making connections between two sets of events

(Jesus' death and the temple's destruction) that could only have been imagined after the war. His gospel appears to have been the earliest full-blown written composition along these lines, but once it was conceived, all of the narrative gospels used this same basic plot.

According to the story line of the narrative gospels, Jesus was destined to come into conflict with the rulers of the world because he appeared in the world as the very son of God. This conflict escalated to a climax in the crucifixion of Jesus as the Christ, but would only be finally resolved when Jesus as the resurrected son of God appeared at the end of time to judge the world and establish a new social order as the reign or kingdom of God. In the meantime, both the resurrection of Jesus and the destruction of the temple were thought to establish the truth of God's great plan.

The first followers of Jesus could not have imagined, nor did they need, such a mythology to sustain them in their efforts to live according to his teachings. Their sayings gospel was quite sufficient for the Jesus movement as they understood it. Even after the narrative gospels became the rage, the sayings gospel was still intact. It was still being copied and read with interest by ever-widening circles. And it was available in slightly different versions in the several groups that continued to develop within the Jesus movement. Eventually, the narrative gospels prevailed as the preferred portrayal for Christians, and the sayings gospel finally was lost to the historical memory of the Christian church.

Were it not for the fact that two authors of narrative gospels incorporated sizable portions of the sayings gospel into their stories of Jesus' life, the sayings gospel of the first followers of Jesus would have disappeared without a trace in the transitions taking place. We never would have known about the Jesus movements that flourished prior to the Christian church. But Matthew and Luke each had a copy of the sayings gospel, and the material each copied from it largely overlapped. It was this fortuitous coincidence that made it possible in recent times to recover the book, even though the sayings now sound like the pronouncements of the son of God instead of the teachings of Jesus.

No modern historian ever imagined that a sayings gospel had once existed, so no one went looking for it. Scholars discovered it inadvertently while poring over the gospels of the New Testament,

4

wondering which had been written first. As they set the gospels side by side for comparison, they noticed two kinds of correspondence. One correspondence was that the story line in Matthew and Luke agreed only when it followed the gospel of Mark. This finding meant that Mark was the earliest narrative gospel and the source for the plot used by Matthew and Luke. But the other correspondence was also of interest. Matthew and Luke contained a large quantity of sayings material not found in Mark and much of this material was identical. This correspondence meant that Matthew and Luke had used a second written document in addition to the gospel of Mark. Scholars called this document Q as a shorthand for *Quelle*, which means "source" in German, for they first thought of it only as the common source for the sayings in the gospels of Matthew and Luke. But once Q was recognized as a source for these gospels, it could be studied on its own. And so the book of the first followers of Jesus has come to light after being lost for almost eighteen hundred years. In keeping with scholarly tradition, I call this lost gospel Q, for it has no other proper name.

By reading Q carefully, it is possible to catch sight of those earliest followers of Jesus. We can see them on the road, at the market, and at one another's homes. We can hear them talking about appropriate behavior; we can sense the spirit of the movement and their attitudes about the world. A sense of purpose can be traced through subtle changes in their attitudes toward other groups over a period of two or three generations of vigorous social experimentation. It is a lively picture. And it is complete enough to reconstruct the history that happened between the time of Jesus and the emergence of the narrative gospels that later gave the Christian church its official account of Christian beginnings.

The remarkable thing about the people of Q is that they were not Christians. They did not think of Jesus as a messiah or the Christ. They did not take his teachings as an indictment of Judaism. They did not regard his death as a divine, tragic, or saving event. And they did not imagine that he had been raised from the dead to rule over a transformed world. Instead, they thought of him as a teacher whose teachings made it possible to live with verve in troubled times. Thus they did not gather to worship in his name, honor him as a god, or cultivate his memory through hymns, prayers, and rituals. They did not form a cult of the Christ such as the one that emerged among the

Christian communities familiar to readers of the letters of Paul. The people of Q were Jesus people, not Christians.

This discovery upsets the conventional picture of the origins of Christianity. The popular conception, based on the portrayal of Jesus in the narrative gospels, is that Jesus appeared as the Jewish messiah to reform the religion of Judaism. He challenged the teaching of the scribes and Pharisees, called the people to repentance, and instructed his disciples to be leaders in a kingdom of God about to be inaugurated. Marching to Jerusalem, Jesus then cleansed the temple and announced its destruction, countered the Jewish authorities there, and was crucified in keeping with a conflict of cosmic and apocalyptic proportions between the Jews and God's plan for his kingdom. At first confused following Jesus' death, the disciples regrouped when he appeared to them as the resurrected Lord and Son of God. They then formed the first church in Jerusalem and started two great Christian missions, one to the Jews and one to the gentiles. They did this in the conviction that the miracle of the resurrection was a sign that Jesus' proclamation of the kingdom of God was true and that God's final judgment upon the world had begun.

None of this is reflected in the sayings gospel Q. In Q there is no hint of a select group of disciples, no program to reform the religion or politics of Judaism, no dramatic encounter with the authorities in Jerusalem, no martyrdom for the cause, much less a martyrdom with saving significance for the ills of the world, and no mention of a first church in Jerusalem. The people of Q simply did not understand their purpose to be a mission to the Jews, or to gentiles for that matter. They were not out to transform the world or start a new religion.

Q's challenge to the popular conception of Christian origins is therefore clear. If the conventional view of Christian beginnings is right, how are we to account for these first followers of Jesus? Did they fail to get his message? Were they absent when the unexpected happened? Did they carry on in ignorance or in repudiation of the Christian gospel of salvation? If, however, the first followers of Jesus understood the purpose of their movement just as Q describes it, how are we to account for the emergence of the Christ cult, the fantastic mythologies of the narrative gospels, and the eventual establishment of the Christian church and religion? Q forces the issue of rethinking Christian origins as no other document from the earliest times has done.

6

This book is about the lost gospel Q and its challenge to the conventional picture of Christian origins. In part I of the book the story of Q's discovery and reconstruction is sketched in broad outline. The full history of scholarly machinations is not given, for this would require a lengthy rehearsal of detailed argumentation from an extensive scholarly bibliography. But the reader will want to know about the major episodes in the scholarly quest for the earliest gospel, why it took scholars so long to recognize Q as a sayings gospel particular to the early Jesus movements, and what to make of a text that exists only in the form of its two citations in Matthew and Luke. A sketch of this history need not be boring, for it dips in and out of a rather romantic search for the Jesus of history that takes some twists and turns that are decidedly humorous in retrospect. This part of the book sets the stage for a closer look at the lost gospel itself.

Part II offers an English translation of Q, together with a reader's guide. This, along with an analysis of Q in part III, is the major contribution of the book.

In part III, observations on the composition of the lost gospel shed light on the content of its teachings and literary history. This in turn will make it possible to trace the activities and experiences of the early Jesus movement through five stages of social history. It is this picture of a robust movement consciously taking its place in a world of competing cultures that challenges the conventional view of Christian origins.

In the course of the presentation in part III, it becomes clear that not all of the sayings in Q can actually be attributed to Jesus. To be sure, all of the teachings in Q are ascribed to Jesus, but many of them address issues that could only have been encountered in the course of later social experiences and they bear the marks of reflection on such experiences. This is not a phenomenon limited to Q or a practice that was peculiar to the people of Q. Scholars have collected several hundred sayings ascribed to Jesus from scattered literature of the first two or three centuries. Of these sayings, only a handful may actually have been spoken by the historical Jesus. Scholars regularly acknowledge this phenomenon by distinguishing between "authentic" and "inauthentic" sayings, defining those sayings that can be plausibly attributed to the historical Jesus as "authentic." But this does not explain the phenomenon of attribution and hardly assuages the average reader's sense of exasperation when told that Jesus did not say what his followers said he said. Thus the practice of attribution needs to be addressed.

Part IV offers the explanation that sayings came to be attributed to Jesus as part of the group's imaginative cultivation of its memory traditions, namely its changing views of Jesus as the founder of the movement. This explanation draws on practices common to many people in antiquity and to major institutions, such as schools, during Greco-Roman times. It is clear that the people of Q are not to be charged with fuzzy memories, ecstatic auditions, or crass deceit because they ascribed new sayings to a Jesus who was no longer alive. Attribution can be understood as a normal means of authorization for certain types of founder figures.

In the case of the people of Q, oriented as they were to the teachings of a teacher, the ascription of teachings to Jesus was a particularly appropriate form of mythmaking. Teachings attributed to Jesus were invested with programmatic status and cultivated as instruction, embellished as rationale, outlined as ethical code, and used as signs of recognition. So solving the problem of "inauthentic" ascriptions does more than explain a feature of ancient sayings collections that people today find unnerving; it will show that Q was much more than a collection of ad hoc instructions for the early Jesus people. Q's purpose in attributing sayings to Jesus and its careful design can be seen as the creation of a highly crafted and profoundly effective myth of origin. This myth of origin claimed epic and divine authority for Jesus as a founder figure without any need to entertain mythological notions of a crucified and resurrected messiah.

Thus Q's challenge to the conventional picture of Christian origins is more far-reaching than the making of a little room for yet another early Christian movement. The Jesus movement documented by Q cannot be understood as a variant form of the Christian persuasion basic to the conventional picture of Christian origins. With Q in view the entire landscape of early Christian history and literature has to be revised.

Part IV proposes such a revision of early Christian history and literature. Scholars are well aware that the writings of the New Testament are a selection from a much larger body of early Christian literature. They also account for the differences among the writings of the New Testament by locating them in different streams of early Christian tradition, which are frequently defined by reference to a known leading figure or author. Thus we have the Pauline tradition, the Johannine tradition, the Petrine tradition, and so on. Because New Testament studies have been guided by an interest in the belief systems of early Christians, scholars refer to the differences among the traditions as "theological." New Testament scholars know that there are many different "theologies" represented in the writings of the New Testament, and this fact provides a point of departure for discussing the many forms of early Christianity.

But charting multiple theologies does not answer Q's challenge. The concept of many theologies leaves in place the assumption of a singular, miraculous, dramatic event or experience that may account for the many forms of early Christianity. By assuming a single origin for all early Christian traditions, which is usually thought to be the overwhelming appearance and resurrection from the dead of the son of God, multiple theologies can be understood merely as various attempts to explicate the mysterious meaning implicit in that divine originating moment. Q's challenge is that a vigorous Jesus movement was generated without recourse to such an originating event, religious experience, or message of salvation. Q demonstrates that factors other than the belief that Jesus was divine played a role in the generation of early Jesus and Christ movements. What may those factors have been?

The early Jesus movements were attractive as arenas for social experimentation called for by the troubled and difficult times. The frequent shifts in military power and political conquest unleashed by the campaigns of Alexander the Great and the ensuing empires, from the Ptolemies and Seleucids to the coming of the Romans, broke the age-old social patterns of life in the eastern Mediterranean. People continued to be identified and treated in terms of their ethnic extractions and traditional cultures, but the social institutions of the old city-states and temple-states that had supported those cultures were gone forever. Uprooted cultural traditions collided in cities that filled with displaced populations. How to get along with each other in an ad hoc world was the critical question. Thus the times were right for thinking new thoughts about traditional values and for experimenting with free association across ethnic and cultural boundaries.

The Jesus movement was attractive as a place to experiment with novel social notions and life-styles. It was generated by a sensitive and considered awareness of the times and a critical posture toward reigning cultural values. Traditional systems of honor based on power, wealth, and place in hierarchical social structures were called into question, as were codes of ritual purity, taboos on intercourse with people of different ethnic roots, and taxation economies. People were encouraged to free themselves from traditional social constraints and think of themselves as belonging to a larger human family. As Q puts it, "If you embrace only your brothers, what more are you doing than others?"

At first no one was in charge of the groups that formed around such teachings. Conversation and mutual support were enough to encourage an individual to act "naturally," as if the normal expectations of acquiescence to social conventions did not apply. As groups formed in support of like-minded individuals, however, loyalty to the Jesus movement strengthened, a social vision for human well-being was generated within the group, and social codes for the movement had to be agreed upon. Why not ask when in need and share what one had when asked, they wondered? Eventually, therefore, the Jesus movement took the form of small groups meeting together as extended families in the heady pursuit of what they called God's kingdom.

To explore human community based on fictive kinship without regard to standard taboos against association based on class, status, gender, or ethnicity would have created quite a stir, and would have been its own reward. Since there was no grand design for actualizing such a vision, different groups settled into practices that varied from one another. Judging from the many forms of community that developed within the Jesus movement, as documented in literature that begins to appear toward the end of the first century, these groups continued to share a basic set of attitudes. They all had a certain critical stance toward the way life was lived in the Greco-Roman world. They all struggled not to be determined by the emptiness of human pursuits in a world of codes they held to be superficial. And they all learned to apply the concept of the kingdom of God to the ethos that developed in their own community. Despite these agreements, however, every group went its own way and drew different conclusions about what to think and do.

Consideration of the experiences and human resources demanded by such social experimentation makes it possible, not only to make room for the people of Q in the early history of the Jesus movement, but to understand all of the groups that formed as manifestations of a common quest for human community appropriate for the times. Part IV locates Q on the map of early Christian literature and integrates the Jesus movement with other traditions that eventually fed into the making of Christianity. All early Christian texts can be placed at specific junctures of a group's social history. Each text can then be studied as an expression of a particular group's thought and discourse at that time. If one charts the various traditions of thought and theology, noting the shifts in social formation they reflect, even the eventual selection of texts represented by the New Testament can be accounted for. Thus the story of Q comes full circle, ending with a brief account of the New Testament texts that made use of Q only to guarantee its erasure from the memory traditions of the Christian church. To understand the privilege granted the narrative gospels in the New Testament of the Christian church is to understand why Q was forgotten in time and why its recovery in recent years has created a bit of consternation among Christian scholars.

Because the challenge of Q cannot be contained within scholarly circles, the book closes with some thoughts on the role of the Christian gospel in contemporary American culture. If Q forces biblical scholars and historians of religion to revise their understanding of early Christian history, a literate public should want to know about it. That in turn will make a difference in the way in which Christians read the narrative gospels. The narrative gospels can no longer be viewed as the trustworthy accounts of unique and stupendous historical events at the foundation of the Christian faith. The gospels must now be seen as the result of early Christian mythmaking. Q forces the issue, for it documents an earlier history that does not agree with the narrative gospel accounts.

I have written the book with this challenge in mind. The issues raised are profound and far-reaching. They are not issues of thought and conscience only for Christians. They make one ask about the reasons for popular attitudes toward the academy and especially for the ease with which the academic study of religion can be dismissed. They make one wonder about the abysmal lack of savvy on the part of the media, critics of the fine arts, and public discourse when the subject of religion and society is broached. And they strike to the heart of an entrenched reluctance in our society to discuss the mythic foundations for attitudes and values, both shared and conflictual, that influence the way we think, behave, and construct our institutions. Q can hardly be discussed without engaging in some honest talk about Christian myth and the American dream. If we take Q seriously, it will turn the quest for Christian origins into a question about our willingness to seriously engage in cultural critique.

PART I

THE

DISCOVERY

OF A LOST

GOSPEL

Finding the Shards

In modern times adventurers, seekers of treasure, and archeologists have discovered many ancient writings in ruins, caves, and old monastery libraries. Some of these finds have been early manuscripts of well-known writings, such as the biblical texts discovered at St. Catherine's monastery in the 1850s or at Qumran in the 1940s. Others have been texts of writings known only by title because of some mention by an ancient author, but were thought to have been lost, forgotten, or burned in the creedal wars of the fourth and fifth centuries. Examples are the discovery of the Epistle of Barnabas at St. Catherine's in 1859 and the Didache, or "Teaching" (of the Twelve Apostles), in the patriarchal library of Constantinople in 1875. Others have come as complete surprises, such as many of the Dead Sea Scrolls from the ancient library at Qumran and the Coptic-Gnostic library at Nag Hammadi discovered during the 1940s.

In the quest to reconstruct the past, every new textual discovery has been greeted with some measure of enthusiasm and many finds have created sensations. New texts are exciting to scholars because of their promise of new knowledge and enticing to others because of a sense that hidden secrets are about to be disclosed. In the case of Q's discovery, however, there has been no announcement, little public excitement, and no sense that anything secret was about to be revealed. That is because Q was not discovered in some ancient cache. A manuscript of Q entitled "The Sayings of Jesus" did not suddenly come to light. Instead, the bits and pieces of this ancient writing were found scattered about in the gospels of the New Testament, and these were very familiar texts. It was by chance, in the course of tracking down the layered traditions of these gospels, that Q slowly emerged. Its existence at the bedrock of the Jesus traditions gradually forced itself upon scholars who hardly noticed the momentous significance of their discovery because the material was already so well known.

The idea that there must have been a text like Q was first thought of over 150 years ago, but its recognition as a document with its own distinctive history had to wait for the present generation of scholars. One reason it took so long is that New Testament scholars have been haunted by the desire to reconstruct the "life" of Jesus. They were therefore preoccupied with the eventful aspects of the gospels, worried about their miraculous features, not about the teachings which they took for granted. Another reason is that, since Q referred to a written source that was used in slightly different ways by two independent authors (Matthew and Luke), reconstructing a single, unified text for study and discussion was at first thought to be impossible. And a third reason is that many New Testament scholars resisted the idea of Q because they thought there was no other example of the genre in early Christian literature and thus could not imagine why early Christians would have written such a text.

However, as the comparative study of the gospels unfolded, the nature of Jesus' teaching eventually became a critical question. Ways to reconstruct the text of Q were developed. Another example of the genre was found, the sayings gospel known as the Gospel of Thomas. And scholars finally turned to questions about Q's composition and content. A brief exploration of the major moments in this long history of scholarship helps in understanding how and why Q finally emerged from the pages of the narrative gospels to challenge their own account of Christian origins. In this chapter the story of Q's discovery as a written text will be told. In the next three chapters the current scholarly excitement about recognizing Q's genre and importance for reconstructing the history of Christian origins will be described.

The story starts early in the nineteenth century, the century known for its quest for the historical Jesus. The quest was made possible by the rational methods of historical criticism learned in the age of enlightenment, but it was driven by a thoroughly romantic Protestant obsession. Protestant critique of the Catholic church claimed that Catholic religion was a pagan adulteration of true Christianity. In order to define true Christianity, Protestant reformers at first located its truth in the scriptures as a way to counter Catholic emphasis on post-biblical tradition as equal in importance for Christian faith and practice. But as the enlightenment dawned, other strategies commended themselves. What if Catholic Christianity could be shown as a historical development that veered away from the original intentions of Jesus and the earliest forms of Christian community and faith? Then the Protestant case would be made. The essence of Christianity would be obvious from the pristine purity of its original form, and Protestant claims to represent the true form of Christianity would have to be acknowledged. So the quest for the historical Jesus was motivated by a Protestant desire to leapfrog over the entire history of Catholic Christianity and land at the beginning where, as it was imagined, the foundations of Christianity had been laid in the life and purpose of its founder.

The problem with this undertaking was that the only records of Jesus' life were the four gospels of the New Testament. At first Protestant scholars thought it enough to note the contrast between the Jesus of the gospel accounts and the history of "pagan" iconography and worship in the Catholic religion. But Catholics had no trouble with the gospels. They had always read them as records of the very events that inspired their religion. Mary was there and the story of the virgin birth. The miracles were there, both in the public appearance of Jesus and in the great events that confirmed the significance of his life—the baptism, transfiguration, crucifixion, and resurrection. Peter was there, as were the twelve apostles, Mary Magdalene, and the great commission to make disciples of all the nations. And there was ample instruction in faith, forgiveness, obedience, and the final judgment. So Protestant scholars had to take another look. Upon a closer reading of the gospels, they had to agree that the gospels contained a good bit of mythology and too many miracles for comfort. This, then, set the agenda for more than a hundred years of detailed investigation. The goal of the quest would be to get behind the myths and miracles of the gospels and reconstruct the story of the man "as he really was."

In retrospect it seems strange that no one thought to question the main story line that resulted from a merger of the four gospels, the very outline of the "life of Christ" that all Christians had in mind. But this was because no one imagined that the evangelists, as the authors of the gospels were called during the nineteenth century, had intended anything other than a biography. A biography of such an important person's life is exactly what a nineteenth-century scholar would have expected of a first-century writer. The problem was that the evangelists lived in pre-enlightenment times, which meant they were "uncritical," and they must have been a bit gullible about the causes of certain events and somewhat mistaken about many of the details. Notice that no two evangelists agreed exactly in their descriptions of the same events and that all of them had trouble keeping their histories free from the miraculous and the mythical. Thus the major issues were set. The quest of the historical Jesus would swirl around the issues of (1) miracles and (2) the fact that the four accounts did not agree in detail.

A discussion of the efforts to remove the sheen of the miraculous from the gospel accounts is not directly relevant to the discovery of Q. That is because Q was uncovered in the course of comparing the four gospels to see which may have been the earliest, not by any of the attempts to explain away the miracles. Nevertheless, because the furor over the miracles frequently drowned out the more laborious quest for the earliest gospel, this background helps clarify why it took so long to recognize Q. The raging battle over the miracles simply overwhelmed enlightenment scholars and resulted in the studies that created sensations. From John Locke's little book on *The Reasonableness of Christianity* (1695), through David Friedrich Strauss's *Life of Jesus* (1835), to Albert Schweitzer's *The Quest of the Historical Jesus* (1906), a book that summed up the century, the quest was the same: how to explain the miracles. Locke thought that, even though reports of miracles in general could not be believed, the miracles of Jesus may actually have happened because they were so unusual, unrepeatable, and unique. Others thought that the common people imagined the miracles because they were so infatuated with this special man. Strauss and others wrote thousands of pages explaining the miracles away as illusions, legends, and myths. Strauss noted that they accrued in the course of early Christian attempts to say how important Jesus' appearance had been. Thus preoccupied with such a quest, scholars found it difficult to concentrate on the question of which gospel was written first. All of the gospels seemed to have so many miracles. And getting rid of the miracles seemed to be highest on the list of priorities if one wanted to get to the life of the man as he really was.

And yet, like a Chinese puzzle, the question of which gospel was the first to be written kept teasing the more critical minds. All scholars agreed that one of the four had to be the first, and most scholars had their favorite to propose. The problem was that arguments supporting the priority of one or the other gospel were so difficult to find. The problem could only be resolved by a rigorous study that used a single set of critical criteria to compare the four with one another. Johann Griesbach provided the tool to do this in his synopsis of the first three gospels published in 1776. Griesbach recognized that the fourth gospel was distinctly different from the first three. In this gospel, Jesus sounded like a passionless god on a temporary mission from another world merely frustrated with the ignorance of humankind in a dull world. The ethereal tone of Jesus' voice in the Gospel of John set it apart from the first three gospels and gave it little claim as historiography. Griesbach therefore placed only the first three gospels side by side for comparison (or *synopsis,* meaning "view together") and thus introduced what was later to be called the "synoptic problem," the question of the order and interrelationships among the three similar accounts.

Griesbach's own solution to the problem was to leave Matthew in place as the first gospel, but switch the order of Mark and Luke, arguing that Mark was an epitome and the last to be written. Others wondered whether it was necessary to switch the order of Mark and Luke, but most agreed that Matthew was first. It seemed right because Mark and Luke had not been "apostles," and Matthew's gospel, after all, was the first gospel in the New Testament, wasn't it?

Arguments such as these came to a halt in the 1830s, when, in a flurry of activity, scholars tackled the synoptic problem with renewed determination. By then it was common scholarly knowledge that the three gospels shared a significant amount of narrative material, but that Matthew and Luke each contained much material that Mark did not have. Karl Lachmann's (1835) contribution to the solution of this problem was the observation that Matthew and Luke agreed in the order of material in their gospels only when they followed Mark. When they did not follow Mark, Matthew and Luke frequently went separate ways even when presenting non-Markan material they both shared. Lachmann also noted that the material in Matthew that was not contained in Mark consisted primarily of the sayings of Jesus, a type of material not characteristic of Mark's gospel. Christian Wilke (1838) drew the obvious conclusion and argued for the "priority of Mark," that Mark must have been the earliest of the three gospels and that it was the Markan account upon which both Matthew and Luke were dependent. Putting all the pieces together, Christian Weisse (1838) proposed the "two-document hypothesis," namely that Matthew and Luke composed their gospels independently, mainly by combining two written sources. One was the Gospel of Mark, the other a source that must have contained the sayings of Jesus. Q had been espied.

Despite the logic of the two-source hypothesis, it was not immediately accepted by the scholarly community. The main reason for resistance had less to do with the idea of a sayings source, however, than with a reluctance to acknowledge the priority of Mark. Preference for Matthew was very strong. Matthew had always enjoyed a position of privilege as the charter for the church. And besides, the Gospel of Matthew was much better suited for the quest of the historical Jesus. Mark was simply too skimpy on the one hand, and too miraculous on the other, to serve as a basis for a plausible life of Jesus. Matthew was made to order. The portrait of Jesus was more acceptable, the purpose of his teachings seemed clearer, and his life unfolded on cue just as a good biography should. When Albert Schweitzer summarized the Jesus quest at the end of the century, and then went on to propose his own life of Jesus, he had no qualms at all about basing his account on the Gospel of Matthew. Even today there are scholars who continue to resist the two-source theory and to favor Matthew as the earliest gospel.

But the two-document hypothesis answered more questions about textual relations among the three gospels than did the theory of Matthean priority and thus, as in any scientific field of research, it had to be taken seriously by critical scholars. And it was taken seriously, although progress in demonstrating its superiority was slow. One has to follow the twists and turns of biblical scholarship for about one hundred years to see the eventual shift in paradigm that allowed Q to be read as a text in its own right. The list of those who made lasting contributions to the testing and refinement of the hypothesis is long and illustrious. H. J. Holtzmann put the Q idea to the test in an exhaustive investigation in 1863 and concluded that it was essentially correct. Bernard Weiss, a careful and conservative New Testament scholar, demonstrated Luke's dependence on Q in 1907. In the same year Adolf von Harnack, the well-known historian of early Christianity, actually published a little book called *The Sayings of Jesus* (English translation 1908) in which, for the first time, a collection of sayings approximate to Q was published apart from its gospel context. Harnack wanted to see how the teachings of Jesus sounded when divorced from a setting of miracle and myth.

By the 1920s, when Rudolf Bultmann and B. H. Streeter each published monumental studies on the synoptic tradition, the two-source hypothesis had largely been accepted by scholars in the liberal tradition. Bultmann used it to establish benchmarks for his *History of the Synoptic Tradition* (1921) and to trace the changes that occurred in individual sayings as the tradition developed. Streeter focused on the manuscript traditions of the gospels, treated them as whole literary units, and produced a detailed comparison of each gospel to the others, all the while focusing on the variant readings of each manuscript tradition. Streeter's study has become a classic and has been recognized as establishing the two-source hypothesis for the modern period of scholarship. He did this by demonstrating that the two-source theory best accounts for both the agreements and the variations in Matthew and Luke at points where each independently used the same source. One might think that, after Streeter, scholars would finally turn to Q as the best and earliest evidence for the first chapter of Christian history. But this was not to happen for another half-century.

At this juncture in the history of Q's discovery, two major obstacles kept the significance of its challenge from coming to fruition. One obstacle was that Q was still thought of mainly as part of the solution to the synoptic problem. Much had been learned about Q, but it was defined solely as a source document for the Gospels of Matthew and Luke, not as a text with its own integrity. By now the standard description was that Q consisted largely of the sayings of Jesus and that its length was at least 225 verses. This judgment was based on the material that appeared in both Matthew and Luke, the so-called minimal text. But Q may have been longer, since Matthew and Luke each contained Q-like material not present in the other gospel. Of the material clearly in common, approximately one-half was all but identical. The language of composition was Greek. And when it was seen that Matthew was responsible for arranging much of the Q material into speeches on specific themes, but that Luke presented the same material in two large blocks, one could account for differences in the order of the sayings. In general, the order of Q material in Luke was found to be closer to the original. So although much had been learned, Q was still mainly considered a collection of isolated sayings. It was far from being recognized as a book of instructions with its own history, much less as a charter for a Jesus movement that did not have a narrative gospel.

The other major obstacle to an advance in Q studies was that such a definition did not produce a unified text of Q, since it was still firmly embedded in the texts of the two gospels. Those who wanted to study Q did not have a single text to read, but had to work with a synopsis of the gospels, comparing readings in two columns, jumping back and ahead to get the sequences straight, and pondering material that may or may not have been part of the original text. Only those having great patience, thorough familiarity with the synoptic tradition, boxes of colored pencils, and a capacity for detailed analysis could even read Q, much less hope to argue for this or that refinement of the text or explore its genre, content, and composition.

After Streeter's work, Q studies were put on hold while New Testament scholars worked on other questions felt to be more pressing. One question, still unresolved since the turn of the century, threatened the Protestant desire to think of early Christianity as a pure, uncontaminated religion. Study after study had shown that early Christianity was not a unique religion but had been "influenced" by the religions of late antiquity. Especially troubling was the similarity of the early Christian message to Jewish apocalyptic thought, a discovery that linked Christianity too closely with Judaism on the one hand, and estranged the modern church from its origins on the other. Also unsettling was the discovery that early Christianity bore a distinct resemblance to the hellenistic mystery cults, particularly where it mattered most, namely in their myths of dying and rising gods and in their rituals of baptism and sacred meals. Whether or not early Christianity differed from the religions of surrounding cultures became a burning issue that diverted attention away from Q and the quest for the historical Jesus.

A second question, unresolved since the middle of the nineteenth century, again surfaced and created even greater scholarly consternation. This was the question of where to locate the foundation of Christian faith in early Christian texts, and how to interpret their meaning for modern Christians. Was the core of Christianity to be found in the person of Jesus and his message according to the gospels, or was it contained in Paul's interpretation of Christian faith with its focus on the "proclamation" (*kerygma*) of the death and resurrection of Jesus? New Testament scholars were not able to say and they found themselves embarrassed by their uncertainty about the "message" at the core of the Christian faith and how that message might be "heard" again in the pages of the New Testament today. Finding ways to locate the central message of Christianity was called the hermeneutical question (from *hermeneia*, "interpretation"), and renewed attention to this pursuit consumed New Testament scholarship before and after the second world war.

Bultmann's program for interpreting the New Testament set the pace. He recognized that early Christians were influenced by the world of late antiquity in which they lived and that they expressed themselves in terms of its mythologies. He therefore proposed a program of demythologization, or a restatement of the meaning of the early Christian message in language that was not mythological. Bultmann thought that the modern philosophy of existentialism was capable of handling such a translation. According to Bultmann, the message of early Christianity was most profoundly expressed in the Pauline kerygma and the Gospel of John. Reduced to existential categories, the message was a pronouncement of freedom from one's past and a call to be radically open to one's future. In essence, the Christian message was an invitation to decide in favor of "authentic" human "existence." This unleashed an epoch of unprecedented debate about the reference of religious language in early Christianity. The question of the historical Jesus was simply sidetracked.

When the time came to again take up the quest for the historical Jesus, however, more than questions about the influence of hellenistic religions and mythological language had to be confronted. A book had been written that created even more havoc than had the hermeneutical issue. This was Karl Ludwig Schmidt's *Der Rahmen der Geschichte Jesu* ("The Framework of the Story of Jesus"), a careful study of the way in which the earliest gospel had been composed. In his hands the Gospel of Mark fell apart and broke up into little pieces, for he was able to show that all of the connecting links between the smaller stories in Mark were of Mark's own doing. This study, published in 1919, effectively brought to an end the old quest for the historical Jesus with its desire for a biography and its unexamined assumption that the basic plot of the narrative gospels was essentially historical record. With the finding that Mark was responsible for the gospel plot, all that was left from the time before Mark were fragments of memory traditions, bits and pieces of oral lore, and perhaps a few collections of parables and stories that someone, for reasons as yet unknown, had hung together by theme. So the old dream was in trouble and new strategies had to be devised if scholars were not going to give up completely the quest for Christian origins. Three new strategies were developed that continue to be used by scholars today.

The first new strategy was called form criticism. If the larger narrative framework of the gospels was the work of later authors, what about the smaller narrative units from which the gospels were composed? Why not analyze the forms in which the Jesus traditions were available to the evangelists and ask about *their* veracity? Perhaps the forms in which these stories were transmitted could tell us how and why they were told. Perhaps some of them would best be explained as memories of things that Jesus had actually said and done. Form criticism took the field of New Testament studies by storm. Major works by Bultmann (1921), Martin Dibelius (1919), and Vincent Taylor (1933) quickly became standards. An entire generation of New Testament scholars turned to the fragments of the pre-gospel Jesus traditions and tried to place them in the earliest stages of Christian memory, if not in the time of Jesus. Parables, miracle stories, pronouncement stories, and small units of sayings were scrutinized to see if any might be imagined as utterances or occurrences in the life of Jesus.

Form criticism dominated New Testament scholarship through the period of the second world war and well into the 1970s. Thus it was not a time for concentrated studies on Q as a document with its own integrity, much less as an important new window onto the social landscape of the early Jesus movement. Just as the Gospel of Mark had fallen into fragments, so was Q still thought of as a collection of small, isolated sayings. These sayings could be analyzed as forms of speech, to be sure. But form-critical analysis also required some social situation or literary context in order to understand the point of an individual saying. Since Q had not been recognized as a literary production with its own social history, the sayings did not have such a setting and thus the study of the sayings in Q could not contribute much to the form-critical project.

After the war scholars began to turn their attention to the gospels as larger units of composition. It was time for putting the pieces back together. Now the point about the evangelists being responsible for the larger narrative frameworks of the gospels could finally be turned to advantage. At first the authors of the gospels were called redactors, or editors, in keeping with the observation that they composed their gospels by arranging and changing earlier written material. But in spite of the desire not to give the evangelists too much credit as creative writers, real composition was finally acknowledged, naive assumptions about reporting history vanished, and the authorial intention of the evangelists came to be called a theology. Seeing how an evangelist arranged the pieces for his gospel, and thus expressed his theology, was called redaction criticism. Scholars learned how to do it, but everyone knew that redaction criticism did not satisfy either the quest for Christian origins or the search for a hermeneutical key to the essence of the Christian message. Redaction criticism merely underscored the fact that early Christians had produced many theologies.

It was not long before redaction criticism gave way to a strictly literary criticism informed by contemporary theories of authorship and composition. This happened in America during the 1960s when religious studies were moving away from theological programs to take up residence in the university. Biblical scholars found themselves in conversation with the full range of the human sciences. What seemed important, finally, was to understand the New Testament in the context of the emergence of Christianity as a complex cultural phenomenon. When read against the background of the feisty social histories of the Greco-Roman age, early Christian texts quickly lost their glaze of normative theological significance and fell into place as literary achievements crafted in the rough and tumble of exciting social experimentation.

A new array of critical approaches to these texts then created a twentieth-century excitement of its own. New Testament scholars learned about discourse, rhetoric, narrative imagination, and the relation of authorship to authority. They explored patterns of social formation, the structures of human societies, the creation of symbolic worlds, and the ways in which myths and rituals worked to forge a group's identity. When used to read the literature produced by early Christians, this new learning brought groups and movements into view that had no place on the older map of Christian beginnings.

Q suddenly seemed important for reasons that had nothing to do with solving the synoptic problem. It caught scholarly attention along with a host of extracanonical writings from the early periods of Christian history, such as the Gospel of Thomas, the Didache, the Apostolic Fathers, the Coptic-Gnostic writings, the apocryphal Acts of the Apostles, and the Gospel of Peter. Q was now on its own, a document from the time before the narrative gospels were written. Many scholars sensed Q's importance and were eager to take it up for study. Unfortunately, basic work still had to be done. The text had to be established, the literary form of the composition was yet to be determined, and the early history of transmission and composition still needed thorough investigation. Studies that contributed to these endeavors began to appear early in the 1970s, then flourished during the 1980s and show no signs of stopping.

Of critical importance for the study of Q was a reconstruction of the minimal text and some consensus about its composition as a recognizable form of literary activity. Text-critical studies have been produced by Siegfried Schulz (1972), Wolfgang Schenk (1981), Athanasius Polag (1982), and Dieter Zeller (1984). Schulz also provided a synoptic edition of the parallel texts from Matthew and Luke with a German translation. This would have been a great advance, except for one feature. He made the mistake of organizing the material by theme and thus erased both the Matthean and Lukan orders. Polag then offered a reconstruction of Q, published in a study of the sayings by Ivan Havener (1987). And in 1988 John Kloppenborg published an edition of the *Q Parallels* in Greek that followed the Lukan order and provided enumerated units, an English translation, an apparatus of scholarly judgments on variant readings, parallels per saying from other early Christian literature, and a Greek concordance.

Kloppenborg's *Q Parallels* is currently the standard text of reference for Q studies in America. But a parallel text is not yet a unified text. To produce a unified text, all of the variant readings must be carefully examined and decisions rendered as to the more original formulation in keeping with a complex set of criteria that includes detailed knowledge of the vocabularies, styles, and ideological preferences of Matthew and Luke as authors. This task is being performed by the International Q Project and the Q Project of the Society of Biblical Literature under the direction of James Robinson at the Institute for Antiquity and Christianity, Claremont. The publication of this project will be a scholarly reconstruction of the Greek text of Q that both Matthew and Luke had at their disposal when writing their gospels. When this critical text appears, the story of Q's retrieval from the layers of textual history that effectively buried it for so long a time will finally come to a close.

With the unified text of Q so close to the surface, coming to terms with its content and composition is already a possibility. The recent excitement over Q has produced a large number of fine studies that acknowledge its integrity and focus on its distinctive contribution to our knowledge of early Christian history. Scholars have been able to identify its genre, elucidate its content, and chart its history of composition. A brief summary of these studies in the next three chapters will set the stage for my own translation of Q in part II. The shards of a lost text have finally been pieced together.

2

An Uncommon Wisdom

When Harnack dared to publish the sayings of Jesus in 1907 he wanted the teachings of Jesus to be read without reference to the narrative gospels. With a single stroke he thought to eliminate the problem of miracle and myth and make it possible for readers to focus on what liberal theologians understood as the essence of Christianity. The genius of Jesus, according to nineteenth-century liberals, was that of a remarkable teacher of an elevated and timeless humane ethic. Thus Harnack thought that these teachings should set the standard for a civilized world. Liberal Christians honored Jesus for his teachings and thought of themselves as fortunate to stand at the end of an illustrious history of enlightenment.

Harnack's plan must have sounded good at the time to large numbers of Christians and scholars, for it drew upon a long inculcation of Christian sensibility that flourished during the late nineteenth century. By then the history of the human race was imagined on the model of evolutionary education. The ages of pagan superstition and cultic religion had finally succumbed to the age of reason. For Protestants, reason and faith merged in the superior ethics of Christianity, and they saw themselves as pedagogues shining in the midst of an unenlightened but educable world. Since Jesus had introduced this ethic into the world as the highest human ideal, he simply could not have been the divine and tragic figure portrayed in the gospel accounts. So Harnack's daring promotion of the teachings of Jesus apart from the narrative gospels must have sounded reasonable to many liberal Christians. But, as it turned out, his book was the last hurrah for the nineteenth-century Jesus.

Harnack should have known that the liberals' Jesus was in trouble, and perhaps he did. He was fighting for reason in the midst of a growing excitement about the presence of apocalyptic language in the preaching of Jesus and the thought that Jesus was driven by the compelling conviction that the world was soon coming to its end. The book that started the excitement was Johannes Weiss's *Jesus' Proclamation of the Kingdom of God* (1892). Weiss was impressed by the pronouncements of a future judgment found in the teachings of Jesus and with Jesus' announcement of a kingdom of God soon to be inaugurated. Weiss put these two themes together, kingdom of God and future judgment, and traced the source of such ideas to the apocalyptic literature of Judaism. He concluded that Jesus was a child of his time, a visionary and proclaimer of an imminent apocalyptic transformation of the world.

Consternation reigned as liberal theologians and historians of religion tried to position themselves in the face of a growing suspicion that apocalyptic language had indeed been the order of Jesus' day. Schweitzer rode in on the crest of this wave and used the apocalyptic perspective to write his famous critique of the nineteenth-century quest. The force of his argument was due to the sense of uncertainty scholars were experiencing because of this shift in paradigm from Jesus as a teacher of humane ethic to Jesus as a radical visionary of the cataclysmic end of the world. Schweitzer's own reconstruction of the life of Jesus was an interpretation of the Gospel of Matthew from the new perspective of Jesus as an apocalyptic prophet. According to Schweitzer, Jesus was mistaken about the imminent end of the world, but noble nonetheless because he had willingly sacrificed himself in an attempt to initiate the final conflagration. No one could simply ignore the apocalyptic buzz and prevail, for to counter the proposal required taking a long, hard look at the gospel texts. Strangely, no one during the nineteenth century had thought it necessary to actually study the sayings of Jesus in rigorous historical perspective. Now it seemed that the presence of the apocalyptic idiom in the teachings of Jesus could hardly be denied. Thus the relationship of the sayings of Jesus to an ethic of enlightenment, a relationship simply assumed by nineteenth-century liberal scholars, became ever more difficult to see. Harnack's liberal Jesus was overpowered by the dramatic entrance of a strange and inhospitable figure into the twentieth-century imagination of Christian origins.

Q was powerless to adjudicate such a conflict of images because it contained sayings that supported both views of Jesus. There were sayings that liberals had frequently cited, such as the injunction to love one's enemies. But Q also contained prophetic and apocalyptic pronouncements, such as the warning always to be ready, "for the son of man is coming at an hour you do not expect." So Q as a collection of sayings did not help, and since both Weiss and Schweitzer had not argued their case by reference to Q, but from their studies of the narrative gospels, Jesus was imagined marching to Jerusalem with fire in his eyes, and that was the figure around which the storm gathered. Harnack's Q was soon forgotten, for it seemed to add nothing to the debate.

At first the main source of scholarly discomfort was embarrassment over the image of Jesus as an apocalyptic prophet. Schweitzer's picture of Jesus included a number of very disconcerting features. Jesus was fanatic about the kingdom of God, mistaken in his announcement of its imminent appearance, wrong to instruct his disciples in their mission, and all but suicidal in his determination to change the course of history by dying willingly for the kingdom's cause. In time, however, the dismay created by Schweitzer's picture of Jesus began to subside, and those who dared to continue the quest found themselves focusing more on the sayings of Jesus than on the dramatic resolve of a hero obsessed with his impossible mission. Slowly it dawned on the scholarly community that the teachings of Jesus still contained a great deal of instruction that was better classed as wisdom than apocalyptic. How could that be? How could an apocalyptic hero also have offered instruction for living in his present messy world?

One can trace the scholarly frustration with finding examples of both wisdom sayings and apocalyptic announcements among the teachings of Jesus from the turn of the century to the present. The languages of wisdom and apocalyptic assume different views of the world, and scholars have found it difficult to imagine how Jesus may have merged them in a single message. Historians have therefore invested enormous energy in the investigation of the ancient near eastern literatures of proverbial wisdom and apocalyptic vision, seeking to understand each worldview and looking for ways in which each may have been related to the other.

Three proposals about proverbial wisdom and apocalyptic sayings in the teachings of Jesus were eventually made during the 1920s and 1930s that commended themselves to the scholarly community. Two of these were made by Rudolf Bultmann and the third by C. H. Dodd. All three assumed that Jesus' message was essentially an apocalyptic preachment. But all three also tried to account for the presence of wisdom discourse among the sayings. None of the three was based on a study of Q.

Bultmann tried two solutions to the problem of wisdom and apocalyptic projections in the teachings of Jesus. He was convinced that Jesus had proclaimed the imminent appearance of the kingdom of God by using an apocalyptic idiom. He therefore took pains to identify elements of prophetic proclamation that could authentically be attributed to Jesus from among the many sayings ascribed to Jesus in the synoptic tradition. He accomplished this in his book on the history of the synoptic tradition (1921) by granting privilege to apocalyptic sayings and explaining most of the wisdom sayings as later ascriptions added by "the church." The wisdom sayings were added, he thought, in order to construct an ethic for the meantime when the end of the world did not immediately transpire. This solved the problem by seeing the apocalyptic sayings as "authentic" and regarding the wisdom sayings as secondary additions to a growing "tradition" of the teachings of Jesus.

The other solution was set forth in a little book called *Jesus* published in 1926. In this book Bultmann wrote as a New Testament theologian, not as a historian with the task of sorting out the authentic sayings from a burgeoning tradition of largely inauthentic attributions. He argued that, since the apocalyptic sayings announced an imminent reign of God without bothering to describe it in detail, and since the wisdom sayings called for an obedience to God without bothering to prescribe what that meant in detail, both could be attributed to the same Jesus and understood as his call for "radical obedience." Existentialism provided the conceptual framework for this interpretation, for radical obedience meant freedom from the constraints of the past and openness to an uncharted future. Scholars concerned about the authority of the New Testament for Christian faith were generally delighted. Scholars trained as historians of religion hardly knew how to respond. Which Bultmann should one take seriously?

These proposals eventually coalesced in the view that the teachings of Jesus were "eschatological." Eschatology is a modern coinage from the Greek adjective *eschatos,* which means "last," "extreme," or "final." By this scholars meant that, even though the end of the world did not occur in keeping with apocalyptic expectations, the new age Jesus initiated was so different from the social world at the time, and from all that had gone before, that the use of apocalyptic idiom was fully appropriate to its announcement. As for Jesus, he could also be described by using the term eschatological. He was an "eschatological" prophet or the "last" prophet, one who stood at the end of Jewish history and announced its end. This terminology tamed the harsh edge of apocalyptic prediction in the teachings of Jesus and added a sense of urgency even to injunctions in the wisdom mode. But many scholars doubted that the listeners of Jesus' day would have understood the sayings as Bultmann suggested and wondered whether they would automatically have made the mental translations necessary for the existential effect.

The third solution to the problem of wisdom and apocalyptic eschatology in the teaching of Jesus addressed this question. The proposal was made in 1935 by C. H. Dodd in a study of the parables of Jesus. The parables contained sayings in the wisdom mode that Bultmann had slighted and that many scholars considered authentic. How might they be understood in keeping with the eschatological assumption? Dodd's first move was to argue that all of the parables were metaphors that referred to the kingdom of God. He then noted that some of them invited the listener to imagine some future advent of the kingdom, but that most were told as if the kingdom could be imagined in the present time. To mediate between the notion of a kingdom reserved for the future and one that was already present, Dodd coined the term "realized eschatology" to suggest that Jesus intended his listeners to imagine the eschatological (future and final) kingdom in the process of being realized in Jesus' own appearance and preaching.

A combination of Dodd's parable theory and Bultmann's program of existentialist interpretation finally occurred in America in the late 1960s, and this union resulted in the development of an influential school of parable interpretation in the 1970s. This school is still popular, and many American scholars have been satisfied to think that the parables answer the quest for the historical Jesus and explain the odd mix of wisdom and eschatology in his teachings. Alas. When the time came, finally, to have another look at Q, the mix of proverbial wisdom with apocalyptic pronouncements was there, but there were very few parables included among the sayings and none that could turn the mix into an easily grasped program of realized eschatology.

What to do? Q required explanation. It was the largest collection of the sayings of Jesus at hand. It therefore had to be taken much more seriously than the selection of parables scholars had been using as their data base. Q was a collection of sayings made by first-century followers of Jesus, not a modern selection of sayings by type that twentieth-century scholars had put together from different synoptic texts and traditions. A first-century collection must have had its own rationale. What if the question of wisdom and apocalyptic in the sayings of Jesus was asked by focusing on Q instead of the parables? What if the imagined historical Jesus as portrayed in the narrative gospels was not allowed to prejudice the study? What if those who made the collection of sayings in Q left some clues to help us understand what *they* thought about Jesus' wisdom and prophetic speech?

A stunning manuscript discovery in 1945 made it possible to get started with such a project. Among the Coptic-Gnostic texts found at Nag Hammadi was, of all things, a collection of the sayings of Jesus called the Gospel According to Thomas (see the new English translation by Marvin Meyer, 1992). The Gospel of Thomas looked very much like Q, and approximately 35 percent of the sayings in Thomas had parallels in Q. Here, then, was a text closely related to Q that proved the existence of the genre in early Christian circles. It also provided yet another text of the sayings of Jesus for comparative study. Since some sayings appeared in both collections, the two texts were somehow related. Surely a study of Thomas would help with the question of Q.

A first breakthrough occurred in 1964 when James Robinson published an article in German on the genre of Q. An English translation was subsequently published in 1971 as "'Logoi Sophon': On the Gattung of Q" ("Sayings of the Sages: On the Genre of Q"). In this article Robinson drew the connection between Q and Thomas; pointed to other early Christian collections of sayings such as the parables in Mark 4, the Didache, and several Coptic-Gnostic writings; and then added examples from the wisdom literatures of ancient Egypt and early Judaism. He concluded that the genre of Q was a common form of wisdom literature. He called it "sayings of the sages" in keeping with such a reference in Proverbs 22:17 and the frequency with which similar formulas appeared in the first lines (*incipits*) of these sayings collections.

If Robinson was right, those who collected the sayings of Jesus in Q and the Gospel of Thomas did so on the model of a wisdom genre. Did this mean that the wisdom sayings were more appropriate to these collections than the apocalyptic sayings and that Jesus' followers had understood them as instructions offered by a sage teacher?

The point about Q being the sayings of a sage was not lost on scholars interested in Thomas and Q. Detailed studies began to focus on the presence and importance of the wisdom sayings in these collections. In addition to sayings that crystallized wisdom in the traditional forms of proverb and maxim, scholars also found stylistic traits, aphorisms, stock images, rhetorical units, and mythological metaphors in the idiom of ancient near eastern wisdom. Perhaps Robinson's identification of the genre of Q was correct, and the idiom of wisdom, not apocalyptic, was fundamental to the collection.

John Kloppenborg thought it was and put Robinson's thesis to the test in a publication called *The Formation of Q* in 1987. Kloppenborg marshalled a large collection of wisdom literature, not only from the ancient near east, but also from Greek traditions and from the mixture of cultures that occurred during the hellenistic era. He was able to show that maxims, proverbs, injunctions, and anecdotes were the idiom of popular philosophy and education during the hellenistic age and that collections of this kind of material functioned as handbooks of instruction. Q did exhibit features typical of the hellenistic handbook of instruction and Kloppenborg argued that Q was composed on such a model. Several blocks of wisdom material in Q clearly took the form of what Kloppenborg called "sapiential instruction." But Q also had features that did not quite fit the model. Wouldn't you know? The difference between Q and the genre of instruction in wisdom had largely to do with the presence of the prophetic and apocalyptic sayings.

That Q contained apocalyptic and prophetic sayings was a serious qualification of the wisdom genre. To make matters worse, others had been working on the organization of material in Q as a literary composition and were emphasizing the importance of prophetic themes. In 1969 Dieter Lührmann published a study called *Die Redaktion der Logienquelle* ("Editing the Sayings Source"). He showed that the theme of judgment functioned as a principle of organization for Q as a whole. This was an advance, for it meant that Q was more than an aggregate collection of disparate sayings, but it did frustrate the thesis that Q was compiled as a collection of wisdom sayings.

Studies appeared in the 1970s and 1980s that put Lührmann's findings to the test and a remarkable agreement began to emerge. With slight variations and refinements, Lührmann's thesis found acceptance and/or confirmation in studies by Arland Jacobson (1978), Dieter Zeller (1984), Philip Sellew (1986), Leif Vaage (1987b), and Migaku Sato (1988). It now appeared that the sayings in Q were organized around the theme of judgment. Prophetic and apocalyptic sayings were not peripheral. They were integral to Q's compositional design.

At this point Kloppenborg made a proposal that turned out to be the second big breakthrough in modern Q studies. Kloppenborg revised Robinson's thesis by suggesting that Q had taken shape in stages, that it had a history of collection and composition. The earliest layer of material was indeed a collection of instructions on the wisdom model. It was this material that could be called "sapiential instruction." The prophetic and apocalyptic sayings could also be seen as a layer of material, a layer Kloppenborg called "the announcement of judgment." The announcement of judgment was indeed the principle of organization of Q at this second stage of its compositional history, but it had not erased large and important blocks of material from the earlier stage of collection.

According to this ingenious proposal both Robinson and Lührmann were right. Robinson was right about the generic model of the sayings collection, and especially about the content of the sayings that Kloppenborg assigned to the earliest layer of collection. But Lührmann was also right about the fundamental importance of the apocalyptic and prophetic sayings for Q's eventual design. To support his thesis, Kloppenborg produced a detailed study of the text, unit by

unit. He summarized the entire history of Q scholarship in an introduction and cited the judgments of others about text-critical details
throughout. He drew upon a wide range of literary-critical and thematic observations to support his thesis that the wisdom material was
formed apart from interest in or knowledge of the theme of judgment,
but that use of the prophetic and apocalyptic materials presupposed
and incorporated the wisdom sayings in Q's present design. Thus the
sequence was established. First there was a collection of sayings organized as sapiential instruction. Later these were incorporated into a
composition that developed the theme of judgment by using
prophetic and apocalyptic discourse. There was no literary evidence
that suggested a reverse sequence. In Kloppenborg's study, Q had finally been treated with respect, regarded as a text with its own integrity, and given the careful reading it deserved.

Kloppenborg's study shed new light on the problem of wisdom
and apocalyptic sayings in the teachings of Jesus. Both idioms were
present in Q, but each functioned differently and entered the history
of composition at a different time. According to Kloppenborg, moreover, the wisdom sayings were typical of the earliest layer of Q. If the
shift from wisdom to apocalyptic could be explained, it would have
tremendous consequences for the quest of the historical Jesus and a
revision of Christian origins. As for Jesus, it would mean that he had
probably been more the sage, less the prophet. And as for Christian
origins, it would mean that something other than an apocalyptic message and motivation may have impelled the new movement and defined its fundamental attraction.

Kloppenborg did not press the point about the historical Jesus,
and he did not argue that, just because apocalyptic sayings were
added to Q at a second stage of composition, they were not taken from
oral tradition as early as that from which the wisdom sayings derived.
But others had already grown suspicious of the apocalyptic hypothesis and were prepared to see the stratigraphy of Q as additional evidence for a nonapocalyptic Jesus. The evidence had been mounting
in studies of the Gospel of Thomas, the parables, the aphoristic quality of the sayings traditions in general, the pre-Markan pronouncement stories, and the nonapocalyptic background of the concept of
the kingdom of God. By now it was well known, for instance, that the
Gospel of Thomas was thoroughly nonapocalyptic in tenor and that it

contained sayings from the very earliest period of the Jesus movements. So Kloppenborg's solution to the presence of wisdom and
apocalyptic sayings in Q fit perfectly the growing consensus that Jesus
was first remembered for his wisdom.

As for Christian origins, it suddenly became clear that the conventional scenario was deeply indebted to the apocalyptic hypothesis.
If Jesus had not been an eschatological prophet, the presence of apocalyptic language in the early traditions of the Jesus movements would
have to be explained some other way. The conventional view of
Christian origins assumed an apocalyptic imagination at the beginning
and a gradual shift to the language of wisdom when the world did not
end as expected. Now the sequence worked the other way around.
The shift was not from apocalyptic announcement to instruction in
wisdom, but from wisdom to apocalyptic. This switch forced a total
reconsideration of Christian origins and of the way in which apocalyptic language had been understood to function. The assumption had
been that preaching an apocalyptic message of judgment could attract
people to a movement that promised salvation from that judgment. It
now appeared that an apocalyptic imagination worked only in support of social values and commitments that were generated by other
attractions and persuasions already at work within the group.

If the entertainment of an apocalyptic imagination was a
secondary development in early Jesus circles, what may have been
the earlier message and attraction of the Jesus movement? If apocalyptic thinking usually emerges in support of social and cultural loyalties already in place, what might those earlier loyalties at the stage
of sapiential instruction have been? And what must have happened
to occasion the shift from a wisdom discourse to an apocalyptic
imagination?

Such questions burgeoned in the wake of Kloppenborg's study
of Q. That they were questions of consequence for Christian origins
was clear. What was not so clear was whether Q could supply the answers. Q would have to be read apart from the patina created by its
long contact with the narrative gospels. The people of Q would have
to come into view, and the social and cultural setting in Galilee would
have to be better understood. Only then would it be possible to catch
the point of Q's instructions and understand the reason for the shift
in Q's discourse from wisdom sayings to apocalyptic pronouncements.

What if Q were situated in its Galilean context and read from a Galilean perspective? What if the sequence from instruction in wisdom to the announcement of judgment in Q's compositional history was a clue to stages in the social history of the Jesus movement? It was worth a try and, lo and behold, when the risk was taken the gospel patina slowly dissolved and a strange new world came into view.

3

Removing the Patina

Biblical scholars always assume a community behind their texts. And New Testament scholars have always thought that the earliest followers of Jesus immediately formed a Christian congregation. That is what Luke reports, and Matthew and John. Mark's ending seems to allow for it. And Paul's letter to the Galatians tells us that Cephas and James were residing in Jerusalem as "pillars" of some group of Jesus people in the mid 50s C.E. If the importance of Jesus was his role in starting the Christian religion, or so the reasoning has been, the first followers must have been Christians. It may not have been easy to start a new religion with fishermen and such, especially when the large-scale plan required coming to see that Jesus was the Christ who came to transform the world by dying for it. But surely the dramatic events of the crucifixion, the resurrection, and the appearances to the women and disciples took care of that. So the first church in Jerusalem must have blossomed overnight, or at least not later than Luke's forty days.

When Q came into view as a text, scholars naturally began to talk about the "community of Q." Just as naturally they thought of the community of Q as the earliest form of Christian congregation. Some even used the term "church" to refer to what must have been the obvious result when people recognized Jesus as the Christ. What did it matter if they recorded his teachings in a document that did not tell all? Surely they must have been Christians.

As interest grew in knowing more about the community of Q, however, studies began to appear that bumped up against features of the text that did not seem to fit the standard scenario etched in the Christian imagination. Not only was there no reference to the death and resurrection of Jesus, no mention of Jesus as the Christ, and no instruction to Peter and the other disciples about continuing Jesus' mission and baptizing converts into the church, the instructions in Q were couched in curious aphoristic discourse, addressed to individuals, and recommended strange public behavior. So the first attempts at describing the community of Q aimed at understanding how these odd features of the text could be made to fit the traditional picture of Christian origins.

Gerd Theissen took note of the strange public behavior called for throughout the document, such as the instructions to sell one's possessions and give to everyone who begs, not to worry about what to eat, about leaving home to follow Jesus, and to give your shirt to the person who grabs your coat. He also noted the connection between injunctions like these and the instructions for working in the harvest where Jesus' followers are told not to carry money or purse. Theissen (1973) first proposed that the Q people were itinerant charismatics who imitated the radical life-style of Jesus, acting out their commitment to his message of the kingdom of God by means of the curious behavior enjoined, such as voluntary poverty and begging. When this did not seem to satisfy the traditional picture of Christian beginnings or to account for all of the sayings in Q, he went on to suggest that the Christian movement consisted of settled Christian communities as well as itinerants (1977). According to this view the Q itinerants were actually missionaries who received their support from the settled communities where they were recognized as Christian prophets. In exchange for supporting the itinerant prophets, the communities received Christian proclamation and instruction. Since that seemed to fit with the picture of Paul's missionary activity, and seemed to agree with Paul's description in Galatians 2:7–8 of two missions (one to Jews and one to gentiles), Theissen's proposal sounded plausible.

Richard Edwards (1976) noted the uneasy mix of wisdom, prophecy, and apocalyptic language in Q and that the "christology" of Q was not yet clearly Christian. The only role for Jesus that might be considered Christian, according to Edwards, was that the people of Q expected his return as the son of man. Edwards therefore argued that the mix of sayings was justified "theologically" and that the early son of man "christology" was called for in light of Jesus' eschatological message and his resurrection from the dead. Since that seemed to fit the standard Christian scenario, no one bothered to ask Edwards how he knew that the people of Q thought that Jesus had been raised from the dead when they made no mention of it.

Eugene Boring (1982) suggested that the Q people were ecstatic prophets who continued to proclaim the kingdom by speaking in Jesus' spirit and name. They could do this because they understood themselves to be filled with the spirit of Jesus as the risen Lord. Q was their handbook of instructions for the mission, and the material in Q was the substance of what they preached. For a while Boring's book was eagerly read, for it all but erased any differences between the people of Q and the standard view of Christian origins. And besides, Boring's appeal to the ecstasy of dramatic spiritual experience was difficult to counter. It complemented so well a long history of Christian desire to anchor religious authority in a miraculous and mysterious event of spiritual transformation. So much the better if that event effected the transformation, not only of Jesus, but of his ecstatic followers as well.

But studies such as these eventually failed to convince the careful readers of Q as the 1980s unfolded. In a 1987 dissertation Leif Vaage made two points that nicely summed up an emerging scholarly consensus about the best approach to Q. Vaage argued for a strict adherence to the text of Q when interpreting any given saying and when reconstructing its social context. He showed that both Theissen and Boring had based their work on a large number of assumptions about Christian origins that were not appropriate to the text of Q. Vaage's own findings, based largely on the harvest instructions, were that Q was interested mainly in behavior and life-style, and that the life-style called for in Q was much closer to patterns of behavior characteristic of Cynics in the hellenistic tradition of popular philosophy than to the descriptions given by Theissen and Boring for Christian charismatic prophets.

Since others had been finding similar discrepancies between the tenor of Q and the traditional interpretation of its sayings, it was clear that the conventional picture of Christian origins was not helping in the attempt to understand Q. The time seemed right for a concerted effort to read Q apart from the standard scenario of Christian beginnings and try to catch sight of the people of Q as they might have looked in their own social world.

In 1988 the Q Seminar of the Society of Biblical Literature turned to the question of the community of Q. Kloppenborg's identification of three layers of textual tradition in Q had already become an acceptable working hypothesis for the seminar, and notations had been created in order to refer to each layer. The earliest layer consisting of "sapiential instruction" was now referred to as Q^1, and the "announcement of judgment" as Q^2. Kloppenborg had also identified a small amount of material that had been added later than the composition of Q^2, such as the story of Jesus' temptation. These later additions were referred to as Q^3. I will use these shorthand designations when referring to the several layers of the Q tradition. In the English translation of the text presented in part II, the material assigned to each of these layers has been set in a different typeface.

At the seminar, Kloppenborg and I each presented a paper on the social history of the people of Q. Careful attention to the layers of tradition in Q's composition made it possible to move from shifts in the group's discourse to stages in the group's social history. Indications of location, dress, behavior, and attitude toward the larger social world could be identified in each stage that agreed with the kind of discourse characteristic for each layer. Analysis of the rhetoric at each stage also brought changes of audience into view, which indicated that the people of Q had experienced changes in their social circumstance. Surprisingly, both Kloppenborg and I agreed in our preliminary descriptions of each stage of the group's social history as well as with regard to the circumstances that must have occasioned the shifts in discourse from stage to stage.

In broad outline, the social history of the people of Q began with an early period of élan, general social critique, and experimentation with countercultural behavior. Their flippant stance toward standard social conventions is captured in such sayings as "Leave the dead to bury their dead," "Do not worry . . . what you will wear," and "Lend without expecting anything in return." This period was followed by an attempt to turn some of their unlikely behavior into rules by which to recognize fellow travelers and exemplify an ethos peculiar to the movement. In the harvest instruction, for instance, there is mention of appropriate attire, a sign of greeting, and proper etiquette when being received as a guest. These early periods and the first attempts at spelling out an ethic are documented in Q^1. At this stage of collection and composition the audience largely consisted of those participating in the movement. But then the group experienced a period of frustration with failed expectations. It was this failure that occasioned the language of judgment which was largely directed toward various sectors of the society that had created obstacles for the movement. This stage of social history is documented in Q^2. At some later time additions were made to the collection that indicate a series of accommodations to other streams of the Jesus movement as well as to some Jewish and hellenistic values that had earlier been eschewed. Q^3 exhibits a relaxation of the tensions that had accompanied earlier stages of social formation.

But who exactly were these people and what precisely was their movement all about? Returning to the text with these questions in mind, features of its discourse were noticed that had been overlooked in earlier studies. One was that the wisdom sayings of Q^1 looked strange when compared with the maxims, proverbs, and injunctions typical for the standard collection of wise sayings. There could be no doubt that the sayings in Q^1 were crafted in the forms of wisdom speech and treated as sage instructions. But they did not trade in truisms, principles, and traditional proverbial wisdom. They were decidedly aphoristic, delighting in extreme cases and in imagery that was more pungent and evocative than observational and instructive. And there was a very large imbalance in favor of imperatives, injunctions, and instruction in specific details of behavior. To call this material sage advice was clearly not sufficient. Something was being recommended other than the wisdom required for well-being either in a conventional society or in a well-defined subcultural group.

To anticipate what we shall find as we enter the world of the text in part III, the aphoristic quality of the sayings in Q^1 is strikingly reminiscent of speech characteristic of the Greek tradition of Cynic philosophy. This kind of sagery did not intend an elucidation of the way the world usually works in order to recommend fitting attitudes and behavior. Instead, poignant insights explored the embarrassing moments of human relations and the pretensions that traditional wisdom

46

overlooks or seeks to cover up with its rationalizations in favor of conventional social values.

New Testament scholars had been aware of the Cynic parallels to a few of the specific attitudes and practices enjoined in Q^1. As we shall see, these included such things as disentanglement from one's family, voluntary homelessness, eschewing normal standards of cleanliness, simple attire, and unashamed begging. But scholars had always discounted these similarities to the Cynics because they did not fit with the traditional picture of the Christian mission. Now, however, more than a few behavioral similarities to the Cynics began to surface. The aphoristic style in Q^1 was very close to the Cynics' way of making pointed comment on human behavior, and the logic involved in recommending extravagant behavior in Q was very close to the rhetoric of a Cynic's repartee when challenged about his own behavior. The forthrightness with which social critique was registered in Q was exactly like that of the Cynics' attitude called *parresia,* or bold, outspoken manner. Aphoristic style, unconventional behavior, and the rhetoric of embarrassment all converged in a critical stance toward the social world that also agreed with Cynic tradition. This stance of social critique was a call for individuals to live against the stream, not a program offered for the reform of society's ills. Thus the Cynic parallels helped us see that social critique in Q^1 was decidedly scatter shot and implicit, not pointed and programmatic as if Judaism, the priests, the Pharisees, or the Romans were to blame for the sorry state of the world. Specific social institutions and particular cultural or religious traditions were not under attack. Natural behavior under the circumstances was what counted, not a system of belief, or a piety, or a reconceptualization of the way the world might work if only certain leaders, institutions, or structures were not in place and in charge. The early Jesus movement was apparently not a reform movement.

The Cynic parallels seemed to subside, however, when turning to the material in Q^2. Here one encountered prophetic idiom as well as explicit appeal to epic lore familiar from the Hebrew scriptures. In contrast to Q^1, the authority of Jesus was greatly enhanced by association with the mythological figure of wisdom, and by imparting to him the kind of knowledge one had to have in order to make the sweeping judgments and announcements attributed to him. A man named John entered the picture with a message of judgment, together with parables that dealt with exclusion and threatened people with the thought that a strict account of their deeds was being kept. The Pharisees were singled out for castigation in an extensive list of charges against them. And the theme of judgment seemed to climax in an apocalyptic announcement of the day of the son of man, an imaginary figure whose judgment would be final at the great trial to come. What could one say about finding these features in Q? Scholars were at a loss. All of these features were familiar themes in the design of the narrative gospels. In the context of the narrative gospels these features had meanings that supported the gospel story. Why were they popping up in Q at the second stage of composition? With Q disentangled from its narrative gospel context these features had no narrative reference to give them significance and were very hard to understand. Some scholars thought we may have been wrong. Perhaps the people of Q had been gospel Christians all along.

Scholarly consternation is a lovely sight to behold, especially when the panic is triggered by a major shift in paradigms. In this case, the picture painted by the narrative gospels had continued to function, unbeknownst, as the dominant paradigm for imagining Christian beginnings. The story provided by the narrative gospels was, in fact, the only model scholars had in mind for thinking about the earliest chapters of Christianity. In spite of knowing that Mark's gospel was a fiction, the setting and logic of his story still served as the frame of reference for understanding the sayings and themes in Q^2, especially those that clearly overlapped with the gospels. According to the narrative gospels most of these themes should have surfaced in Q^1 as reminiscences of Jesus. According to the gospels, wasn't Jesus baptized by John? Was he not an eschatological prophet of the kingdom of God? Did he not call for the transformation of Israel? Did he not tangle with the Pharisees and threaten them with divine judgment? Was he not crucified by the Jewish authorities? The recent studies of Q suggested otherwise, that Jesus was first remembered as a Cynic sage and only later imagined as a prophet who uttered apocalyptic warnings. So what was a poor, confused scholar to do? When confronted with data that does not fit the dominant paradigm, scholars reassess and repeat the experiment. Either the data must be wrong or the paradigm will have to change. Take care, proceed with caution, leave no stone unturned. Such are the signals heard from within.

Detailed studies have therefore been devoted to item after item in a list of troublesome Q^2 themes during the last five years. These are precious studies, for they exhibit a remarkably fresh and candid approach to sayings that had always been taken for granted and interpreted from the gospel point of view. The method has been thorough with respect to the text of Q, critical in the comparison of Q with the gospels, and open with regard to the way such language worked in the cultures of the time. In every case these studies have produced results that are similar. A theme that is common both to Q and to the gospels takes on different meanings in each literary context. When read in Q these themes are better understood if their gospel connotation is avoided. Thus the sayings in Q should be studied apart from the narrative gospels.

As we shall see in part III, this is the case with the prophet motif, the apocalyptic idiom, the terminology of the kingdom of God, the theme of discipleship, the castigation of the Pharisees, and a few allusions to death by crucifixion and killing. Interpreting themes such as these solely in the context of the Q document, without reference to the gospels, supported the growing suspicion that the people of Q were not Christians: the people of Q did not think of Jesus as a messiah, did not recognize a special group of trained disciples as their leaders, did not imagine that Jesus had marched to Jerusalem in order to cleanse the temple or reform the Jewish religion, did not regard his death as an unusual divine event, and did not follow his teachings in order to be "saved" or transformed people.

The process of defamiliarization has been painful for some. The rewards, however, have been rich indeed. Finally Q can be understood apart from its gospel context. The people of Q can now be seen as a lively Jesus movement. The Jesus movement can now be placed in its own Galilean environment. And as for Galilee, our understanding of its social and cultural world has also been forced to change. Q and the Jesus movement fit quite nicely into the picture now being painted by archeological and sociological analyses of first-century life and times in Galilee.

You also will be asked to look at the sayings in Q with new eyes. The fresh translation of Q material in part II will help and the explication of the text in part III is designed precisely as a revision of the more familiar, traditional Christian view. But the traditional picture of Galilean culture also needs to change. In this case, the scholars' advantage is too great, too comprehensive to share easily in the course of ad hoc textual observations. Most readers will have an image of Judaism in Palestine, based on the Christian gospels, that will frustrate the attempt to make sense of Q and will seriously inhibit their own process of defamiliarization. This image consists of a set of assumptions about the social, political, and religious world in which the story of Jesus was set. Even if Q is taken out of the narrative frame of the gospels, this image of Jewish life in Galilee tends to remain in the background and can only be challenged by a full historical redescription. Thus the following chapter provides some basic, up-to-date information about the social and cultural climate of first-century Galilee.

4

Galilee Before the War

In the world of the Christian imagination Galilee belonged to Palestine, the religion of Palestine was Judaism, so everyone in Galilee must have been Jewish. Since this picture is wrong, and since Q can make no sense as long as it prevails, the reader needs to have a truer picture in mind. This chapter presents a sketch of what scholars are discovering about Galilee as a discrete social and cultural location, and about the situation that prevailed in the first century C.E. It is the historical once upon a time that sets the stage for the story of Q.

A glance at the following map will show that Galilee was not contiguous to Judea. It was even further removed from Jerusalem than Samaria, the home of age-old religious traditions that had always been in competition with loyalties centered in Jerusalem. During the three or four centuries prior to the time of Jesus, tensions had escalated between the Samaritans, who were resident in the land when the Jews returned from exile in Babylon in 539 B.C.E., and the Jewish leaders, who determined to rebuild their temple in Jerusalem. Sometime during the fourth century a parting of the ways took place when, as the stories recall, the Samaritan king Sanballat wanted to join with the Jews and help construct a temple at Jerusalem, but was rebuffed. Later in the mid second century B.C.E. the Jews won their independence from the Seleucids of Antioch, the successors in that region to the legacy of Alexander the Great, and established the Maccabean-Hasmonean dynasty of priest-kings in Jerusalem. They then set out

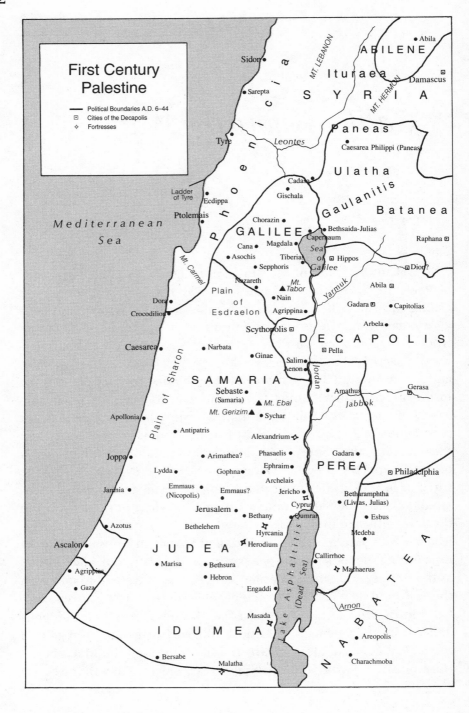

First Century
Palestine

— Political Boundaries A.D. 6–44
▣ Cities of the Decapolis
◇ Fortresses

on a program of conquest and annexation to regain control of all the territory associated with the golden age of David and Solomon. The Samaritans to the north were conquered and their temple destroyed in 135 B.C.E. The Idumeans to the south of Judea were also conquered and forced to be circumcised, a rather irrevocable mark to a very revocable allegiance. And Galilee was not annexed until about 100 B.C.E. The reports of these wars show that there was strong popular resistance against Jewish domination. The fighting was fierce. The conquered peoples did not regard their annexation as a homecoming, and loyalty to Jerusalem could not be taken for granted.

As for Galilee, it had never been fully incorporated into the cultural entity that Christians imagine as "Israel." It was a land of mixed peoples, a crossroads, and a kind of buffer zone on the borders of petty kingdoms that had their centers to the north in Syria, to the east in the Transjordan and Damascus, and to the south in Samaria and Jerusalem. For centuries these petty kingdoms had been pawns in the large-scale contests that centered even farther away in the empires of the upper Tigris-Euphrates to the north and Egypt to the south. From the perspective of those who sat in power in Egypt and Babylon, the petty kings in Antioch, Damascus, the Philistine plain, and Jerusalem were worth having on one's side. But Galilee was hardly worthy of a moment's consideration. It had no capital city, no king, no temple, and no hierarchy of priests. In the constant shifts in political power, with armies marching up and down the highways of the Levant, Galilee was a no-man's-land reserved for initial skirmishes in larger undertakings. It was a kind of beachhead where the surge of political crosscurrents constantly kept the people on their toes.

It is not surprising that loyalty to kings and their gods was not a Galilean virtue. Even the old stories of Israel's conquest of the land told of the failure to take completely the regions of Galilee from those who already lived there, peoples who refused to join in the tribal confederations. We tend to think of Galilee as a natural part of the land of Israel because the kingdoms of David and Solomon included it, and because the extent of their kingdoms became the ideal realm for any Jewish state centered in Jerusalem. But Galilee belonged to the kingdom of David and Solomon for less than one hundred years. After that it was part of the kingdom of Israel with its own "northern" traditions and its capital at Shechem, the provincial center later to be known as Samaria. Then it was annexed as a province by Assyria, transferred to Neo-Babylonia, and invaded by the Persians. The stories of the Jews who returned from deportation to Babylon belong to the history of Jerusalem and Judea, not to Samaria and the district of Galilee. The stories say that the Jews found the Samaritans unworthy to help build the temple at Jerusalem because they had intermarried with the people of other cultures. And as for Galilee, it was known among Jews as "the land of the gentiles."

After Alexander, the hellenizing programs of the Ptolemies and Seleucids dotted the landscape on all sides of Galilee with newly founded cities on the Greek model. Greek cities were founded in Phoenicia, southern Syria, the Decapolis (region of "ten cities" to the east of the Sea of Galilee), northern Palestine, and the coastlands to the west. Theaters, schools, stadia, porticoed markets, administrative offices, foreign legions, and transplanted people with franchise as "citizens" took their place as signs of the hellenistic age. Samaritans and Galileans did not resist. They did not generate a revolution like that of the Maccabees in Judea.

Jewish resistance to hellenistic forms of governance and culture was centered in Judea. The Maccabees resisted in the interest of conserving a specific image of Jewish culture based on the ancient near eastern model of the temple-state. The temple-state was ruled by a king who was invested with executive power, and a high priest who represented purity, or the culture's codes of propriety. In the eyes of the Maccabees, the leaders of the Jerusalem establishment were in danger of accommodating Greek culture and turning Jerusalem into a hellenistic city. The situation came to a head in 167 B.C.E. when the infamous Seleucid king, Antiochus IV Epiphanes, put Syrian troops in Jerusalem to suppress resistance to his hellenizing program. The Maccabee brothers started a guerrilla campaign against two fronts, Syrian hegemony (the wrong kings) and the Jerusalem aristocracy (the wrong high priests). They fought under the banner of the "traditions of the fathers" and were eventually successful against the Syrian armies and the Jerusalem establishment. They were less successful in the battle of cultures.

After winning independence for Jerusalem, the Maccabees assumed for themselves the roles both of king and high priest and established the Hasmonean dynasty (140 B.C.E.). They took their military victories as a sign that the time had come to restore the kingdom of David and Solomon. That, however, was not an easy thing to do, even for kings prepared to use armies on the model of the hellenistic tyrant. Their project of expansion required an additional forty years of military activity, with Galilee the last to be annexed in 100 B.C.E. Thus their rule over "the land of Israel" lasted only from 100 to 63 B.C.E. when a second momentous political complication set the stage for the final chapter of what we now call the second temple-state. In 63 B.C.E. Pompey entered the picture to settle an internecine conflict for the Hasmonean throne and turned Palestine into a Roman province. This meant yet another superimposition of military, political, economic, social, and cultural presence with which Galileans had to contend.

With such a history, it may come as a surprise to learn that Galilee supported a vibrant and productive society. It was a land of rolling hills and fertile valleys, bordered to the north and west by mountainous terrain, to the east by the Sea of Galilee and the Jordan river, and to the south by the mountains of Samaria. Thus it was somewhat protected from the brunt of armies that preferred, if possible, to use the major north-south routes, one to the east called the "King's Highway," or the major road along the sea coast to the west. Of course, armies always needed food and Galilee was known as a little bread basket. But for the Galileans there were always the mountains to the north for hiding, should there be need to escape from military forays with designs upon them or their produce.

In the case of traders, however, the traffic was constant. There were roadways through Galilee that gave access in all directions to the wider world of travel and trade: to Damascus, Tyre, Ptolemais, Caesarea, Samaria, Jerusalem, the Transjordan, and the Decapolis. These roads linked up with the major routes mentioned above that connected the Levant with Egypt, Syria, and the Tigris-Euphrates valley. They also provided access to active seaports on the Mediterranean. Thus Galilee was fully exposed to the ebb and flow of goods, ideas, and reports of events that generated social and cultural change in the Greco-Roman age.

Galilee was known for its sunny and temperate climate and its lands watered by springs. The shores of the Sea of Galilee were something of a resort and the lake sustained important fisheries. Galilee was famous for its grains, olive oil, wines, fruits, nuts, dates, and fish, all of which were produced in sufficient quantity to export. The land was thickly populated with peasants, small farmers, handworkers, and day laborers living in small villages and medium-sized towns. There is archeological evidence that the villages and towns of Galilee formed networks of exchange for a diversified market of foods, goods, and craftwork. The picture one gets is that Galilee with its self-supporting economy was a good place to live, if only the kings and their armies did not sweep through too often.

Who, then, were these people? In the ancient near east and the lands along the eastern Mediterranean Sea, social identity was marked by the land, culture, and people to which one belonged. One spoke of tribes, peoples, and nations, and for each there was a distinct location that centered the shrines and symbols of one's cultural tradition. When meeting a stranger the first disclosure of importance would be one's ethnic identity. The Greek term was *ethnos* meaning race, nation, people, tribe, etc. Thus it made some difference whether one was Egyptian, or Syrian, Cyprian, Hellene, Roman, and so forth. In Palestine distinctions of importance were made, for instance, among Jews (from Judea, the land of Judah, with its temple in Jerusalem), Idumeans, Samaritans, Phoenicians, and Syrians, each with their acknowledged lands and cities. But who was a Galilean? The name *Gelil* meant "district" and so referred to a geographical region rather than a land associated with a particular ethnic extraction or culture. *Gelil ha goim* was the "district of the nations," the part of the mythic land of Israel that Jews and Samaritans shared with other peoples.

Judging from its history, and with an eye on a good historical atlas, the changing borders of lands contiguous to Galilee indicate that it had been open to a variety of Semitic peoples from the lower Levant, including those from the coastal districts, the valleys of the upper Jordan drainage, and the Bedouin lands stretching to the east. Archeological evidence shows an ebb and flow of population. So it must have been a land where peoples and their cultures frequently met and mixed. The long history of conquests by ancient near eastern empires also must have contributed to the mix of peoples and cultures in Galilee. And the foundation of cities during the hellenistic period populated the Levant with colonists from afar.

Since Galilee was not known as a land of origin for a specific ethnic identity with its cultivation of hoary traditions, or for its cultural production of literature and institutions of religion, some scholars have concluded that it was largely rural in mentality and peasant in population, a sort of illiterate, sleepy backwater isolated from the political and ideological currents that determined loyalties in the bouncy history of Palestine and the Levant. But such an assessment does not match the picture that is now coming into view. One has to account for the savvy and self-confidence of a mixed people who managed to create a landed way of life and sustain it in the face of repeated subjections to foreign rulers eager for the control and taxation of its production.

It is true that no Galilean city ever played a role comparable to centers of regional loyalties, petty kingdoms, and commercial enterprise such as Samaria, Tyre, or Damascus. Sepphoris, one of Galilee's larger towns and the seat of governance under the Hasmoeans and Herodians, is not even mentioned in the histories of Israel. And there is no history of loyalty to any god of royalty, or had Galilee a history of wars to cleanse the land of unclean people or power. But that does not mean that Galileans did not love their land, had no shrines, and did not know how to celebrate life together. It does not mean that their towns and villages did not function, or that the people were not wide awake and fully apprised of the wider world around them.

Three hundred years of hellenistic influence just before the time of Jesus is an especially important factor. Hellenistic influence has been downplayed by scholars in the interest of buttressing the picture of Jesus appearing in the midst of a thoroughly Jewish culture. Unfortunately for this view, archeological evidence of hellenization in Galilee continues to increase. Since language is such a basic index of cultural influence, it is significant that southern Galilee was largely Greek-speaking in the first century, though of course bilingual. Although the Ptolemies and Seleucids had not colonized Galilee by founding a new city in the middle of the region, Galilee was literally surrounded by cities on the hellenistic model. The towns of the Decapolis were newly founded hellenistic cities. One of them, Scythopolis, was on the southern border of Galilee and another, Gadara, was just across the Jordan, a day's walk from Nazareth or Sepphoris. All of these cities were proud of their hellenistic institutions, including theaters, sporting arenas (*gymnasia*), and schools. Gadara produced famous philosophers and poets of the Cynic school, including Melea-ger (100 B.C.E.), Philodemus (110–40 B.C.E.), and Oenomaus (120 C.E.). Tiberias, built by Herod Antipas on the shore of the Sea of Galilee in 19 C.E., was founded on the hellenistic model. And Sepphoris, an hour's walk from Nazareth, was a thoroughly hellenized city. It was rebuilt by Herod Antipas during Jesus' time and archeological investi-gations have unearthed a theater and the now-famous mosaic of Dionysus. The dates for these important pieces of evidence are, un-fortunately, still disputed, ranging from the first to the second century C.E. But even if they belong to the second century they should not be discounted, for they demonstrate the extent to which hellenistic cul-ture was taken for granted in Galilee despite an increasing influx of Jews in the period after the Roman-Jewish war of 66–73 C.E.

What, then, can be said about a Jewish presence in Galilee be-fore the war? Jews may have moved into Galilee at any time after the exile, and especially during the hellenistic age, as part of the move-ment of peoples characteristic of the times. If so, a rather strange cir-cumstance must be imagined for Jews living in Galilee. Normally, Jews in the diaspora (living outside of Judea) formed communities of mutual support. In Egypt, for instance, they built "houses of prayer" where they met to cultivate their Jewish culture at a distance from their temple and land. But would Jews in Galilee have formed dias-pora congregations or built buildings for that purpose? The custom-ary answer has been yes, and in the course of the first century the term synagogue does begin to appear as a name for Jewish congrega-tion both in Palestine and throughout the Roman empire. But the Greek word *synagogue* simply means "congregation" and so must have referred at first to the people coming together, not to the place or building where they gathered. In the Levant, at any rate, congregation had taken place for millennia at shrines, city gates, and city squares. It was during Roman times that the term synagogue became attached to the place or building in which meeting occurred and a Jewish syn-agogue (building) was a standard feature in cities throughout the em-pire. The problem is that, according to archeological evidence, synagogue buildings in Galilee appear only in the third century C.E. This documents the influx of Jews after the war, but says nothing about the situation before the war. Before the war Josephus tells of synagogues in Caesarea, Dora, and Tiberias. So there were synagogues in cities adjacent to Galilee on the diaspora model, and Herod's Tiberias may have had one, also on the diaspora model. But before the Roman period it seems highly unlikely that Jews moving to Galilee would have considered themselves living in the diaspora or have formed congregations on its model.

That is because there was another model for Jewish congregation indigenous to Judea and by extension to northern Israel. Whereas the diaspora model was a form of local and independent Jewish congregation, the *ma'amadoth,* or priestly-scribal "stations" in the village square, were official outposts of the temple system of governance and taxation, situated in villages central to a region. They served as courts and housed scribes who oversaw the life and production of the people. They also provided a place where calls to prayer were coordinated with the temple services in Jerusalem. After the annexation of Galilee in 100 B.C.E., it is possible that a similar system was introduced into the new territory. Certainly there were official scribes in Galilee during the period of governance from Jerusalem. And Jews who had taken up residence there may have gained some prominence and control of some local Galilean town courts or congregations of elders, the form of governance typical for villages and towns in antiquity.

So Jewish presence in Galilee after 100 B.C.E. was no doubt obvious and may have set a new cultural tone. At the very least, all Galileans were now required to acknowledge Jerusalem as the royal city in charge of Galilean affairs instead of Antioch. Galileans must have paid their temple taxes. Josephus reports that they took advantage of the thrice-yearly pilgrimage requirements to Jerusalem in order to seek a hearing for their grievances. And Jews in Galilee must have paid some attention to the laws and codes related to Jewish identity and practice. But it would be wrong to picture Galilee as suddenly converted to a Jewish loyalty and culture.

Even if one were to imagine that local lore had kept alive memories of belonging to the old kingdom of Israel, the distinctions among Galileans, Samaritans, and Jews have to be kept in mind. The Samaritans had certainly kept alive the old traditions of "northern" Israel focused on Shechem/Samaria, but they were not for that reason Jews. And Galilee was not Samaria just as Samaria was not Judea. So even the Semitic component of the Galilean population needs to be carefully nuanced lest the fact of Jewish presence in Galilee allow the myth of a common Jewish culture to continue.

And the Pharisees? Ah yes, the Pharisees. Even conservative Christian scholars have begrudgingly had to admit that there is only the spottiest evidence for the presence of Pharisees in Galilee before the Roman-Jewish war, and nothing to suggest that they had any position of power there. The Pharisees were active in Jerusalem and represented a form of Jewish thought and piety that took on increased importance in the course of the first century, but scholars have not been able to identify any official function for them whether within Galilee or at Jerusalem. Views of them have ranged from political party, scribal retainers of the temple bureaucracy, teachers in schools such as those of Hillel or Shammai, to members of a religious society or sect. No theory seems to satisfy. Jacob Neusner (1973) is probably right that it is best to see them as individuals who espoused and practiced a simple code of purity rules as the mark of a Jewish way of life. They developed this code in the midst of a confusion of cultures and at a time when it was clear that the Jewish temple-state was coming to its end. For the study of the Jesus movement, and especially for an understanding of the charges leveled against the Pharisees in Q, it is extremely important to know that the Pharisees were not officials in charge of Jewish synagogues. That is the picture Christians have had in mind and there is absolutely no basis for it whatsoever.

And the Romans? Tensions did mount under the Romans. Their attempt to resolve the conflict between Hasmonean rivals for the priest-kingship of Jerusalem and its domain which now stretched from Idumea to Galilee only unleashed a sorry history of atrocities that lasted from 63 to 37 B.C.E. The rivals, Aristobulus II and Hyrcanus II, formed factions, and a leading Idumean family of strong men, the Herodians, played the middle as generals in the army. Finally exasperated, the Romans appointed Herod the Great to be king over Palestine, leaving the selection of high priests to the Jews. Herod ruled from 37 to 4 B.C.E. He succeeded in establishing the *pax romana* in Palestine, but his rule was harsh and unpopular, and it set the stage for a bit of unrest around the time of Jesus.

Incidents at Sepphoris can be used to illustrate the nature of the violence and unrest that played itself out on Galilean soil during this period. In 55 B.C.E. Herod was a general in Galilee serving under his father, Antipater, who had just been named procurator of Palestine. Herod and his father had taken sides with Hyrcanus II, and the Romans had blessed this union by recognizing Hyrcanus as high priest while shifting executive and military power to Antipater as their appointee. While in Galilee, Herod set out to track down and kill a certain Hezekiah, the leader of a band of robbers operating on the Syrian border. He did this apparently to ingratiate himself with the Roman legate in Syria, Sextus Caesar, and for a time the Herods seemed to have all under control. However, their fortunes turned in 40 B.C.E. when the surviving son of Aristobulus II took control of Jerusalem with the help of Parthian troops. Phasael, Herod's brother, committed suicide in Galilee and Herod himself fled to Rome. There the Romans appointed him king and sent him back to Galilee to restore order.

Upon return, Herod's first move was to occupy Sepphoris and turn it into a military base from which to march on Jerusalem. Josephus reports that the people of Sepphoris fled the city as Herod approached. Then, after Herod's death in 4 B.C.E., Judas the Galilean, son of the slain Hezekiah, stormed the military installation at Sepphoris to get at the armory. The Roman legate from Antioch responded by burning Sepphoris to the ground and, according to Josephus, sold the people into slavery. In accordance with Herod's desire, Augustus had divided Palestine into three districts, one for each of his sons, with Archelaus as Ethnarch of Judea and Samaria, Philip as Tetrarch of northern Transjordan, and Herod Antipas as Tetrarch of Galilee and Perea, or southern Transjordan. Archelaus was no match for the assignment, and from 6 C.E. until the Roman-Jewish war Judea-Samaria was ruled by Roman procurators, governors in charge of procuring tribute. But Herod Antipas and Philip enjoyed relatively long and quiet reigns, Herod ruling Galilee from 4 B.C.E. to 39 C.E. During his rule Herod Antipas first rebuilt Sepphoris, presumably on the hellenistic model, and then founded Tiberias on the Sea of Galilee, certainly on the Greek model.

Sepphoris was again caught in the middle of international intrigue during the prelude to the Roman-Jewish war. The political and social situation in Jerusalem had deteriorated to the level of riots, plundering, and factions engaged in guerrilla warfare for control of the temple precincts. Vespasian, the Roman general, was appointed legate in Palestine to quell the unrest, and Josephus was sent from

Jerusalem to raise an army at Sepphoris as a defense against Vespasian's forces. Josephus found that the Galileans refused to get involved, and he was unsuccessful in his attempt to raise an army for the defense of Jerusalem. Later, when writing the history of the war as a leading Jewish intellectual who now wished to mollify Roman attitudes toward the Jews, Josephus explained that the Galileans were too "peaceful." The modern historian detects, instead, a Galilean disaffection with the warring kings and the troubled times. Galileans had no reason to be loyal either to the Romans, or to the Herodians, or to the temple establishment in Jerusalem. If that is so, we need to find reasons for the attraction of the Jesus movement other than those that Christians have traditionally had in mind.

In the Christian imagination Jesus appeared on a thoroughly Jewish scene that was ripe for religious reform. New Testament scholars have therefore looked for circumstances in Galilee that would explain the popular reception of Jesus' message and the rapid expansion of the Jesus movements. Every proposal must combine an interpretation of Jesus' message with a picture of popular mentality in order to account for the attractiveness and motivation of the movement. There are four major types of explanation: (1) reformation, (2) revolution, (3) sectarian formation, and (4) utopian program. None of them fits Q, and none fits the circumstances in Galilee.

The theory of reformation arises from the history of Christian theology. According to this view, Judaism was badly in need of reform because the temple-state was based on a priestly system of sacrificial religion that was primitive, embarrassing, and wrong. Or, focusing upon the Pharisees, the religion of Judaism has been characterized as exclusivistic, legalistic, and wrong. Or, reading the Hebrew scriptures as the Old Testament of the Christian Bible, the Jews had not listened to the prophets, were a disobedient people, and were greatly in need of the messiah lest they fall under the wrath of their righteous God. But neither righteous indignation, nor Pharisaic burden, nor revulsion at the thought of a sacrificial cult are appropriate descriptions of a Galilean mentality to which Jesus may have appealed. And there is nothing in Q to support a message directed to any of these concerns.

The theory of revolution is a twentieth-century notion. It assumes that Jesus' conflict with the Jerusalem establishment was generated by a messianic mission and interprets the gospels in the light of

Josephus' accounts of the Jewish factions that fought for control of the temple in the Roman-Jewish war. Most explications of this scenario ride on the caveat that, of course, Jesus' "revolution" was different because it was nonviolent and aimed at spiritual reform. But this theory doesn't work. Mark's gospel was written in the 70s and his account of Jesus in Jerusalem is anachronistic, for he plays on the recent memories of the war to gain plausibility for his story. And the revolts from 66 to 73 C.E. reported by Josephus can hardly be used as examples of any earlier incidents of popular protest or of aristocratic intrigue with designs upon control of the temple system. The theory is especially flawed, however, because of its faulty assumption that a call for revolt against the Romans and/or the temple establishment in Jerusalem would have motivated Galileans to rally around Jesus. There is nothing in Q to suggest anything of the kind.

The theory of sectarian formation is rooted in a long history of the Christian claim to be the new or true "Israel," or people of God. According to this theory, the early church emerged from within Judaism as the fulfillment of Israel's promise, as its righteous remnant, or as those who faithfully recognized Jesus as the messiah. Its twentieth-century version is couched in the apocalyptic hypothesis according to which "the Jews" were undone by signs of divine displeasure and impending judgment. All were both fearful and expectant before the coming of the messiah. Voilà. Jesus appeared and those who recognized him naturally constituted the remnant of the worthy. The problem with this scenario is that neither apocalyptic hysteria nor the sense of being a righteous remnant is a plausible motivation for generating a movement in Galilee. An apocalyptic message only works as a motivation to form a sect from within the world of Jewish religious identity to which one already belonged. There is no hint of the formation of a Jewish sect in Q^1. And even in Q^2 where apocalyptic idiom occurs, the primary loyalty is to a Jesus movement based on some other attraction.

The theory of a utopian program is a recent scholarly proposal. The notion is that the situation in Galilee had become desperate for the peasants. Persistent poverty, plundering, and a system of double taxation (to Rome as well as to the Jerusalem temple) had rendered many homeless and reduced the people to starving. Jesus appeared with a vision of the kingdom of God. He talked about the evil of riches. He said that God would provide food and clothing. He performed healings and the crowds gathered around. Unfortunately for this theory, archeological studies of Galilee and the economic history of the Levant do not support such a picture. The notion of double taxation assumes that Roman tribute was superimposed upon an already heavy tax levied by the temple-state. It is of course true that heavy taxation of produce and the payment of tribute were standard features of the aristocratic empires in antiquity. It is also true that Roman governance was mainly a matter of securing order and taking tribute. But the Roman practice in general was to use the local system of levies, not to create new ones, and to take their bite off the top as a kind of taxation. So whether there was a system of double taxation under Herod is quite unclear. It is even less clear what happened to the temple tax system in Galilee under Herod Antipas, who had no official connection with the temple establishment in Jerusalem. In the face of such uncertainties, and lacking evidence for destitute conditions in Galilee, it is best not to assume that Jesus' main attraction was the announcement of a utopian ideal.

What then? If the Jesus movement was not generated by a passion to reform Judaism or by a revolt against foreign powers or by an economic revolution, what was its attraction? Something other than charismatic display, ecstatic religious experience, or a message of eternal salvation must have generated the movement because there is nothing in the text of Q that reflects interest of this kind. So what may its attraction have been?

Two lines of investigation are still open. One is that clues about the motivations of the people of Q may surely be found in the text of Q if we give it a fresh, close reading. The other is that a clearer picture of the social circumstances in Galilee may provide a setting that can help explain such motivations. As the story of Q unfolds it will become clear that two features of its sociology are inextricably intertwined. One is a rather strong challenge to individuals to dare a natural and simple life-style. The other is a seriousness that developed about loyalty to a group. The question, then, is whether such a *group*, based on such an unconventional call to *individual* freedom, could have been its own attraction. The answer seems to be yes, but in order to see why this was so we need to enlarge the picture of life in Galilee to include a number of cultural considerations.

The conquests of Alexander and the subsequent spread of hellenic culture have been idealized and romanticized in western thought, as has the *pax romana*. But the cultural contributions of the Greeks, and the social orders achieved by the Romans, were not unmixed blessings. That is because the Greco-Roman age also brought to an end the civilizations of the ancient near east that had been in place for three millennia or more. The social system basic to these cultures was what we now call the temple-state, a model that had been honed to perfection and replicated over and over again, whether in a more stable elaboration such as Egypt enjoyed, or as the more vulnerable near eastern kingdom. The temple-state centered, defined, and maintained the society's myths, rituals, codes of recognition, patterns of thought and behavior, social hierarchies, national boundaries, system of education, round of festivals, social ethics, laws, and the meaning of a people's labor, production, and exchange. In the wake of Alexander, temple-states crumbled and the social structure supporting these cultures was destroyed.

As for the Greek city-state, highly touted as the better way under the banner of freedom, citizenship, and autonomy, it lost its noble functions and credibility under the Macedonian heirs to Alexander's fortunes, who used it as a means of colonization and imperial control. The hellenistic city brought to the Levant Greek learning, but it did not offer franchise to the native populations, so it could not serve as a substitute for what had been destroyed. Thus the traditional hierarchies of royal power, priestly purity, and official scribal activity were gone. These were the institutions that had held together the ancient temple-states, the official structures that merged to create a single social and cultural organism. And as for the Romans, their contribution to the well-being of peoples in the Levant was a soulless superimposition of law and order, a network of military surveillance and economic exploitation that was incapable of commanding the loyalty of the peoples they governed.

Thus we are coming to understand that the Greco-Roman age was experienced as an erosion of illustrious traditions and as a fragmentation of societies whose loss was keenly felt by all the peoples of the eastern Mediterranean lands. Foreign governance within a people's home country, and the widespread displacement of people from their native lands, left many traditional social and religious functions unattended. People were left to their own devices, whether at home in an alien environment or living abroad in ghetto-like clusters throughout the empires. An explosion of human energy was unleashed in the quest to salvage what one could of one's illustrious traditions, and an amazing outpouring of human ingenuity was invested in the quest to fill the voids created by the disintegration of the older social systems.

As people moved, some cultural artifacts were portable, such as the memories, lore, myths, and literature that people cherished. These they took with them wherever they went. Other monuments to a culture could be recreated, such as shrines that transplanted in miniature a place to say one's prayers and make one's offerings to familiar heroes and gods. A shrine could be as simple as the erection of a statue at home, or a *stela,* a stone inscribed with the virtues of a god, in some public place. A shrine could be as ornate as a temple complete with imported priests, oracles, festivals, and processions. Private resident donors, city councils, and ethnic associations were often involved in the process of recognizing a foreign god and accommodating its cult. The so-called mystery religions of Isis, Osiris, Attis, Adonis, Mithra, and the Syrian goddess are examples of diaspora cults which claim to represent archaic religions and cultures rooted in other lands.

But portable artifacts and diaspora cults could not reconstitute the fully-orbed societies in which a people's cultural tradition had been inculcated. Living in an expansive multicultural world meant rubbing shoulders with others, putting pieces of one's own culture on display, and experimenting with new ways to negotiate one's place in the larger scheme of things. Three manifestations of human creativity characteristic for the Greco-Roman age will help paint the cultural setting within which the attraction of the Jesus movement can be understood.

One important phenomenon of the Greco-Roman age was the appearance of the religious and philosophical entrepreneur, sometimes called the divine man, sometimes the sophist or sage. The entrepreneur stepped into the void left vacant by the demise of traditional priestly functions at the ancient temple sites and addressed the confusion, concern, and curiosity of people confronted with a complex world that was felt to be at the mercy of the fates. Artemidorus' *Oneirocriticon,* a handbook for "Dream Interpretation," documents a profession that worked for a fee. Interpreters of dreams accumulated a large archive of lore about dreams, principles of interpretation, and useful examples of typical dreams. Interpretation focused on concerns common to people living in uncertain times—success and failure, whether a human relationship would bring well-being, and what to do in the event of loss, ill health, or untoward circumstances. Other entrepreneurs set up oracles. An example is the famous snake oracle of Alexander Abunoteichus whom Lucian portrayed as a fraud. A huge collection of magical papyri attests the profession of those who knew how to concoct potions and formulae for every eventuality. Professional physicians and charismatic healers complemented the official shrines known for their healing miracles, such as those of the god Asclepius at Epidaurus, Cos, and elsewhere. Astrologers also were regarded as professionals, as were diviners who could read the flutters of birds or the entrails of a sacrificed animal and so predict the future. And then there were the itinerant teachers who stepped forth to sell their philosophies and advice to anyone in search of guidance. Called sophists by those who sought to discount their teachings, and divine men by those who idealized them, the figure of the lone sage exemplified the individual's quest for wholeness and self-sufficiency in the midst of a world devoid of social services and supports.

A second characteristic of the Greco-Roman age was the formation of small social units variously called fellowships (*koinoniai*), festive companies (*thiosoi*), or *collegia*. These were created by people seeking support in pursuit of common interests ranging from ethnic comradeship and cultural conservation, through funeral societies, religious conventicles, and monastic communities, to include a variety of craft guilds organized for economic protection in the wild and wooly world of international trade. Because fellowships tended to be ethnically based, and thus seem to have been an apparently natural development, and because we are so accustomed to organizations such as clubs, lodges, and ethnic community centers in our own society, it may be difficult for us to grasp the significance of this novel development in social formation. It deserves recognition as a very important development in the social history of western culture. Fellowships substituted for societies that had been destroyed. Their novelty resided in a combination of the free association of individuals with membership controlled by elections, fees, and rules. To belong to such an association was therefore quite a different matter than belonging to a family, tribe, temple-state, or nation. Experimentation in the organization and function of such a fellowship was called for by the wide range of purposes to which this simple model was put. The model determined only that the members meet regularly (the average was approximately once a month), usually for a common meal, after which business and socializing became the order of the day.

A third characteristic of the Greco-Roman age was a burgeoning preoccupation with ideas, philosophies, and the writing of literature. This phenomenon may also be understood as a quest to understand a world grown problematic because of social uncertainties. Much of this intellectual activity was expressly devoted to an exploration of social issues. National epics and local histories had to be revised and romanticized in order to compete with the illustrious histories of other peoples. A new ending had to be found for epics that had celebrated the ancient temple sites. Archaic epochs were embellished as models of ideal societies in order to gain critical leverage for assessing contemporary regimes and social arrangements. The laws of Solon and Moses, the royal bearing of Hercules, David, and Osiris, and the human representations of Gilgamesh, Adam, Prometheus, and the Seven Sages were all re-searched for guidance applicable to the present state of affairs. Treatises flourished on the topics of kingship and tyranny, the ideal ruler, and the basis for laws and humanistic ethics. In general, questions related to authority and power, virtue and justice, law and well-being, were burning issues that controlled much of the philosophical discourse and literature of the time.

What if we let Galilee have its place in the Greco-Roman world? What if the people of Galilee were not isolated from the cultural mix that stimulated thought and produced social experimentation in response to the times? What if Galileans were fully aware of the cultural and intellectual forces surging through the Levant? What if we acknowledged that the compact and convoluted history of foreign conquests in Galilee had created disaffection for many Galileans, and a predisposition for social and cultural critique? What if the mix of indigenous, hellenistic, Jewish, and Roman cultures had disturbed the social equilibrium enough to challenge the traditional diffidence of the people in Galilee? What if we thought that Galileans were capable of entertaining novel notions of social identity? What then? Why then we would be ready for the story of the people of Q.

PART II

THE TEXT OF THE LOST GOSPEL

5

The Book of Q

Thivis chapter presents the text of the lost gospel. The English translation is based on the Greek texts in Matthew and Luke, which are available in John Kloppenborg's *Q Parallels* (1988). In order to arrive at a unified Greek text, I have consulted the scholarship on the reconstruction of the original text as well as the work of the Q project at Claremont. I have aimed at a fresh translation, trying to catch the original tenor in the everyday language of our own time, in order to avoid the familiar ring many of these sayings have acquired from their biblical context.

In this chapter I present two versions of the lost gospel: the original book of Q and the complete book of Q. The original book is composed only of Q^1 material. The complete book of Q incorporates all three levels of Q material. In the complete version, I have provided headings both for major sections of the text and for its smaller segments. The segments have the notation QS and are numbered for easy reference. The numeration bears no relation to biblical chapter and verse, and it differs slightly from Kloppenborg's divisions of the text. For those who may be interested in locating the Q material in the Bible or in comparing my reconstruction of the text with Kloppenborg's segmentation, a chart of correspondences is given in appendix B.

As the story of Q unfolds in part III, reference will constantly be made to the three layers of Q's compositional history. These layers are distinguished in the text by means of different typefaces, as follows:

Q^1 material, the earliest layer in the collection, is set in bold.

Q^2 material, the second layer, with compositional design, is set in regular, or lighter, type.

Q^3 material, the latest additions to the text, is set in italic.

Within the text there are notations as follows:

<> = Scholarly conjecture where textual material is no longer extant.

[ ] = Translator's note to the reader.

My advice is to read only the original book of Q before going on to the discussion of Q^1 material in chapter 6. It would then be helpful to read only the Q^2 material in the complete book the second time through, in order to savor its distinctive flavor. Q^2 material will be discussed in chapters 7 and 8. Finally, the whole text of the complete book should be read from beginning to end, paying attention to the shifts in mood as they occur and taking note of the overall design. The final shape of the text will be discussed in chapter 9.

THE ORIGINAL BOOK OF Q

<These are the teachings of Jesus.>

<Seeing the crowds, he said to his disciples,>

"How fortunate are the poor; they have God's kingdom.

How fortunate the hungry; they will be fed.

How fortunate are those who are crying; they will laugh."

"I am telling you, love your enemies, bless those who curse you, pray for those who mistreat you.

If someone slaps you on the cheek, offer your other cheek as well. If anyone grabs your coat, let him have your shirt as well.

Give to anyone who asks, and if someone takes away your belongings, do not ask to have them back.

As you want people to treat you, do the same to them.

If you love those who love you, what credit is that to you? Even tax collectors love those who love them, do they not? And if you embrace only your brothers, what more are you doing than others? Doesn't everybody do that? If you lend to those from whom you expect repayment, what credit is that to you? Even wrongdoers lend to their kind because they expect to be repaid.

Instead, love your enemies, do good, and lend without expecting anything in return. Your reward will be great, and you will be children of God.

For he makes his sun rise on the evil and on the good; he sends rain on the just and on the unjust."

"Be merciful even as your Father is merciful.

Don't judge and you won't be judged.

For the standard you use [for judging] will be the standard used against you."

"Can the blind lead the blind? Won't they both fall into a pit?

A student is not better than his teacher. It is enough for a student to be like his teacher."

"How can you look for the splinter in your brother's eye and not notice the stick in your own eye? How can you say to your brother, 'Let me remove the splinter in your eye,' when you do not see the stick in your own eye? You hypocrite, first take the stick from your own eye, and then you can see to remove the splinter that is in your brother's eye."

"A good tree does not bear rotten fruit; a rotten tree does not bear good fruit. Are figs gathered from thorns, or grapes from thistles? Every tree is known by its fruit.

The good man produces good things from his store of goods and treasures; and the evil man evil things.

For the mouth speaks from a full heart."

"Why do you call me, 'Master, master,' and not do what I say?

Everyone who hears my words and does them is like a man who built a house on rock. The rain fell, a torrent broke against the house, and it did not fall, for it had a rock foundation.

But everyone who hears my words and does not do them is like a man who built a house on sand. The rain came, the torrent broke against it, and it collapsed. The ruin of that house was great."

When someone said to him, "I will follow you wherever you go," Jesus answered, "Foxes have dens, and birds of the sky have nests, but the son of man has nowhere to lay his head."

When another said, "Let me first go and bury my father," Jesus said, "Leave the dead to bury their dead."

Yet another said, "I will follow you, sir, but first let me say goodbye to my family." Jesus said to him, "No one who puts his hand to the plow and then looks back is fit for the kingdom of God."

He said, "The harvest is abundant, but the workers are few; beg therefore the master of the harvest to send out workers into his harvest.

Go. Look, I send you out as lambs among wolves.

Do not carry money, or bag, or sandals, or staff; and do not greet anyone on the road.

Whatever house you enter, say, 'Peace be to this house!' And if a child of peace is there, your greeting will be received [literally, "your peace will rest upon him"]. But if not, let your peace return to you.

And stay in the same house, eating and drinking whatever they provide, for the worker deserves his wages. Do not go from house to house.

And if you enter a town and they receive you, eat what is set before you. Pay attention to the sick and say to them, 'God's kingdom has come near to you.'

But if you enter a town and they do not receive you, as you leave, shake the dust from your feet and say, 'Nevertheless, be sure of this, the realm of God has come to you.'"

"When you pray, say,

'Father, may your name be holy.

May your rule take place.

Give us each day our daily bread.

Pardon our debts, for we ourselves pardon everyone indebted to us.

And do not bring us to trial [into a trying situation].'"

"Ask and it will be given to you; seek and you will find; knock and the door will be opened for you.

For everyone who asks receives, and the one who seeks finds, and to the one who knocks the door will be opened.

What father of yours, if his son asks for a loaf of bread, will give him a stone, or if he asks for a fish, will give him a snake?

Therefore, if you, although you are not good, know how to give good gifts to your children, how much more will the father above give good things to those who ask him!"

"Nothing is hidden that will not be made known, or secret that will not come to light.

What I tell you in the dark, speak in the light. And what you hear as a whisper, proclaim on the housetops."

"Don't be afraid of those who can kill the body, but can't kill the soul.

Can't you buy five sparrows for two cents? Not one of them will fall to the ground without God knowing about it. Even the hairs of your head are all numbered. So don't be afraid. You are worth more than many sparrows."

Someone from the crowd said to him, "Teacher, tell my brother to divide the inheritance with me." But he said to him, "Sir, who made me your judge or lawyer?"

He told them a parable, saying, "The land of a rich man produced in abundance, and he thought to himself, 'What should I do, for I have nowhere to store my crops?' Then he said, 'I will do this. I will pull down my barns and build larger ones, and there I will store all my grain and my goods. And I will say to my soul, Soul, you have ample goods stored up for many years. Take it easy. Eat, drink, and be merry.' But God said to him, 'Foolish man! This very night you will have to give back your soul, and the things you produced, whose will they be?' That is what happens to the one who stores up treasure for himself and is not rich in the sight of God."

"I am telling you, do not worry about your life, what you will eat, or about your body, what you will wear. Isn't life more than food, and the body more than clothing?

Think of the ravens. They do not plant, harvest, or store grain in barns, and God feeds them. Aren't you worth more than the birds? Which one of you can add a single day to your life by worrying?

And why do you worry about clothing? Think of the way lilies grow. They do not work or spin. But even Solomon in all his splendor was not as magnificent. If God puts beautiful clothes on the grass that is in the field today and tomorrow is thrown into a furnace, won't he put clothes on you, faint hearts?

So don't worry, thinking, 'What will we eat,' or 'What will we drink,' or 'What will we wear?' For everybody in the whole world does that, and your father knows that you need these things.

Instead, make sure of his rule over you, and all these things will be yours as well."

"Sell your possessions and give to charity [alms]. Store up treasure for yourselves in a heavenly account, where moths and rust do not consume, and where thieves cannot break in and steal.

For where your treasure is, there your heart will also be."

He said, "What is the kingdom of God like? To what should I compare it? It is like a grain of mustard which a man took and sowed in his garden. It grew and became a tree, and the birds of the air made nests in its branches."

He also said, "The kingdom of God is like yeast which a woman took and hid in three measures of flour until it leavened the whole mass."

"Everyone who glorifies himself will be humiliated, and the one who humbles himself will be praised."

"A man once gave a great banquet and invited many. At the time for the banquet he sent his servant to say to those who had been invited, 'Please come, for everything is now ready.' But they all began to make excuses. The first said to him, 'I've bought a farm, and I must go and see it. Please excuse me.' And another said, 'I've just bought five pair of oxen and I need to check them out. Please excuse me.' And another said, 'I've just married a woman and so I can't come.' The servant came and reported this to his master. Then the owner in anger said to his servant, 'Go out quickly to the streets of the town and bring in as many people as you find.' And the servant went out into the streets and brought together everybody he could find. That way the house was filled with guests."

"Whoever does not hate his father and mother will not be able to learn from me. Whoever does not hate his son and daughter cannot belong to my school.

Whoever does not accept his cross [bear up under condemnation] and so become my follower, cannot be one of my students.

Whoever tries to protect his life will lose it; but whoever loses his life on account of me will preserve it."

"Salt is good; but if salt loses its taste, how can it be restored? It is not good for either the land or the manure pile. People just throw it out."

THE COMPLETE BOOK OF Q

Introduction

QS 1. TITLE

<These are the teachings of Jesus.>

QS 2. THE SETTING FOR THE INSTRUCTIONS

[The Q^2 addition of the John material erased the original introduction to Jesus and his teachings. See QS 7.]

John's Preaching

QS 3. THE APPEARANCE OF JOHN

<John appeared in the countryside along the Jordan river.>

QS 4. JOHN'S ADDRESS TO THE PEOPLE

He said to the people who were coming out to be plunged [into the river], "You offspring of vipers! Who warned you to flee from the coming fury? Change your ways if you have changed your mind. Don't say, 'We have Abraham as our father.' I am telling you, God can raise up children for Abraham from these stones. Even now the ax is aimed at the root of the trees. Every tree that does not bear good fruit is cut down and thrown into the fire."

QS 5. JOHN'S PREDICTION OF SOMEONE TO COME

"I am plunging you in water; but one who is stronger than I is coming, one whose sandals I am not worthy to touch. He will overwhelm you with holy spirit and fire. His winnowing fork is in his hand to clear his threshing floor and gather the wheat into his granary. The chaff he will burn with a fire that no one can put out."

The Temptations of Jesus

QS 6. JESUS TEMPTED BY THE ACCUSER

Then Jesus was led into the wilderness by the spirit for trial by the accuser [diabolos, the prosecuting angel of the heavenly court]. He fasted for forty days and was hungry. The accuser said, "If you are the son of God, tell this stone to become bread." But Jesus answered, "It is written, 'No one lives by bread alone.'" Then the accuser took him to Jerusalem and placed him at the highest point of the temple and said to him, "If you are the son of God, throw yourself down, for it is written, 'He will command his angels to protect you,' and 'They will carry you with their hands so that your foot will not strike a stone.'" But Jesus answered him, "It is written, 'You shall not put the lord, your God to the test.'" Then the accuser took him to a very high mountain and showed him all the kingdoms of the world and their splendor, and he said to him, "All these I will give you if you will do obeisance and reverence me." But Jesus answered him, "It is written, 'You shall reverence the lord your God and serve him alone.'" Then the accuser left him.

Jesus' Teaching

QS 7. INTRODUCTION

<Seeing the crowds, he said to his disciples,>

QS 8. ON THOSE WHO ARE FORTUNATE

"How fortunate are the poor; they have God's kingdom.

How fortunate the hungry; they will be fed.

How fortunate are those who are crying; they will laugh.

How fortunate you are when they reproach you as good-for-nothings because of the son of man [a Semitic idiom for "human being," capable of being used as a circumlocution, thus, "because of me" or "because of Jesus"]. Rejoice, be glad, you have a great reward in heaven. That is exactly how they treated the prophets."

QS 9. ON RESPONDING TO REPROACH

"I am telling you, love your enemies, bless those who curse you, pray for those who mistreat you.

If someone slaps you on the cheek, offer your other cheek as well. If anyone grabs your coat, let him have your shirt as well.

Give to anyone who asks, and if someone takes away your belongings, do not ask to have them back.

As you want people to treat you, do the same to them.

If you love those who love you, what credit is that to you? Even tax collectors love those who love them, do they not? And if you embrace only your brothers, what more are you doing than others? Doesn't everybody do that? If you lend to those from whom you expect repayment, what credit is that to you? Even wrongdoers lend to their kind because they expect to be repaid.

Instead, love your enemies, do good, and lend without expecting anything in return. Your reward will be great, and you will be children of God.

For he makes his sun rise on the evil and on the good; he sends rain on the just and on the unjust."

QS 10. ON MAKING JUDGMENTS

"Be merciful even as your Father is merciful.

Don't judge and you won't be judged.

For the standard you use [for judging] will be the standard used against you."

QS 11. ON TEACHERS AND STUDENTS

"Can the blind lead the blind? Won't they both fall into a pit?

A student is not better than his teacher. It is enough for a student to be like his teacher."

QS 12. ON HYPOCRISY

"How can you look for the splinter in your brother's eye and not notice the stick in your own eye? How can you say to your brother, 'Let me remove the splinter in your eye,' when you do not see the stick in your own eye? You hypocrite, first take the stick from your own eye, and then you can see to remove the splinter that is in your brother's eye."

QS 13. ON INTEGRITY

"A good tree does not bear rotten fruit; a rotten tree does not bear good fruit. Are figs gathered from thorns, or grapes from thistles? Every tree is known by its fruit.

The good man produces good things from his store of goods and treasures; and the evil man evil things.

For the mouth speaks from a full heart."

QS 14. ON PRACTICAL OBEDIENCE

"Why do you call me, 'Master, master,' and not do what I say?

Everyone who hears my words and does them is like a man who built a house on rock. The rain fell, a torrent broke against the house, and it did not fall, for it had a rock foundation.

But everyone who hears my words and does not do them is like a man who built a house on sand. The rain came, the torrent broke against it, and it collapsed. The ruin of that house was great."

What John and Jesus Thought About Each Other

QS 15. THE OCCASION

After Jesus said these things, he went into Capernaum. And a centurion [Roman army officer in charge of 100 soldiers], when he heard about Jesus, came to him begging him, "My servant is lying paralyzed at home about to die." Jesus said to him, "I will come and heal him." The centurion answered him, "Sir, I am not worthy to have you enter my home. Just say the word and my servant will be healed. For I am a man under orders, with soldiers under me. I say to one 'Go,' and he goes; to another, 'Come,' and he comes, and to my slave, 'Do this,' and he does it." When Jesus heard this he was amazed and said to those who were following him, "I tell you, I have not found such confidence in Israel." And he said to the centurion, "Go." And when the centurion returned home, he found the servant well.

QS 16. JOHN'S INQUIRY

John heard about this and sent his disciples to ask, "Are you the one to come, or should we look for another?" Jesus said, "Go and tell John what you hear and see: the blind recover their sight, the lame walk, lepers are cleansed [healed and therefore made 'clean'], the deaf hear, the dead are raised, and the poor are given good news.

And fortunate is the one who is not disturbed [at hearing these things] about me."

QS 17. WHAT JESUS SAID ABOUT JOHN

When John's disciples left, Jesus began to speak to the crowds about John:

"What did you go out into the wilderness to see? A reed shaking in the wind? [The implied answer is no.] Then tell me what you went out to see. A man in soft clothes? Look, those who wear soft clothes live in palaces. So what did you expect? A prophet? Yes, of course, and much more than a prophet. This is the one referred to in the writings, 'Look, I am sending my messenger before you. He will prepare your path ahead of you.' I am telling you, no one born of a woman is greater than John; yet the least in God's realm is greater than he."

QS 18. WHAT JESUS SAID ABOUT THIS GENERATION

"To what shall I compare this generation? It is like children sitting in the marketplace and calling to each other: 'We played the pipes for you and you did not dance.' 'We sang a dirge and you did not wail.' For John did not come eating or drinking, and they are saying, 'He is demon possessed.' The son of man [that is, Jesus; see QS 8] has come eating and drinking, and they say, 'Look at him, a glutton and a drunkard, a friend of tax collectors and sinners.' But in spite of what they say, wisdom's children show that she is right."

Instructions for the Jesus Movement

QS 19. ON BECOMING A FOLLOWER OF JESUS

When someone said to him, "I will follow you wherever you go," Jesus answered, "Foxes have dens, and birds of the sky have nests, but the son of man has nowhere to lay his head."

When another said, "Let me first go and bury my father," Jesus said, "Leave the dead to bury their dead."

Yet another said, "I will follow you, sir, but first let me say goodbye to my family." Jesus said to him, "No one who puts his hand to the plow and then looks back is fit for the kingdom of God."

QS 20. ON WORKING FOR THE KINGDOM OF GOD

He said, "The harvest is abundant, but the workers are few; beg therefore the master of the harvest to send out workers into his harvest.

Go. Look, I send you out as lambs among wolves.

Do not carry money, or bag, or sandals, or staff; and do not greet anyone on the road.

Whatever house you enter, say, 'Peace be to this house!' And if a child of peace is there, your greeting will be received [literally, 'your peace will rest upon him']. But if not, let your peace return to you.

And stay in the same house, eating and drinking whatever they provide, for the worker deserves his wages. Do not go from house to house.

And if you enter a town and they receive you, eat what is set before you. Pay attention to the sick and say to them, 'God's kingdom has come near to you.'

But if you enter a town and they do not receive you, as you leave, shake the dust from your feet and say, 'Nevertheless, be sure of this, the realm of God has come to you.'"

Pronouncements Against Towns That Reject the Movement

QS 21. THE UNRECEPTIVE TOWN

"I am telling you, Sodom will have a lighter punishment on the day of judgment than that town."

QS 22. THE GALILEAN TOWNS

"Woe for you, Chorazin! Woe for you, Bethsaida! If the forceful deeds performed among you had been done in Tyre and Sidon, they would have changed their ways long ago, sitting in sackcloth and ashes. In the judgment Tyre and Sidon will have a lighter punishment than you.

And you, Capernaum, do you think you will be praised to high heaven? You will be told to go to hell."

Congratulations to Those Who Accept the Movement

QS 23. ON THE ONE WHO RECEIVES THE WORKER

"Whoever welcomes you welcomes me, and whoever welcomes me welcomes the one who sent me."

QS 24. ON THE ONE WHO RECEIVES REVELATION

Jesus declared, "I am grateful to you, father, master of heaven and earth, because you have kept these things hidden from the wise and understanding and revealed them to babies. Truly I am grateful, father, for that was your gracious will.

Authority over all the world has been given to me by my father. No one recognizes the son except the father; and no one knows who the father is except the son and the one to whom the son chooses to reveal him."

QS 25. ON THE ONE WHO HEARS AND SEES

"How fortunate are the eyes that see what you see! for I'm telling you that many prophets and kings longed to see what you see and did not see it, and to hear what you hear and did not hear it."

Confidence in the Father's Care

QS 26. HOW TO PRAY

"When you pray, say,

'Father, may your name be holy.

May your rule take place.

Give us each day our daily bread.

Pardon our debts, for we ourselves pardon everyone indebted to us.

And do not bring us to trial [into a trying situation].'"

QS 27. CONFIDENCE IN ASKING

"Ask and it will be given to you; seek and you will find; knock and the door will be opened for you.

For everyone who asks receives, and the one who seeks finds, and to the one who knocks the door will be opened.

What father of yours, if his son asks for a loaf of bread, will give him a stone, or if he asks for a fish, will give him a snake?

Therefore, if you, although you are not good, know how to give good gifts to your children, how much more will the father above give good things to those who ask him!"

Controversy with This Generation

QS 28. ON KINGDOMS IN CONFLICT

He exorcised a demon that had made a man mute, and when the demon had been thrown out, the dumb man spoke and the people marveled. But some said, "He exorcises demons by Beelzebul, the ruler of demons."

Knowing their thoughts, he said to them, "Every kingdom divided against itself is destroyed, and every house divided against itself will not stand. And if Satan also is divided against himself, how will his kingdom stand?

You say that I exorcise demons by Beelzebul. If I exorcise demons by Beelzebul, by whom do your sons exorcise them? Why not ask them and see what they say?

But if I exorcise demons by the finger of God, then God's rule has caught up with you.

When a strong man, fully armed, guards his own palace his possessions are safe. But when someone stronger than he attacks and conquers him, the stronger demolishes his defenses and then plunders his goods."

Making Sure Whose Side You Are On

QS 29. THOSE FOR AND THOSE AGAINST

"Whoever is not with me is against me, and the one who does not gather with me scatters."

QS 30. THE RETURN OF AN EVIL SPIRIT

"When an unclean spirit [demon] leaves a person, it wanders through arid regions seeking rest without finding it. Then it says, 'I will return to my house from which I came.' And when it comes it finds the house swept and tidy. Then it goes and brings seven other spirits more wicked than itself, and they go in and settle there. And the last state of that person is worse than the first."

QS 31. HEARING AND KEEPING THE TEACHING OF GOD

As he was saying these things, a woman from the crowd spoke up and said to him, "How fortunate is the womb that bore you, and the breasts that you sucked!" But he said, "How fortunate, rather, are those who listen to God's teaching and observe it!"

Judgment on This Generation

QS 32. THE SIGN OF JONAH

Some said to him, "Teacher, we wish to see a sign from you."

He answered them, "A wicked generation looks for a sign, but no sign will be shown to it, except the sign of Jonah.

For as Jonah became a sign to the Ninevites, so will the son of man be to this generation.

The queen of the south [the queen of Sheba] will arise at the judgment and condemn this generation. For she came from the ends of the earth to hear the wisdom of Solomon, and look, something greater than Solomon is here.

The men of Nineveh will arise at the judgment and condemn this generation. For they repented at the preaching of Jonah, and look, something greater than Jonah is here."

True Enlightenment

QS 33. THE LAMP AND THE EYE

"No one lights a lamp and puts it under a bushel basket, but on a lampstand. And those in the house see the light.

The lamp of the body is the eye. If your eye is good your whole body will be full of light. But if it is bad your whole body will be full of darkness. If the light in you is darkness, how great is that darkness."

Pronouncements Against the Pharisees

QS 34. O YOU PHARISEES

"Shame on you Pharisees! for you are scrupulous about giving a tithe [tenth] of mint and dill and cumin to the priests, but you neglect justice and the love of God.

These things you ought to have done, without neglecting the others.

Shame on you Pharisees! for you clean the outside of the cup and the dish, but inside you are full of greed and incontinence. Foolish Pharisees! Clean the inside and the outside will also be clean.

Shame on you Pharisees! for you love the front seats in the assemblies and greetings in the marketplaces. Shame on you! for you are like graves, outwardly beautiful, but full of pollution inside.

Shame on you lawyers! for you load people with burdens heavy to bear, but you yourselves refuse to carry even a light load.

Shame on you! for you erect memorials for the prophets, the prophets your fathers killed. Thus you witness and consent to the deeds of your fathers; for they killed the prophets and you build monuments for them.

For this reason the wisdom of God said, 'I will send them prophets and wise men, some of whom they will kill and persecute,' in order to hold this generation accountable for the blood of all the prophets shed from the foundation of the world, from the blood of Abel to the blood of Zechariah who perished between the altar and the sanctuary. Truly, I tell you, this generation will be held accountable.

Shame on you lawyers! for you have taken the key of knowledge away from the people. You yourselves do not enter the kingdom of God, and you prevent those who would enter from going in."

On Anxiety and Speaking Out

QS 35. ON SPEAKING OUT

"Nothing is hidden that will not be made known, or secret that will not come to light.

What I tell you in the dark, speak in the light. And what you hear as a whisper, proclaim on the housetops."

QS 36. ON FEAR

"Don't be afraid of those who can kill the body, but can't kill the soul.

Rather fear the one who is able to destroy both body and soul in Gehenna [hell fire].

Can't you buy five sparrows for two cents? Not one of them will fall to the ground without God knowing about it. Even the hairs of your head are all numbered. So don't be afraid. You are worth more than many sparrows."

QS 37. ON PUBLIC CONFESSIONS

"Every one who admits in public that they know me, the son of man will acknowledge before the angels of God [heavenly court]. But the one who disowns me in public, the son of man will disown before the angels of God.

Whoever makes a speech against the son of man will be forgiven. But whoever speaks against the holy spirit will not be forgiven.

When they bring you before the assemblies of the people [synagogues or town meetings], don't worry about what you are to say. When the time comes, the holy spirit will teach you what you are to say."

On Personal Goods

QS 38. FOOLISH POSSESSIONS

Someone from the crowd said to him, "Teacher, tell my brother to divide the inheritance with me." But he said to him, "Sir, who made me your judge or lawyer?"

He told them a parable, saying, "The land of a rich man produced in abundance, and he thought to himself, 'What should I do, for I have nowhere to store my crops?' Then he said, 'I will do this. I will pull down my barns and build larger ones, and there I will store all my grain and my goods. And I will say to my soul, Soul, you have ample goods stored up for many years. Take it easy. Eat, drink, and be merry.' But God said to him, 'Foolish man! This very night you will have to give back your soul, and the things you produced, whose will they be?' That is what happens to the one who stores up treasure for himself and is not rich in the sight of God."

QS 39. ON FOOD AND CLOTHING

"I am telling you, do not worry about your life, what you will eat, or about your body, what you will wear. Isn't life more than food, and the body more than clothing?

Think of the ravens. They do not plant, harvest, or store grain in barns, and God feeds them. Aren't you worth more than the birds? Which one of you can add a single day to your life by worrying?

And why do you worry about clothing? Think of the way lilies grow. They do not work or spin. But even Solomon in all his splendor was not as magnificent. If God puts beautiful clothes on the grass that is in the field today and tomorrow is thrown into a furnace, won't he put clothes on you, faint hearts?

So don't worry, thinking, 'What will we eat,' or 'What will we drink,' or 'What will we wear?' For everybody in the whole world does that, and your father knows that you need these things.

Instead, make sure of his rule over you, and all these things will be yours as well."

QS 40. ON HEAVENLY TREASURE

"Sell your possessions and give to charity [alms]. Store up treasure for yourselves in a heavenly account, where moths and rust do not consume, and where thieves cannot break in and steal.

For where your treasure is, there your heart will also be."

The Coming Judgment

QS 41. THE HOUR

"Be sure: If the owner of a house knew when a thief was coming, he wouldn't leave his house to be broken into.

You also must be ready. For the son of man is coming at an hour you do not expect."

QS 42. ON FAITHFULNESS

"Who then is the faithful and wise servant, when one is held responsible to serve the household meals at the proper time? Fortunate is the servant whom the master finds doing just that. I tell you for sure, his master will promote him and give him charge of all his possessions. But if that servant says to himself, 'My master is delayed' and begins to mistreat his fellow servants and to eat and drink with the wayward crowd, the master will come on a day when he does not expect him, at an hour he does not know. He will punish him severely and consign him to the destiny of those who are unfaithful."

QS 43. FIRE AND DIVISION

"I came to strike fire on the earth, and how I wish that it were already aflame!

Do you think that I have come to bring peace on earth? No, not peace, but a sword.

For I have come to create conflict between a man and his father, disagreement between a daughter and her mother, and estrangement between a daughter-in-law and her mother-in-law. A person's enemies will be one's own kin."

QS 44. SIGNS OF THE TIMES

He said to the crowds, "When you see a cloud rising in the west you say 'It is going to rain'; and so it does. When a south wind is blowing you say, 'It will be hot'; and so it happens. If you know how to read the signs of the sky, why can't you judge the signs of the times? Why don't you judge for yourselves what is right?"

QS 45. SETTLING ACCOUNTS

"Make an effort to settle with your accuser while you are with him on the way to court. If you don't, he will drag you to the judge, the judge will hand you over to the guard, and the guard will throw you in prison. I am telling you, you will never get out until you have paid the very last penny."

Parables of the Kingdom

QS 46. THE MUSTARD AND THE YEAST

He said, "What is the kingdom of God like? To what should I compare it? It is like a grain of mustard which a man took and sowed in his garden. It grew and became a tree, and the birds of the air made nests in its branches."

He also said, "The kingdom of God is like yeast which a woman took and hid in three measures of flour until it leavened the whole mass."

The Two Ways

QS 47. THE NARROW GATE AND CLOSED DOOR

"Strive to enter by the narrow door, for many, I tell you, will try to enter by it and will not be able.

Once the owner of the house has locked the door, you will stand outside, knock at the door, and say, 'We ate and drank with you, and you taught in our streets.' But he will say to you, 'I do not know where you are from. Get away from me, all you unrighteous people.'"

QS 48. EXCLUSION FROM THE KINGDOM

"Many will come from east and west and sit at table in the kingdom of God.

There will be wailing and clenching of teeth when you see Abraham, Isaac, Jacob, and all the prophets in the kingdom of God and you yourselves excluded.

Look, the last will be first, and the first will be last."

QS 49. LAMENT OVER JERUSALEM

"O Jerusalem, Jerusalem, killing the prophets and stoning those who are sent to you! How often would I have gathered your children together as a hen gathers her brood under her wings, and you refused.

Look, your house is left desolate. Now, I tell you, you will not see me until you say, 'Blessed is the one who comes in the name of the Lord.'"

The True Followers of Jesus

QS 50. ON HUMILITY

"Everyone who glorifies himself will be humiliated, and the one who humbles himself will be praised."

QS 51. THE GREAT SUPPER

"A man once gave a great banquet and invited many. At the time for the banquet he sent his servant to say to those who had been invited, 'Please come, for everything is now ready.' But they all began to make excuses. The first said to him, 'I've bought a farm, and I must go and see it. Please excuse me.' And another said, 'I've just bought five pair of oxen and I need to check them out. Please excuse me.' And another said, 'I've just married a woman and so I can't come.' The servant came and reported this to his master. Then the owner in anger said to his servant, 'Go out quickly to the streets of the town and bring in as many people as you find.' And the servant went out into the streets and brought together everybody he could find. That way the house was filled with guests."

QS 52. ON THE COST OF BEING A DISCIPLE

"Whoever does not hate his father and mother will not be able to learn from me. Whoever does not hate his son and daughter cannot belong to my school.

Whoever does not accept his cross [bear up under condemnation] and so become my follower, cannot be one of my students.

Whoever tries to protect his life will lose it; but whoever loses his life on account of me will preserve it."

QS 53. SAVORLESS SALT

"Salt is good; but if salt loses its taste, how can it be restored? It is not good for either the land or the manure pile. People just throw it out."

Community Rules

QS 54. WHEN TO REJOICE

"What do you think? If a man had a hundred sheep and lost one of them, wouldn't he leave the ninety-nine and go look for the one that was lost? And if he should find it, I tell you, he will rejoice more over that one sheep than over the ninety-nine that did not go astray.

Or which woman, if she had ten drachmas [silver coins] and lost one, would not light a lamp, sweep the house, and look until she finds it? And when she finds it, she invites her friends and neighbors in saying, 'Rejoice with me for I have found the drachma which I'd lost.'"

QS 55. EITHER/OR

"No one can serve two masters. Either he hates the one and loves the other, or he is loyal to one and despises the other. You cannot serve God and wealth [*mammon*]."

QS 56. THE KINGDOM AND THE LAW

"The law of Moses and the prophets [of Israel] were authorities until John. Since then the kingdom of God has been overpowered by violent men.

It is easier for the heavens and the earth to pass away than for one stroke of the law to lose its force.

Everyone who divorces his wife commits adultery, and the one who marries a divorced woman commits adultery."

QS 57. ON SCANDALS

"Scandals are sure to come; but shame on the one through whom they come. It would be better for him if a millstone were hung around his neck and he were thrown into the sea than for him to lead astray one of these little people."

QS 58. ON FORGIVENESS

"If your brother sins, warn him. If he listens to you, forgive him. Even if he sins against you seven times in a day, you must forgive him."

"If you have faith like a grain of mustard, you could say to this mulberry tree, 'Begone and plant yourself in the sea,' and it would obey you."

The Final Judgment

"The days are coming when they will say to you, 'Look, he is in the wilderness.' Do not go out. Or 'Look, he is sequestered in some house.' Do not follow them. For just as lightning flashes and lights up the sky from one side to the other, so it will be on the day when the son of man appears.

Just as it was in the days of Noah, so it will be on the day of the son of man. They ate, they drank, they married, they were given in marriage right up until the day when Noah entered the ark. Then the flood came and took them all.

In the days of Lot it was the same—they ate, they drank, they bought, they sold, they planted, they built. But on the day when Lot left Sodom, fire and sulfur rained down from heaven and destroyed them all.

This is how it will be on the day when the son of man appears.

I am telling you, on that night there will be two in the field. One will be seized and the other left. Two women will be grinding together. One will be taken and the other left.

Where the corpse is, there the eagles [vultures?] will gather."

QS 61. SQUARING ACCOUNTS

"That day is like a man who took a trip. He called his servants together and gave them full responsibility for his possessions. To one he gave five talents [a large sum of money], to another two, to another one. When he returned the master ordered his servants to settle their accounts. The first said, 'Sir, your five talents have earned another five talents.' The master said to him, 'Well done, good servant. You have been reliable in financial matters; I will put you in charge of more important affairs.' The second approached and said, 'Sir, your two talents have earned another two talents.' The master said to him, 'Well done, good servant. You have been reliable in financial matters; I will put you in charge of more important affairs.' The third approached and said, 'Sir, I was afraid, because you are a hard man. You withdraw what you did not deposit, and you reap where you did not sow. Here is your talent which I safely hid away for you.' His master said to him, 'You good-for-nothing servant. You knew that I reap what I did not sow? Why then didn't you invest my money so that when I returned I might get it back with interest?' 'Take the talent from him and give it to the one who has the ten talents.'

I tell you, everyone who has will receive more, and from the one who does not have, even what he has will be taken away."

QS 62. JUDGING ISRAEL

"And you who have followed me will sit on thrones, judging the twelve tribes of Israel."

PART III

THE
RECOVERY
OF A
SOCIAL
EXPERIMENT

6

Dancing to the Pipes

Q is packed with bright, memorable sayings. Some are pithy aphorisms, such as "Don't judge and you won't be judged." Others ride on picturesque images like gathering figs from a thornbush or what happens to tasteless salt. Exhortations that recommend striking behavior abound, as in the injunction to offer the other cheek when slapped. Succinctly phrased observations on the everyday world collide with clever conclusions about the wily ways of human pursuits. Anecdotes, parables, colorful condensations of epic lore, and pointed apocalyptic pronouncements fill the horizon of an imaginative world that stands to challenge the status quo. Q bristles with critical judgments on truths held to be self-evident and social conventions that most people would have taken for granted. Q's challenge to its readers was to have another look at their world and dare to dance to a different tune.

However, sorting through these sayings to find the reasons for such talk is a difficult exercise. At first one has the impression of a motley collection of ad hoc material put together in a helter-skelter fashion. One hardly knows what to make of it as a whole. The older theory about Q's composition was based on this impression. It held that these sayings traveled separately in oral tradition, that each saying was considered an important pronouncement in its own right, and that each was added to various collections made at different times for the purpose of convenience and the preservation of sayings held to be sacred because Jesus had said them. Compositional design was therefore not to be expected.

This theory still has some value, for it recognizes that Q was reworked at several stages in a community that collected and cultivated these sayings over a long period. Many of the sayings seem out of place, appearing to reflect different periods in the life of the community. Some sayings suggest a very early period in the community's life ("Don't worry, you are worth more than the birds"), while others deal with issues and questions that could only have arisen later ("Rejoice when they reproach you; that is exactly how they treated the prophets"). And some sayings appear to have been added to the collection in order to address the situation of the community in the period after the Jewish war ("Jerusalem, Jerusalem, your house is left desolate"). But as soon as one sees that the sayings cluster and that clustering shows signs of purpose, a closer analysis is necessary.

Recent studies have shown that it is possible to be quite precise about the reasons for the clusters and their arrangement in the larger collection. One can see blocks of material organized by theme, sayings that illustrate or comment upon others, and small units of what the Greeks would have called a complete argumentation. Frequently, the way sayings are grouped or ordered makes a point. Sometimes a saying offers a specific interpretation of a preceding unit of material, or draws a conclusion that redirects the significance of a theme and points to the next cluster. If one pays careful attention to shifts in features such as grammar, tenor, formal characteristics, and implied audience, strategies can be discerned that indicate compositional design rather than simple aggregation.

Discrete stages in the literary history of such a collection are much more difficult to identify. That is because, in the nature of the case, rearrangements in the order of proverbial material frequently erase the design of previous collections. And, since it is always the arrangement of proverbial material that provides the literary context for interpreting a particular figure of speech, earlier connotations are easily lost.

A breakthrough occurred when it was seen that seven clusters of sayings in Q share distinctive features that are missing in the rest of the material. Some of these clusters are carefully composed rhetorical units, and all of them address a coherent set of issues with the same audience in view and the same concerns in mind. When analyzed, these compositions do not need the rest of Q in order to make sense as a set of instructions. Further study established that the scribes responsible for Q as a whole had reason not to entirely erase the design of this earlier collection. That fortuitous accident of scribal history, retaining earlier instructional material that happened to be in the form of small compositions, makes it possible to isolate an earlier layer of tradition in Q and thus an earlier stage in the history of the Q community. These seven clusters are now recognized as the remains of the earliest collection of sayings in the Q tradition, the layer of Q material called Q^1. They are precious nuggets indeed.

A thorough account of the scholarly excavation of these foundation stones is hardly possible, for the labor has been painstaking and the arguments intricate. But we need to understand the reasons scholars have marshalled for being so sure about the assignment of these clusters to the early layer of the Q tradition. Some of these reasons have to do with the identification of "seams," places where it is obvious that sayings were added or joined to others when elaborating or expanding upon themes. In order to be certain about seams, a mastery of Greek syntax is required, but even in English translation thematic shifts are easily seen, and careful attention to the sequence of material will often reveal the logic of primary and secondary considerations in the development of themes and the conjunction of blocks or units of speech. An example is the reference to Sodom in QS 21, a saying that picks up on the immediately preceding Q^1 saying about an unreceptive town and shifts to the Q^2 theme of judgment on Galilean towns elaborated in the sayings that follow.

Identifying seams where material was added to prior material is a standard procedure in the study of sayings collections and instructional handbooks of antiquity. Seams tell us that collections were frequently changed in the process of transmission by means of notations, additions, deletions, and the reorganization of material. Sayings collections, called *gnomologia* (from *gnome*, meaning "maxim"), were not considered sacred literature that should be left intact and passed on just as it had been received.

A second set of reasons has to do with the coherence of a given layer of material in the development of a tradition. Reading through the document as a whole, different types of material that share similar features begin to emerge. Features of importance for determining the coherence of a layer of tradition include themes (such as the announcement of judgment in Q^2), style (such as the imperatives in Q^1), and rhetorical strategies (such as the appeal to nature as an argument in Q^1). The form of address to a particular audience can also help identify a layer of material as can a certain attitude toward the world. The similarity of literary genres and the order and organization of material are also clear signs of the coherence of a particular layer of tradition. In the case of Q, three distinct layers have been identified, which are called Q^1, Q^2, and Q^3. Two of these, Q^1 and Q^2, are clearly coherent in style and content. Q^2 is also coherent in organization. Q^3 consists only of fragmentary additions, but these fragments do share a distinctive set of themes. Thus each layer can be understood as a stage in the reinterpretation of the teachings of Jesus.

A third set of reasons for knowing that the aphoristic material in Q^1 is earlier than the prophetic pronouncements in Q^2 or the mythology of Q^3 has to do with matters pertaining to sequence in the growth of a tradition. In order to establish sequence, scholars pay attention to the logical and rhetorical effect of the seams between layers of coherent material. The effect of seams on the meaning of adjoining units, and consistent patterns of framing one type of material by another type of material, frequently reveal attempts to resignify previous sayings. It is often the case that authors of later additions show knowledge of and interest in the material they framed, whereas the authors of earlier material do not show any knowledge of the later material. If the earlier material does not need the later material to make its point, the direction of development is given. Since Q^2 presupposes and depends on Q^1, whereas Q^1 makes perfectly good sense as the discourse of a community without Q^2, the stages of composition must have run from Q^1 to Q^2.

Common sense can also be called upon to reconstruct the sequence of these layers of tradition. For example, it is not reasonable to think that the playful style of repartee characteristic of Q^1 entered the tradition after its discourse had taken on the serious and hostile stance toward the world characteristic of Q^2.

This chapter focuses on the sayings in Q^1. The plan is to identify the nature of this discourse, recreate the social and conceptual world to which the style belonged, and use the content of its instruction to reconstruct the earliest period of the Q movement. The seven clusters assigned to Q^1 are the following:

1. Jesus' Teaching
   QS 8 ON THOSE WHO ARE FORTUNATE
   QS 9 ON RESPONDING TO REPROACH
   QS 10 ON MAKING JUDGMENTS
   QS 11 ON TEACHERS AND STUDENTS
   QS 12 ON HYPOCRISY
   QS 13 ON INTEGRITY
   QS 14 ON PRACTICAL OBEDIENCE

2. Instructions for the Jesus Movement
   QS 19 ON BECOMING A FOLLOWER OF JESUS
   QS 20 ON WORKING FOR THE KINGDOM OF GOD

3. Confidence in the Father's Care
   QS 26 HOW TO PRAY
   QS 27 CONFIDENCE IN ASKING

4. On Anxiety and Speaking Out
   QS 35 ON SPEAKING OUT
   QS 36 ON FEAR

5. On Personal Goods
   QS 38 FOOLISH POSSESSIONS
   QS 39 ON FOOD AND CLOTHING
   QS 40 ON HEAVENLY TREASURE

6. Parables of the Kingdom
   QS 46 THE MUSTARD AND THE YEAST

7. The True Followers of Jesus
   QS 50 ON HUMILITY
   QS 51 THE GREAT SUPPER
   QS 52 ON THE COST OF BEING A DISCIPLE
   QS 53 SAVORLESS SALT

Embedded in these blocks of Q^1 material are a number of terse sayings that give the collection its distinctive tone. An example is the saying in QS 39 that "life is more than food." Every smaller unit of composition has at least one terse saying. Some are formulated as maxims, others as imperatives, but all have the quality of aphoristic speech. Most of these aphorisms function within their units as core sayings around which the unit clusters, or on which supporting considerations build. When viewed together, moreover, these sayings make a comprehensive set of sage observations and unorthodox instructions. They delight in critical comment upon the everyday world and they recommend unconventional behavior.

These sayings put us in touch with the earliest stage of the Jesus movement when aphoristic discourse was the norm. I shall refer to this period in the social history of the movement as stage 1. The blocks of material in Q^1 build upon this aphoristic core by adding arguments to confirm its insights and by developing rules for living creatively in the light of its critical assessment of the everyday world. I shall refer to the social experience reflected in the *blocks* of Q^1 material as stage 2. To catch the flavor of discourse from the pre-Q^1 period of the Jesus movement (stage 1), it will help to list the following aphorisms (paraphrased in some cases in order to highlight the point and encourage a fresh look):

How fortunate the poor; they have the kingdom. (QS 8)

Everybody embraces their kin. (QS 9)

The standard you use will be the standard used against you. (QS 10)

Can the blind lead the blind? (QS 11)

A student is not better than his teacher. (QS 11)

A good tree does not bear rotten fruit. (QS 13)

Foxes have dens, birds have nests, but humans have no home. (QS 19)

The harvest is abundant, the workers few. (QS 20)

Everyone who asks receives. (QS 27)

Nothing is secret that will not be revealed. (QS 35)

People are worth much more than the birds. (QS 36)

Life is more than food. (QS 39)

The body is more than clothing. (QS 39)

Where your treasure, there your heart. (QS 40)

Everyone who glorifies himself will be humbled. (QS 50)

Whoever tries to protect his life will lose it. (QS 52)

If salt is saltless, it is good for nothing. (QS 53)

These sayings are not uniquely brilliant, but they are pungent. Some observations are keen, others are mildly humorous, and some are laughable in the sense that the inversion of standard practices or attitudes has been pressed to the point of absurdity. Life in general is under review and conventional values are under critique.

The sayings about the good tree and the salt are examples of using proverbial lore to score an unnerving point. Everyone would have known about good trees bearing good fruit and salt as a positive metaphor for sealing friendships and "seasoning" a human relationship. But to make the observation that a good tree does *not* bear bad fruit, or that salt is worthless if it loses its saltiness, tends to raise the eyebrows and calls for circumspection. The saying about asking and receiving, on the other hand, invites a bit of introspection, as does the saying about the standard. At first these truisms seem rather banal. But on second thought one starts wondering whether they always apply. Since none of them specifies the circumstances that must pertain in order for these sayings to always be true, they work to solicit a heightened awareness whenever one is involved in the give and take of human intercourse.

Overall, the message of these sayings is that customary pretensions are hollow. Claim to superior status based on such things as wealth, learning, possessions, secrets, rank, and power is exposed as questionable if not ridiculous. The perspective is that of the underdog, and the vision is that of those who can see through the emptiness, who already know that the emperor has no clothes. There is no sign of hostility toward those caught in the usual binds, and there is no suggestion of a program to change the system that supports questionable values. There is, however, a hint of pensiveness that attends the critique, a desire that those who hear it will come to share their perspective. The exposé is also poignant because implicit in the critique is the assumption that there must be a better way to live.

The better way is not spelled out with these aphorisms. One has only the sense that simplicity is better than pretension, that realistic assessment is a better guide than status, and that life would be more rewarding if lived another way. In general it is clear that sympathies lie with the poor, the least, the humble, the servant, and those consigned to positions without privilege, more than with their social opposites. But more than this cannot be said without additional information.

The aphoristic sayings just cited are phrased as maxims, which means they counted as statements that were considered generally true of the social world in view. If one now looks for aphoristic sayings that are phrased as imperatives, not maxims, a somewhat clearer picture of the better way to live begins to emerge. Instructions actually predominate in Q^1, and most of the blocks of Q^1 material are composed in support of instructions set forth as imperatives. Many of these imperatives are succinctly phrased and are aphoristic in character. Some of them appear to turn the observations in the maxims around and recommend a mode of behavior appropriate to the critical stance. This means that the better way of life was actually enjoined as livable. If we look for aphoristic imperatives that function as core pronouncements or clearly illustrate the theme in a cluster of Q^1 sayings, the following sayings emerge (using paraphrase again to make the point):

Rejoice when reproached. (QS 8)

Love your enemies. (QS 9)

Bless those who curse you. (QS 9)

If struck on one cheek, offer the other. (QS 9)

Give to everyone who begs. (QS 9)

Judge not and you won't be judged. (QS 10)

First remove the stick from your eye. (QS 12)

Leave the dead to bury their dead. (QS 19)

Go out as lambs among wolves. (QS 20)

Carry no money, bag, or sandals. (QS 20)

Greet no one on the road. (QS 20)

Eat what is set before you. (QS 20)

Ask and it will be given to you. (QS 27)

Don't be afraid. (QS 36)

Don't worry about your life. (QS 39)

Make sure of God's rule over you. (QS 39)

Sell your possessions and give to charity. (QS 40)

These admonitions build upon observations about life in the larger world and the need to be careful about accepting conventional codes of honor and ethics at face value. As instructions, the admonitions assume that the social world is an arena in which the people of Q will encounter those who are living by traditional rules. It is a jungle out there and the behavior enjoined is risky. One can expect to meet up with wolves and those who may curse and reproach you. The advice is to be cautious but also courageous. One should not respond in kind, but take the reproach in stride and with confidence that one is right. One should discard unnecessary trappings and live the simple, unencumbered life. When asked, give; when in need, ask. The challenge is not to be consumed with worry.

One wonders at the crisp formulations of such a curious challenge. The forthright imperatives evince a sense of seriousness, but why one should take them seriously is not expressly stated. In order to understand their attraction and significance we need a fuller picture of the way of life that is being recommended. If we expand the data base somewhat, by noting the way in which these core aphorisms are elaborated in the larger blocks of Q^1, a number of themes surface for repeated emphasis. The list includes such items as the following:

Voluntary poverty (QS 38, QS 39, QS 40)

Lending without expectation of return (QS 9)

Critique of riches (QS 8, QS 38, QS 40)

Etiquette for begging (QS 9, QS 27)

Etiquette for troublesome encounters in public (QS 20)

Nonretaliation (QS 9, QS 10, QS 20)

Rejoicing in the face of reproach (QS 8)

Severance of family ties (QS 19, QS 52)

Renunciation of needs (QS 8, QS 19, QS 39, QS 40)

Call for authenticity (QS 13, QS 35, QS 53)

Critique of hypocrisy (QS 12)

Fearless and carefree attitude (QS 36, QS 39)

Confidence in God's care (QS 26, QS 27)

Sense of vocation (QS 19, QS 20)

Discipleship without pretension (QS 11, QS 14, QS 38, QS 50, QS 52)

Singlemindedness in the pursuit of God's kingdom (QS 19, QS 39, QS 40, QS 52, QS 53)

These themes point to a way of life that historians recognize as a pattern of behavior highly recommended by popular philosophers during the hellenistic and Greco-Roman periods. Q[1] enjoins a practical ethic of the times widely known as Cynic.

New Testament scholars have often remarked on the Cynic parallels to much of the material in Q[1]. Since such similarity often comes as a surprise to Christian readers of the gospels, accustomed as they are to hearing the words of Jesus against the background of the prophetic speech of the Hebrew scriptures, few have concluded that the Cynic analogy should be taken seriously. A Cynic look-alike Jesus would, in any case, present something of an embarrassment due to the fact that the Cynics are remembered mostly for their unlovable ways. The modern caricature of the ancient Cynics usually calls to mind the unsavory figure of Diogenes of Sinope and dwells upon his habits of biting sarcasm and public obscenities. To be cynical in modern parlance is also fraught with negative connotation. Cynicism is equated with disengaged negativity, giving up rather than confronting the challenges of life. To be cynical is never thought to be helpful when questions about the meaning of life are seriously under review.

The modern caricature of the ancient Cynics is inaccurate and the modern use of the word cynic to describe the ancient Cynics is unfair. A more balanced view would see the Cynics as the Greek analogue to the Hebrew prophets. Cynics played a very important social role as critics of conventional values and oppressive forms of governance for approximately one thousand years, from the fifth century B.C.E. to the sixth century C.E. Their popular philosophy produced such figures as Antisthenes, Diogenes, Crates, Bion, Teles, Meleager, Musonius Rufus, Dio Chrysostomos, Demonax, Peregrinus Proteus, Sostratus, and Theagenes—all important figures in the history of Greek thought. Their gifts and graces ranged from the endurance of a life of renunciation in full public view, through the courage to offer social critique in high places (called *parresia*, or "boldness of speech"), to the learning and sophistication required for the espousal of Cynic views at the highest level of literary composition. Justly famous as irritants to those who lived by the system and enjoyed the blessings of privilege, prosperity, and power, the Cynics were highly regarded for their achievement in honing the virtue of self-sufficiency (*autarcheia*) in the midst of uncertain times. Epictetus' third discourse is a remarkable revelation of a Stoic's high esteem for the Cynic's calling as an important social role even during the imagined halcyon age of the Roman imperium.

The crisp sayings of Jesus in Q^1 show that his followers thought of him as a Cynic-like sage. Cynics were known for begging, voluntary poverty, renunciation of needs, severance of family ties, fearless and carefree attitudes, and troublesome public behavior. Standard themes in Cynic discourse included a critique of riches, pretension, and hypocrisy, just as in Q^1. The Cynic style of speech was distinctly aphoristic, as is that in Q^1. And Cynics were schooled in such topics as handling reproach, nonretaliation, and authenticity in following their vocation, matters at the forefront of Jesus' instructions in Q^1. If Jesus was remembered as a Cynic-like sage, we need to make sure we understand why the Cynics behaved as they did.

The public image was that of the lone beggar who had renounced the comforts of life to pit himself against the elements and practice the virtues of living with little. The Cynic wore a telltale cloak and carried a pouch for the day's morsels and the morrow's coins. A stick and sandals were also allowed, but that was all. A favorite form of anecdote, called *chreia*, used these props to characterize the Cynic's resolve, depict him in the most destitute of straits, and explore the wit required to live with hunger, cold, and public reproach. Thus, when one of his students complained of the cold, Antisthenes told him to fold his cloak double. When a child used his hands to get a drink of water, Diogenes threw his cup away and said that a child had bested him in the contest for living simply. When someone slapped him in reproach, Diogenes asked himself out loud why he had forgotten to wear his helmet that day. We have hundreds of anecdotes that follow this form. The ancient Greeks got their point and delighted in their cleverness.

These popular philosophers of a natural way of life did not wander off to suffer in silence. Their props were a setup for a little game of gotcha with the citizens of the town. Those who dared to give the Cynic any attention at all usually found themselves in contradiction. It mattered little whether a bystander or a passerby was generous or abusive. A scurrilous remark could be turned to advantage by exposing the underlying cultural taboo as ridiculous. An offer to help would also receive a put-down by triggering some remark about those who have and those who do not. Either way, the Cynic's purpose was to point out the disparities sustained by the social system and refuse to let the system put him in his place. According to one story, bystanders had commended a person for giving Diogenes a handout, whereupon he said, "Have you no praise for the one who was worthy to receive such a gift?" Thus the marketplace was the Cynic's platform, the place to display a living example of freedom from social and cultural constraints, and a place from which to address townspeople about the current state of affairs.

As might be expected, the Cynic was a favorite target for ridicule. That, of course, was just what the Cynic wanted. Public performance and close encounter with the barefaced straights was exactly what the Cynic vocation called for. The Cynic response often seemed harsh and aggressive, but to make his point there was always a touch of humor as well. The challenge for a Cynic was to see the humor in a situation and quickly turn it to advantage. A large number of Cynic anecdotes feature this ability. Some examples are the following stories about Diogenes of Sinope recorded by Diogenes Laertius in his *Lives of Eminent Philosophers*:

> When told that people were laughing at him, Diogenes said, "But I am not laughed down."
>
> When asked why he was begging from a statue, he said, "To get practice in being refused."

When asked what kind of wine he preferred, he replied, "The kind another pays for."

When someone said that life was bad, he replied, "Not life itself, but living as you do."

In our time there is no single social role with which to compare the ancient Cynics. But we do recognize the social critic and take for granted a number of ways in which social and cultural critique are expressed. These compare nicely with various aspects of the Cynic's profession. For example, we are accustomed to the social critique of political cartoonists, stand-up comedians, and especially of satire in the genre of the cabaret. All of these use humor to make their point. We are also accustomed to social critique in a more serious and philosophical vein, such as that represented by political commentary. And there is precedent for taking up an alternative life-style as social protest, from the utopian movement of the nineteenth century, to the counterculture movement of the 1960s, to the environmentalist protest of the 1980s and 1990s. The list could be greatly expanded, for much modern entertainment also sets its scenes against the backdrop of the unexamined taboos and prejudices prevailing in our time. Each of these approaches to a critical assessment of our society (satire, commentary, and alternative life-style), bears some resemblance to the profession of the Cynic sage in late antiquity.

Those who study the Cynic's wit soon discover that humor was more than an adornment to their game. Gotcha had rules, and the rules demanded that the Cynic see and take advantage of the humor in a situation. To play the game and win, the Cynic would have to accept a reproach by letting it stand as a statement that was true, a description of his behavior with which he would have to agree. "Well, you are right. I did do that. I did say that." But then, by a series of rapid mental gymnastics, the Cynic would (1) seize on some feature of his opponent's statement that revealed an assumption with which the Cynic did not agree, (2) shift to another way of looking at the situation (or to a different set of circumstances in which the statement would not apply), and (3) come up with a retort that exposed the challenger's statement as a naive cliché.

A fine example of this strategy is found in the story about Diogenes who, when reproached for entering unclean places (probably

118

a euphemism for a house of prostitution), said, "But the sun enters the privies without being defiled." The retort lets the statement of his challenger stand but shifts attention to a case in which "entrance" into an "unclean" place does not result in becoming unclean. For a moment the confusion of categories strikes one as funny. It also creates a sense of uncertainty about the assumptions underlying the challenger's reproach.

In the anecdotes cited earlier, the critical twists from challenge to response shift in idiom (laughing at/laughing down), purpose (begging to get/begging as an exercise), classification (kinds of things/kinds of human exchange), and quality (life in general/a certain lifestyle). The lack of fit when applying a common taboo to an inappropriate situation, or the gap between a challenge and the Cynic's response, creates humor. But the humor covers a devastating, if momentary, insight into the partiality of conventional perceptions and thereby offers a critical perspective on their underlying logic.

Noting the Cynic's wit should not divert our attention from their sense of vocation and purpose. Epictetus wrote that the Cynic could be likened to a spy or scout from another world or kingdom, whose assignment was to observe human behavior and render a judgment upon it. The Cynic could also be likened to a physician sent to diagnose and heal a society's ills. If asked for his credentials, the Cynic might well claim to be a messenger sent by the gods. Epictetus, at least, had no hesitation in finding such language fully appropriate, although for a Greek such a reference to divine vocation could easily be made without creating mystique or claiming supernatural status.

Thus there was method in the Cynics' madness. In fact, leading Cynics were often regarded as philosophers, and Cynicism was frequently accorded rank among the schools of Greek philosophy. The Stoics sometimes claimed the Cynics as their precursors in order to trace their own school of thought back to Socrates. But everyone knew that Cynic intellectuals did not organize schools in the grand tradition and were not impressed with abstract conceptual systems put forth to explain an ordered universe. They were much more interested in the question of virtue (*arete*), or how an individual should live given the failure of social and political systems to support what they called a natural way of life. They borrowed freely from any and every popular ethical philosophy, such as that of the Stoics, to get a certain point across. That point was the cost to one's intelligence and integrity if one blindly followed social convention and accepted its customary rationalizations.

Cynics had no trouble appealing to the intelligence of the people. They trusted the capacity of the average person to see through the rhetoric of common discourse and assess a human situation at its grubby level of personal desire and manipulation. Their task was not to pose as teachers of truths people did not know, but to challenge people to live in accordance with what they did know. They constantly called attention to the accidental nature of social status and the ephemeral rewards of material success. They criticized social structures of hierarchy, domination, and inequity by poking fun at the superficial codes of honor and shame that supported them. They took every opportunity to deflate the egos of the privileged. And they delighted in exposing the ulterior motive of calculated action.

What counted most, they said, was a sense of personal worth and integrity. One should not allow others to determine one's worth on the scale of social position. One already possessed all the resources one needed to live sanely and well by virtue of being a human being. Why not be true to the way in which the world actually impinges upon you? Say what you want and what you mean. Respond to a situation as you see it in truth, not as the usual proprieties dictate. Do not let the world squeeze you into its mold. Speak up and act out.

Verve was therefore the Cynic virtue. It was generated by a sense of self-reliance, but involved the capacity for taking a lively interest in any and every encounter with another human being. Verve could also be used as a standard to diagnose human well-being, rank human achievement, and assess the merits of social systems and their cultural symbols. Nevertheless, the Cynic critique of cultural conventions finally came to rest, not on society as a system, but on the shoulders of the individual who was willing to live "according to nature." The invitation was to take courage and swim against the social currents that threatened to overwhelm and silence a person's sense of verve.

Such a philosophy was custom-made for Galilean circumstance during the late hellenistic period. The age-old Galilean strategies for accommodating foreign rulers would have been hard pressed under the accelerated shifts in governance that were taking place. Shrugs with respect to the loyalties demanded by foreign kings, priests, and generals were no longer sufficient to survive with sanity in the face of the layered and pervasive political forces in power. Add to that the widespread malaise and sense of social uncertainty of the time, and Galilee as the land of the nations turns out to be a likely spot for a Cynic-style social critique.

The Jesus people are best understood as those who noticed the challenge of the times in Galilee. They took advantage of the mix of peoples to tweak the authority of any cultural tradition that presumed to set the standard for others. They found a way to encourage one another in the pursuit of sane and simple living. And they developed a discourse that exuded the Cynic spirit. The aphorisms in Q^1 set the Cynic-like tone, and the injunctions reveal a strong sense of vocation that corresponds to the Cynic way of life. The Jesus movement began as a home-grown variety of Cynicism in the rough and ready circumstance of Galilee before the war.

Several inferences about the movement can be drawn from this core of aphoristic material. Beliefs were not a major concern. Behavior was what mattered and the arena for the action was in public. The public sphere was not subjected to a systematic analysis, however, as if society's ills had been traced to this or that particular cause. The social world was under review, to be sure, for the behavior recommended was intentionally nonconventional, mildly disruptive, and implicitly countercultural. But there is no indication that the purpose of this behavior was to change society at large. The way society worked in general was taken for granted, in the sense of "What more can one expect?" Instead, the imperatives were addressed to individuals as if they could live by other rules if they chose to do so. It is important to see that there was no sense of external, institutional threat to motivate this change in life-style. It is especially important to see that the purpose of the change was not a social reform. The Jesus people were not organizing to fight Roman power or to reform Jewish religion.

A movement based on such a personal challenge was nevertheless capable of generating a social vision. The blocks of material in Q^1 to which we now turn are proof that many responded to the movement and that an association of like-minded persons began to form. Because of the aphoristic core, there is still a distinct undercurrent of élan in this material, some hints of humor, and a decidedly self-assured attitude that pervades the whole. But when one reads the blocks of material as units designed to argue for attitudes that should be normative for the group, the mischievous, zesty tone of the aphoristic core diminishes. As soon as this feature is seen, the Cynic analogy begins to fade.

Cynics formed a class of persons who shared a kind of mutual respect. But to be a Cynic hardly meant belonging to a movement that involved meetings or the formation of a group guided by a social notion. In the case of the Jesus people, however, signs of social formation can be detected even among the core aphorisms of Q^1, and membership in a movement fully determines the tenor of the block compositions that build upon that core. This feature of the Jesus movement appears to be distinctive.

The signs of social formation at the earliest stage of the tradition (stage 1) are (1) the shift that seems to have taken place from aphoristic discourse ("How fortunate the poor") to maxim-like generalizations ("Where your treasure, there your heart"), (2) the high incidence of imperative injunctions ("Sell your possessions and give to charity"), (3) the use of the second-person plural to address readers, (4) a heightened interest in the effect of challenging encounter on the quality of human relationships, and (5) a hint of fascination with what might be called an egalitarian view of social roles and ranking.

Turning to the stage 2 units of composition, a heightened self-awareness about belonging to a movement is obvious, and a social vision can be discerned. And now an odd thing happened. Injunctions formulated in the earlier aphoristic style evolved into rules for the group and were supported by arguments. This is most curious, for an aphoristic view of the social world, and a challenge to live against its codes, are hardly an adequate foundation for constructing positive community rules and ethical principles. Nevertheless, such a development is exactly what took place in the Jesus movement.

The block of material concerning food and clothing in QS 39 provides a clear example of this development. The unit is composed on the model of a pattern of argumentation that hellenistic teachers of rhetoric called a thesis or elaboration. In this case an especially demanding Cynic-like injunction was set forth in the form of a thesis and argued as a principle. To see the argument at work, one needs to know that in ancient rhetoric, maxims, analogies, and examples counted as proofs and that stacking them up in a certain way was considered a complete argumentation. Analogies were usually taken from the natural order, while examples were taken from life. If a complete argumentation was well done, it was thought to be persuasive. QS 39 is a complete argument on the thesis that one should not worry:

> Thesis: One should not worry about life (food) or body (clothing).
>
> Reason: Life is more than food and the body is more than clothing.
>
> Analogy: Ravens do not work for food; God provides for them. You are worth more than birds.
>
> Example: No one can add a day to life by worrying.
>
> Analogy: Lilies do not work, yet are clothed.
>
> Example: Solomon in all his splendor was not as magnificent as the lilies.
>
> Analogy: Notice the grass. If God puts beautiful clothes on the grass, won't he put clothes on you?
>
> Conclusion: One should not worry about food and drink.
>
> Example: All the nations worry about such things.
>
> Exhortation: Instead, make sure of God's rule over you, and all these things will be yours as well.

New notions and features of discourse enter the tradition in this argumentation in support of the movement's ethos. Especially important are (1) the reference to the rule or kingdom of God, (2) the express appeal to nature as a manifestation of the divine, and (3) the use of an example from epic history (Solomon). These features show that reflection on the movement had occurred and that a way had been found to give a reasoned account of its otherwise odd persuasions ("Don't worry about food and clothing"). It is important to see that the processes of social formation and rationalization go hand in hand, and that this is not the only block of material in Q^1 in which such intellectual activity can be detected.

Every block of Q^1 material exhibits the same strategy: QS 8 moves from the aphoristic "How fortunate the poor" to a tripartite characterization of the Jesus people (the poor, the hungry, and those with reason to mourn), and finally to a blessing on those who suffer rejection because of their association with the Jesus movement. QS 9 contains the Cynic-like injunction to "bless those who curse you," and then develops it into an elaborate explication of what it means to "love your enemies." QS 10 turns the cautionary injunction "Don't judge and you won't be judged" into an ethical principle with theological consequences. QS 11 takes the Cynic-like observation about the blind leading the blind as an occasion to introduce a warning not to think of oneself as more sage than one's teacher. QS 12 hovers on the border between a charge against hypocrites with sticks in their eyes and an injunction to take care of one's own blind spots before criticizing a "brother." QS 13 turns the unnerving observation about trees and their fruit into a moralistic admonition to match what you say with what you really think. QS 14 illustrates the import of a sharp riposte, "Why call me master and not do what I tell you?" with a parable about building a house that can last. If the core of the prayer in QS 26 is the request for daily bread, a Cynic theme, it has been embedded in a thoroughly theologized social piety. In QS 27 the beggar's delight, "Ask and it will be given to you," has been transformed into a comforting community maxim about the assurance of God's care. In QS 38 a Cynic-like put-down, "Sir, who made me your judge or lawyer?" leads to a moralistic parable about the tragic fate of a rich man who did not make the right "judgment" about his goods. And the thoroughly Cynic injunction in QS 40 to sell one's possessions and give to charity was turned into a promise of treasure in heaven. So QS 39 is not the only block of Q^1 material that bears the marks of reflection upon a Cynic-like movement in the process of social and ethical formation.

What, pray tell, was going on? There is only one term in all of Q^1 that refers to the movement and its purposes. That is the term kingdom of God (*basileia tou theou*), a term that connotes both the power and authority of God to rule or execute a judgment, as well as a realm or domain within which God's rule was fully actualized. The rule of God is what the Q people said they were representing in the world. For us, the problem with the term is that the Q people used it in a wide range of reference and took its meaning for granted. Scholars have therefore had a very difficult time understanding its range of connotation and finding a suitable translation. The kingdom of God is mentioned in seven sayings at the Q[1] level, as presented (sometimes paraphrased) in the following list:

> How fortunate the poor; theirs is God's kingdom. (QS 8)
>
> No one who puts his hand to the plow and then looks back is fit for God's kingdom. (QS 19)
>
> If you enter a town and they welcome you, eat what is set before you, attend to the sick, and say that "God's kingdom has come near to you." (QS 20)
>
> But if you enter a town and they do not welcome you . . . say, "Nevertheless, be sure of this, that God's rule has come to you." (QS 20)
>
> When you pray, say, "Father . . . , may your kingdom take place, give us each day our daily bread." (QS 26)
>
> Make sure of his rule over you, and these things will be yours as well. (QS 39)
>
> What is God's kingdom like? It is like a grain of mustard. . . . It is like yeast which a woman hid in three measures of flour. (QS 46)

The first thing to notice is that none of these references paints an apocalyptic view of the world, the traditional scholarly understanding of the kingdom of God as discussed in chapter 2. Neither do any assume an apocalyptic view of the world as a larger frame of reference in order to enhance the significance of the activity to which the term refers. Thus the old apocalyptic hypothesis can safely be set aside. Only in the parables of the mustard seed and the yeast does the rule of God become the object for consideration, and there it is compared to the natural process of growth. In all other instances the meaning of the term is taken for granted, and its mention is ancillary to the making of other points. The other points all have to do with common human circumstances. In each case the rule stands for something that can be accomplished, something that contrasts with the conventional, meriting a change of attitude or behavior worthy of a new vision. God's kingdom can be announced, desired, affirmed, claimed, and signaled in a given human exchange. Thus the link between the notion of the rule of God and the pattern of Q's countercultural practices is very, very strong.

This use of the term would not have sounded strange to hellenistic ears. During this period the overarching models for the discussion of social issues were those of the city, largely derived from the Greek tradition, and the kingdom, largely derived from ancient near eastern traditions. The focus of debate was the question of legitimate rule. The terms were set by classical Greek philosophy and its discussions of politics and governance. The issues had finally settled on the difference between *nomos* and *physis* as alternative foundations for society. *Nomos* meant legislation or social convention, understood as the laws enacted by the city's *demos*, or council of citizens. *Physis* meant nature, ultimately the divine order reflected in the *cosmos*. But in the post-Alexander age, issues of political import could not be grasped adequately on the model of the archaic polis, or city-state. Kings, tyrants, and generals were too much in evidence for that and, as we have seen, the Greek polis had become a vehicle for colonization, imperial expansion, and the control of foreign lands and peoples. The *demos* had met its Alexander, and the polis had encountered the ancient near eastern temple-state. So the classical terms of the debate had to shift to questions about legitimate power and privilege.

The debate finally focused on the differences between a king and a tyrant. The ideal king was one who lived and ruled in full embodiment of the highest ethical standards. Essays were written on the theme of ruling wisely and righteously. Treatises explored the possibility of combining law as legislation and law as royal edict by imagining divine kings living according to the law of nature at the archaic fountainhead of legal and epic traditions. The terminology of rule burgeoned, including such terms as rule (*basileia*), sovereignty (*arche*), authority (*exousia*), command (*hegomonia*), and power (*dynamis*).

But no one was fooled about the persons or governments actually in power during the Greco-Roman period. So these discussions about the ideal king and his kingdom took two interesting turns. One was an explosion of creative imagination that we would call myth-making. If the present forms of rule were far from the ideal, and the people knew it, something other than philosophical speculation was called for. The ideal kingdom had to be imagined as an alternative order with some relation to the present status quo. The past was plumbed for golden ages, the natural order was imagined as being governed by laws, the cosmos was viewed as the eternal city in which all human beings lived as "cosmopolitans," and hope for better times was sustained by projections of the ideal kingdom into the future.

The other turn took place in the schools of popular ethical philosophy. As frequently happens, ideal models of a social system can be used as reflectors to think through basic questions about the system. Once abstracted, however, a social model can also be used to reflect upon the individual's place in the structure of the system and on the individual as a microcosm of the system. Not surprisingly, therefore, given the malaise created by the devolution of traditional social systems and the dislocation of people from familiar structures of law, the language of rule or kingship came to be used as a metaphor for personal self-control. The term king no longer had to refer to an actual ruler, and kingdom no longer had to refer to a political domain. "King" became a metaphor of a human being at its "highest" imaginable level, whether of endowment, achievement, ethical excellence, or mythical ideal. "Kingdom" became a metaphor for the "sovereignty" manifest in the "independent bearing," "freedom," "confidence," and self-control of the superior person, the person of ethical integrity who thus could "rule" his "world" imperiously.

Stoics internalized the image of the king and idealized the individual who ruled his passions and controlled his attitudes even in circumstances where others governed his existence. Their strategy was to be hopeful about the constructive influence of such individuals on society. A popular Stoic maxim was "The only true king is the wise man." Cynics were not as sanguine about the philosopher's chance of influencing social reform, but they also used the royal metaphor to advantage. In their case, taking control of one's life required extrication from the social scene. They lived "according to nature," they said, and the natural order was imagined as a realm of divine rule in opposition to the prevailing social order. As Epictetus put it, the Cynic's staff was his "scepter," his mission was to represent the great king Zeus, and the Cynic's "sovereignty" was the imperious bearing with which he "ruled" in the public arena by telling and showing others how they should live.

The use of the term kingdom of God in Q[1] matches its use in the traditions of popular philosophy, especially in the Cynic tradition of performing social diagnostics in public by means of countercultural behavior. The aphoristic imperatives recommended a stance toward life in the world that could become the basis for an alternative community ethos and ethic among those willing to consider an alternative social vision. Thus the spread of connotation must be kept in mind when encountering the term God's kingdom in Q. The language of the kingdom of God in Q captures precisely the ambiguities involved in the range of connotation from ruling as behavior to rule as domain: from individual to group, behavior to ethos, practice to conceptual order, human society to divine order. The thought had not yet occurred at the Q^1 level, as it did later at the Q^2 stage, that the location of God's kingdom was to be found precisely in the social formation of the movement. But it is clear that an overlap had already occurred between the concept of the rule of God as an alternative realm or way of life everywhere available to daring individuals, on the one hand, and the ethos of the movement as the particular manifestation of God's kingdom on the other. That is why the language of the rule of God in Q^1 refers not only to the challenge of risky living without expectation that the social world will change but also to the exemplification of a way of life that like-minded persons might want to share.

The God in question is not identified in terms of any ethnic or cultural tradition. This fits nicely with Galilean provenance, and since the metaphors of God's rule are largely taken from the realm of nature, the conception of God in Q^1 is also compatible with the Cynic tone of the teachings. The match between the Cynics and the Q people is not exact, however, mainly because the Cynics had no interest in emphasizing the divine aspect of either the natural order or the rule they represented. The people of Q, on the other hand, did emphasize that the rule they represented was the rule *of God*. There is little more to be learned about the nature of this God from the sayings about his kingdom, but other sayings about God in Q^1 (paraphrased below) represent him as a father:

> Love your enemies, do good, and lend, without expecting anything in return. Your reward will be great and you will be children of God. For he makes his sun rise on the evil and on the good; he sends rain on the just and on the unjust. (QS 9)

Be merciful even as your Father is merciful. (QS 10)

Father, . . . give us . . . pardon us . . . do not bring us to trial. (QS 26)

If you who are not good know how to give good gifts to your children, how much more will the father in heaven give good things to those who ask him. (QS 27)

If God puts beautiful clothes on the grass . . . , won't he put clothes on you . . . ? Your father knows that you need these things. (QS 39)

The concept of God as a father was widespread at the time, so the Jesus people were not laying claim to any particular tradition of religious thinking or inventing a new theology. Their conception is universal in the sense that all of nature is God's domain and all kinds of people are under his care. And yet, the way in which the Q people talked about God strikes a note of seriousness that is not evident in the earlier aphoristic materials. This seriousness is not about coming to a proper understanding of God, for the father is merely the guarantor of the better way of life demonstrated by the movement. The seriousness is about the movement itself and the care of its members. God is emphasized as being a father because the members of the movement are in need of a father's care. The Q people are not yet thinking of themselves as a family, but they are getting close.

In Q^1 the embryonic social formation of the movement has to be inferred from the nature of the discourse. In Q^2, on the other hand, a vivid picture of the Jesus movement comes into view as a fully self-conscious movement. Before we move to that stage of the group's history, however, there is one more important window into the early period of socialization that Q^1 provides, and this is the instruction about working for God's kingdom in QS 20. This instruction contains the saying about being sent out as lambs among wolves, a formulation that retains its Cynic flavor and is best understood as an address to individuals. However, it also contains a saying about a large harvest with few workers, a saying that implies some kind of program. And appended to the harvest saying is the injunction to beg the master of the harvest to send out laborers. Recent studies of this instruction have argued convincingly that of these two sayings, the one about the lambs and wolves is the earlier. This means that the developmental sequence discernible in Q^1 as a whole is also true of this instructural unit. An originally Cynic-like challenge to go out into the public arena and confront the wolves was changed into an instruction befitting a movement with a collective sense of mission. But what kind of a mission might that have been?

The injunction to "beg the master of the harvest to send out workers into his harvest" assumes a stage in the movement when house groups had developed and thought of themselves as the appropriate form of the Jesus people. In fact, the speech as a whole pivots on a single issue. It is the question of appropriate behavior in the event of being "welcomed" or "not received" when entering a house in another town. The instructions for the road are that one should *not* wear a pouch or sandals, should not carry a staff, and should not greet anyone. Reception at a house depends on a "child of peace" being there and is signaled by an exchange of the traditional greeting, "Peace." Behavior is spelled out in terms of conventional rules of hospitality: Eat what they provide; do not offend the host by accepting another's hospitality and going on to another house. While with one's host, one should "attend to the sick" and tell them that "God's rule has come near to you." However, there is no instruction about what to do at the house should the traveler not be welcomed. Such instruction is offered only in regard to a city that does not receive the worker, in which case a gesture, apparently of accusation, is to be performed (shaking the dust from one's feet on leaving). This means that the movement had experienced rejection in public.

The instructions for the road are particularly interesting because they are concerned with just those items that typify the Cynic's garb and manner. Why are these items forbidden? Some scholars have thought that the Q people may have wanted to outdo other Cynics in their renunciation of basic needs. But the instruction may have been not to dress (any longer?) like a Cynic. Either way, a contrast is being made, and the rest of the instructions may tell us why. The reason seems to be that the public arena was no longer the place where the most important activity was occurring within the movement. At this time there were houses where Jesus people sought hospitality and talked about the rule of God. The instructions suggest that the Q people had become interested in the etiquette of cordial relations among houses of hospitality and spelled out rules for the behavior of workers when traveling to other towns. Begging had been modulated into requesting hospitality as a representative of the movement. One gets the impression of a network of house groups interested in staying in touch.

It is clear that these instructions were formulated as guidance for a movement that had spread throughout Galilee, and that Jesus people who were not personal acquaintances might be found in other towns. Spreading would have taken place in the normal course of contact and travel wherever talk about God's rule caught the attention of persons willing to listen. Apparently, many were quite attracted to the Jesus people and their talk about the rule of God. Their diagnosis of the social situation must have made sense and their challenge to risk reproach by taking in hand what one could of one's own life must have sounded right. But as groups formed in different places and the teachings of Jesus became the topic of conversation, recognition of kindred spirits became an issue, and the arena of activity shifted from the public sphere to the house group. The earlier Cynic-like life-style, geared as it was for a critical encounter with the world, would have become inappropriate. What it meant to live in accordance with the rule of God would now have to be worked out in relation to persons and problems within the group. Thus the codification of Cynic-like injunctions as community rules in Q^1 can be understood as a response to the problems of social formation. As we shall see, these problems surface in Q^2 as the primary cause for a marked shift in both the discourse and the life-style of the Jesus movement.

7

Singing a Dirge

Asudden shift in tone awaits the reader of Q². The new temperament is so strongly profiled that a comparison with the sayings in Q¹ is unavoidable and the contrast in mood overwhelming. It is a shift for which one has not been prepared, and the effect is stunning.

The aphoristic style of Q¹ falls away almost to the point of disappearing. Aphoristic imperatives are gone, as is the sense of confidence in God's care derived from the way in which nature provides for basic needs. In its place one hears the voice of a prophet pronouncing judgment on a recalcitrant world, a prophet who does not refrain from castigation and the sledge of apocalyptic threat.

The shift in tone is matched by a panoply of new forms of speech. In contrast to Q¹ the reader now encounters narratives, dialogue, controversy stories, examples taken from epic tradition, descriptive parables, warnings, and apocalyptic announcements. If one looks for corresponding changes in the rhetoric and style of discourse one is not disappointed. Instead of exhortation ("Don't worry"), there is pronouncement ("The last will be first, and the first will be last"). Instead of imperatives ("Love your enemies"), there is direct statement ("I came to strike fire on the earth"). Indirect address ("Who then is the faithful servant") is interspersed with direct address ("You must be ready"). Formulas of reciprocity, such as "The standard you use is the standard used against you," are tightened and shift their setting of consequence from what happens in the public sphere to what

131

will happen in the kingdom of God. And all of these judgments and verdicts are rendered with an authority that does not brook appeal.

New ideas also are encountered. The expanded horizon introduces figures from the epic tradition. A man named John enters the picture. There is reference to the wisdom of God and the holy spirit. There are two miracle stories and warnings about what to say when put on trial. The rule of God is now spoken of as a kingdom to be fully revealed at some other place and time, presumably at the end of time. And a final judgment is described replete with thrones, court scenes, banishments, and a threatening figure called the son of man.

A listing of the major blocks of material in Q^2 illustrates the shift that took place and the constant presence of the theme of judgment.

1. John's Preaching

   QS 3 THE APPEARANCE OF JOHN
   QS 4 JOHN'S ADDRESS TO THE PEOPLE
   QS 5 JOHN'S PREDICTION OF SOMEONE TO COME

2. What John and Jesus Thought About Each Other

   QS 15 THE OCCASION
   QS 16 JOHN'S INQUIRY
   QS 17 WHAT JESUS SAID ABOUT JOHN
   QS 18 WHAT JESUS SAID ABOUT THIS GENERATION

3. Pronouncements Against Towns That Reject the Movement

   QS 21 THE UNRECEPTIVE TOWN
   QS 22 THE GALILEAN TOWNS

4. Congratulations to Those Who Accept the Movement

   QS 23 ON THE ONE WHO RECEIVES THE WORKER
   QS 25 ON THE ONE WHO HEARS AND SEES

5. Controversy with This Generation

   QS 28 ON KINGDOMS IN CONFLICT

6. Making Sure Whose Side You Are On

   QS 29 THOSE FOR AND THOSE AGAINST
   QS 30 THE RETURN OF AN EVIL SPIRIT

7. Judgment on This Generation

   QS 32 THE SIGN OF JONAH

The theme of judgment is very closely related to an apocalyptic imagination. The threat of coming up short in a final judgment flows like an undercurrent from the preaching of John to the parable of the talents. Many of the prophetic pronouncements, images of destruction, and the parables of exclusion take their seriousness from this apocalyptic backdrop even when it is not made explicit. It is also the apocalyptic framework that forced a reconception of God and made it possible to imagine the rule of God as a realm to be fully revealed only at the end of time.

The inverse is also true, however, and this is an important point to understand. The apocalyptic imagination is very closely related to the theme of judgment. If one compares the apocalyptic language in Q^2 with the way it is commonly used in the apocalyptic literature of the time, the features that are missing in Q^2 are remarkable. There is very little interest in imagining the rule of God as a glorious kingdom of the end time. In Q^2 the final trial is focused upon personal vindication or condemnation, making sure who is in and who is out of the kingdom. The last judgment does not function to vindicate a sectarian group at the expense of the destruction of its enemies. Also, there is no hint of fascination with an end-time scenario in order to imagine what it will take to rescue the righteous from an impossible world or create a better world to replace it. For the people of Q there was little comfort to be derived from the thought of a final judgment. There is no hint of a personal piety grounded in an apocalyptic hope for an eventual transformation. There is no indication that the Q community closed its borders on the world and stiffened to prepare for a dramatic change of circumstance. The apocalyptic imagination served only one purpose for the people of Q, and that was to guarantee the threat of judgment that they wanted to bring down upon people who had frustrated their mission. That was all. Thus, in spite of the potentially overwhelming apocalyptic frame of reference in Q^2, there is actually much more interest invested in the substantive issues of self-definition and loyalty to the movement than there is in seeing these issues solved at a final judgment. It is obvious that the people of Q were distressed and incensed, and that they had targeted certain people such as the Pharisees for their fire. But they were not in the process of becoming an enclave, conventicle, or apocalyptic community. They put the language of apocalyptic to use only in order to put muscle into their judgments upon the present state of their world. The beauty of an apocalyptic projection was that it could turn a contemporary critique or a charge into a threat with a tinge of ultimacy: "You will surely get your just deserts."

What was the problem that called forth such wrath and created such a shift in discourse between Q^1 and Q^2? It must have been related to something which happened in the social history of the people of Q, and some clues are present in the shift in discourse itself. In contrast to Q^1 where all the sayings are addressed to the followers of Jesus as a group and serve to instruct them as individuals in their project of representing God's kingdom in the world, Q^2 includes a large number of sayings that address the world at large. Some of these sayings are indirectly addressed to outsiders, as if hoping that the whole world might overhear what is being said. Such is the case with the sayings in QS 32 to the effect that this generation is "wicked." But many sayings address those outside the movement directly as if they were present for the speeches. Examples would be the sayings in QS 22 and QS 34: "Woe for you, Chorazin"; "Shame on you Pharisees." What is said about those addressed in this way is significant.

There is mention of the "offspring of vipers" and "this wicked generation" that did not change its mind (QS 4, QS 32), of "this generation" that did not join in the dance or the mourning (QS 18), of cities like Chorazin, Bethsaida, and Capernaum that were too haughty to change their ways (QS 20, QS 22), and of lawyers and Pharisees who refused to enter God's kingdom because of their positions of privilege, and who kept others from entering as well by means of their own rules for staying pure (QS 34). These are sharp sayings, and they are shouted for the whole world to hear, like Roman candles shot against the night sky exploding and blanketing the entire region of Galilee with their sparks. But the nature of their message, rhetoric, and style belies the authors' ruse. It is very clear that the authors knew they were shouting into the wind.

You can almost see them in the process of formulating what they wished they had said to those who had raised their ire: "O you Pharisees, look at all the ways you have been wrong." But the manner of the charge is not calculated for persuasion. If there ever had been a real confrontation it was now a thing of the past. The premises on which the charges are based are exactly those that had been rejected when the real debate broke down. The people of Q held their position but lost the argument. Real Pharisees were no longer in earshot, at least not any who were worth their Jewish salt. The scolding as it now stands sounds like a one-sided shouting match, and no one puts up with a shouter unless the family resemblance won't let you leave. Unfortunately for the people of Q, their audience had already turned away. Rejection, then, turns out to be the cause of the wrath as well as the point of the charge. Is it possible to understand how the people of Q got themselves into such a mess?

Judging from the life-style characteristic for Q^1, the Jesus people could have experienced rejection for any number of reasons. The people of Q could have appeared silly, or tiring, a bit unnerving, or even too dangerous for close association, but rejection for such reasons should have been taken in stride. Many of the Q^1 instructions are addressed precisely to the situation of reproach in public, and none of them recommends wrath. So something else must have happened.

Taking notice of two additional features of Q^2 will put us on the right track. One is the indication that loyalty to the movement had become a very serious issue. The definition of a faithful follower had been raised and worry about the movement losing members had become an all-consuming concern. The other is that the evidence for social stress comes to focus upon the pain experienced in the rupture of human bonds and relationships. There is mention of tension internal to the group and division within families. There are also threats of exclusion from the kingdom of God. Noting that the concern about loyalty, the matter of division, and the castigation of an unsympathetic world are all indications of social stress, an extremely troubled phase of the movement's social history unfolds.

One can mark the increase in concern about loyalty by paying attention to the way in which mutual recognition was measured. In the very earliest stages of the movement (stages 1 and 2) it was sufficient to talk about "keeping" Jesus' words. That was what the movement was about, and those who did "keep" the words, who were interested and willing to talk and act in accord with them, were easily recognized as being Jesus people. As the movement spread, however, mutual recognition became more of a problem. As Q^1 shows, houses of hospitality formed and a sense of mission emerged. The standard for recognition ("keeping" the words of Jesus) did not change, but a growing emphasis on the importance of doing so is noticeable. And yet, who among the Jesus people could put such a concern into one's own words? And with what authority? The experimental nature of the movement would have made it difficult for any would-be leader to stand up and say, "If you do not keep Jesus' words you are not helping the cause," or "You are not really one of us," or "You are out." But Jesus might be imagined to have said such things. After all, the figure of Jesus as founder of the movement and the voice of Jesus as authority for the community's instructions were already taken for granted.

However, to imagine Jesus giving additional instruction about himself, saying how important his own teachings were, or saying that one had to keep them in order to be a true follower, would have greatly advanced the importance of Jesus in comparison to earlier understandings of his significance as a teacher. The resulting image of Jesus would have had tremendous consequences for the kind of authority Jesus had for the movement, recasting his role from that of a Cynic-like teacher who espoused a way of life that any and all might try, to that of an authoritative model, judge, and keeper of accounts. For now Jesus would refer to himself as his own authority, set forth his teachings as community code, and accept as a matter of course his own importance as the one who intended from the first to set the standard for what the movement must become. And so it happened that concern for measuring loyalty to the teachings of the movement turned Jesus into the founder of the movement.

This enhancement of the authority of Jesus took place by degrees. The first development in this direction can be seen already in the statements that Jesus makes about himself at stage 2 of this social history. It will be helpful to notice the import of these sayings in Q^1 before going on to the subsequent developments in Q^2. Thus, fully in keeping with the genre of instruction, we have the following formulations in Q^1:

Why do you call me master and not do what I say? (QS 14)

Everyone who comes to me and hears my words and does them is like a man who built a house on rock. (QS 14)

Look, I send you out as lambs among wolves. (QS 20)

Sir, who made me your judge or lawyer? (QS 38)

Notice that Jesus refers to himself as the instructor of sayings and injunctions that have become standards for the self-definition of the movement. This registers the first and most fundamental shift in the enhancement of Jesus' image and authority. QS 38 is most interesting in this regard, for it names an issue over which Jesus' words do not have authority, and thus reveals the desire to limit Jesus' authority to matters of instruction for and loyalty to the movement. As for QS 14, the instructions Jesus refers to as "what I say" are none other than the sayings contained in Q^1 as a whole.

A second advance in the self-authorization of Jesus' instructions can be seen in two other clusters of sayings, both of which appear to be later developments in the compositional history of Q:

How fortunate you are when they reproach you . . . because of me. (QS 8)

Whoever does not hate his father and mother will not be able to learn from me. (QS 52)

Whoever does not accept his cross and so become my follower cannot be one of my students. (QS 52)

These sayings fit best in the period between the collection of most Q^1 materials and the revision in Q^2. I shall call this intermediate period stage 3. The saying in QS 8 is a statement modeled on the preceding three pronouncements of "fortunate" status or "honor" and must have been added at some later time. It breaks the pattern of the first three pronouncements and provides the basis for adding yet another saying about the prophets at the Q^2 level of composition, a motif to which we shall return. QS 52 is a cluster of sayings at the very end of Q^1, likely candidates in a likely place for additions to the collection just prior to the programmatic revisions characteristic for Q^2. These sayings signal the direction in which the Q^2 people were to move as they measured loyalty to their movement.

Note that the behavior enjoined in QS 8 and QS 52 is still a matter of personal performance in keeping with the movement's standards of recognition. One is to "rejoice when reproached," disentangle family ties, accept one's "cross" (meaning, "bear up under condemnation"), and not allow the fear of being killed to affect loyalty to the movement. Although all of these are extreme cases of having one's mettle tested, thus reflecting a time of distress for the Jesus people, none was unusual for the Cynic tradition on which the Jesus movement drew. All occur in the Cynic tradition as examples of testing personal integrity. The saying in QS 52 about losing one's life in order to preserve it had a long proverbial history behind it, and the cross had become a metaphor for the ultimate test of a philosopher's integrity.

The injunction to take up one's cross in order to be a true follower of Jesus need not be taken as an oblique reference to Jesus' own death, the cause and occasion for which are not at all certain despite the customary assumption of crucifixion. Even if the saying were so taken, however, it would only mean that the people of Q viewed Jesus' death in the same light as that accorded other well-known examples of courage in the face of threats to one's life. Thus Jesus' crucifixion would have served the people of Q as an example of the integrity required of any of his followers, an integrity that was still being measured by commitment to the way of life enjoined within the movement.

And yet, a slight but important shift in focus from the teachings to the teacher can be detected in QS 8 and QS 52. In these sayings loyalty to the movement is expressed, not in terms of keeping Jesus' words, but in terms of behavior befitting a true follower of Jesus, or staying true to the movement "because of" Jesus. Jesus is viewed as the founder-teacher who exemplified his own teachings and thus made a personal investment in the movement. And being a "true follower" can easily shift yet another notch to include the notion of loyalty to Jesus himself. Consider now the following statements from Q[2]:

> Fortunate is the one who is not disturbed [at hearing these things] about me. (QS 16)

> Whoever welcomes you welcomes me, and whoever welcomes me welcomes the one who sent me. (QS 23)

> How fortunate are the eyes that see what you see. (QS 25)

> If I exorcise demons by the finger of God, then God's rule has caught up with you. (QS 28)

> Whoever is not with me is against me, and the one who does not gather with me scatters. (QS 29)

> Everyone who admits in public that they know me, the son of man will acknowledge before the angels of God. The one who disowns me in public, the son of man will disown before the angels of God. (QS 37)

These statements are not the only ones in Q^2 that address the question of loyalty to the movement, but they suffice to show that the question of loyalty had become an extremely important issue, and that loyalty to the movement could now be expressed in terms of loyalty to Jesus, not just in terms of keeping his words. Keeping his words was still the fundamental sign of recognition, but Jesus was now imagined to speak in roles other than that of a teacher. Jesus had become the founder of a movement with a programmatic mission. Faithfulness to the movement could be expressed in terms of admitting that one "knew" Jesus. Admitting that one was a Jesus person was now a matter of some consequence.

This concern for loyalty to the movement is matched by signs of social distress. Tensions within the movement are indicated by the saying on scandals in QS 57 and the instruction to forgive a brother if he has a change of heart in QS 58. But changes of heart have apparently not been the rule. Families have been torn asunder and the divisions have been rationalized as fully in keeping with the importance and purpose of the movement. Painful? Yes, but to be expected:

> Do you think that I have come to bring peace on earth? No, not peace, but a sword.
>
> For I have come to create conflict between a man and his father, disagreement between a daughter and her mother, and estrangement between a daughter-in-law and her mother-in-law. A person's enemies will be one's own kin. (QS 43)

This pronouncement turns painful experience into programmatic purpose. It is quite different than the Cynic-like saying in Q^1 about rejecting one's family in order to be a follower of Jesus (QS 52). In Q^2, families have been split over loyalty to the movement. This means that rejection is now working the other way around. And the signs of division do not stop there. The children in the marketplace have said no to the music of the movement. The missionaries have experienced rejection. The story of the Beelzebul accusation in QS 28 is about rejection, conflict, and labeling Jesus and his followers as agents of a foreign (Syrian) god. Jesus' retort about "your sons" turns the challenge back upon his questioners and directs the issue of conflict to the social world that Jesus shares with them. There are instructions in

QS 37 and QS 45 about what to do in case one is called before the village authorities. And there are several examples taken from the epic tradition of the Hebrew bible in QS 32, QS 34, and QS 60 that are used to illustrate the divisive consequences of refusing to listen to sage and/or prophetic advice.

The language of divisive conflict is very closely related to another theme that is even more important for our purposes. This is the theme of inclusion versus exclusion, a theme that presupposes the notion of boundaries and borders. The people of Q^2 had not organized their movement to become a society with membership requirements and officers, much less with rites of entrance. But the rule of God that they represented was certainly in the process of being reconceived as a discrete domain or kingdom, and there was now a great deal of talk about "entering into" the kingdom or being excluded from it. The "least in the kingdom" are greater than John (QS 17). The lawyers have shut the kingdom of God against the people and prevented the people from going in (QS 34). The faithful servant will be given charge of the master's estate (QS 42). One should "strive to enter by the narrow door" (QS 47). And "in the kingdom of God . . . the last will be first, and the first will be last" (QS 48).

Reading more closely, one sees that loyalty to the Jesus movement had run up against the challenge of Jewish propriety and the question of belonging to the people of God as the children of Abraham, or Israel. And the Jesus people had taken this challenge seriously. The evidence for this includes the repeated appeals to biblical traditions, the preaching of John about the children of Abraham, the import of the Beelzebul accusation, and the list of counter charges leveled against Pharisees and lawyers (or scribes).

As this challenge to the movement stiffened, the debate apparently came to focus on the difference between the life-style of the Jesus people and the Jewish codes of purity advocated by the Pharisees. The term Pharisee appears to have been a label meaning "purists" referring to their type of piety. The Pharisees had worked out an innovative response to the troubled times in Palestine from a thoroughly Jewish perspective. The temple establishment had lost its legitimacy and the sacrificial system its efficacy, but one could still be true to the Jewish heritage by following a code for ritual purity as an individual. Thus the Pharisaic code also defined a life-style. Their code consisted of a small list of rituals such as tithing, prayers, fasting, and giving to charity, in combination with a number of cleanliness rules, such as washings and the selection of foods. These codes were not "laws," for they had no institutional base of promulgation. Pharisees were simply a class of individuals who lived by this code as a way to define themselves as Jewish. Whether or not there were many Pharisees living in Galilee, their code would have been well known as one way to mark Jewish identity. The Jesus people ran afoul of the Pharisaic code and were challenged for doing so. They in turn singled out the Pharisees as their chief critics.

Conflict with the Pharisees does not mean that the Jesus movement intended a reform of Judaism, or that it was generated by a claim to represent a biblical heritage or ideal. Neither does it mean that the Jesus movement was made up only of Jews who happened to be living in Galilee. But some members of the Jesus movement must have been Galilean Jews, because the issue of loyalty came to be phrased as a Jewish question, was taken very seriously, and was eventually answered in Jewish terms.

One can easily understand how this situation might have developed if loyalties to the Jesus movement began to wear and tear at the fabric of families and villages in which Jewish sensibilities were strong. One can imagine a family worried about the involvement of some of its members in the Jesus movement. Attempts at dissuasion could have and must have taken many forms. But insisting upon traditional family loyalties, throwing up Pharisaic standards, and making arguments for preserving Jewish identity were apparently the ploys that struck home. They were in any case the ones that got a response from the Q people. And they triggered a spate of countercharges that determined the emerging self-identification of the Jesus movement. The indications are that the inner family, inner village debates on matters such as these were very lively and vociferous before all parties agreed to disagree.

The charges against the Pharisees and lawyers in QS 34 are especially interesting in this regard. The issues under debate were just what one might expect—washings, giving to charity, tithes, justice, honor, and knowledge. The list combines items typical for the Pharisaic code of ritual purity with items for which scribal representatives of the temple system of courts and taxation would be known. Such standards had apparently been held up as exemplary by families and village leaders seeking to chide their Jesus people into postures of propriety. Apparently the people of Q were not impressed. They regarded the Pharisaic codes as foolish and the lawyers' justice as burdensome. True to their Cynic heritage, the Jesus people were still capable of engaging in a bit of caustic riposte. The Pharisees were like tombs (so much for their desire to be honored), and the lawyers treated people like beasts of burden (so much for their claims to know the law and administer justice). And so the "debate" must have gone, ad hoc volleys largely missing their targets but nonetheless expressing firm convictions on either side of the match. But then the ante was upped. Lo and behold, the people of Q linked the Pharisees and lawyers to the history of what their fathers did to the prophets. The Q people even crafted an oracle of the wisdom of God saying that this present generation would be held accountable for the blood of all the prophets (QS 34). That is some ante. Suddenly we are swept into a world of fantastic imagination, stupendous claim, and grand mythologization. It is clear that the offense had registered and that the defense would be to beat the Jewish exemplars at their own game.

The Jesus movement must have been worth it in the eyes of those who now turned to the intellectual labor of mythmaking. They had to find ways to read the biblical epic as if it registered a devastating criticism of the Pharisees. In sorting through the scriptural traditions they also looked for self-justifying arguments, examples in support of their own movement. This amounted to an implicit claim upon cultural heritage represented by the epic tradition, a claim that would only have made sense if the Jesus people had become a distinct group and were now willing to see themselves reflected in the traditions of Israel. Some at least were thinking that the Jesus movement had become more than a forum for social critique, more than a support group for persons wanting to stand tall in unsettling times. A community had formed to seek its own identity in contrast to other social, ethnic, and cultural configurations.

But what a "reading" of the biblical traditions. There is very little evidence for actual literary activity in regard to the scriptures as texts, and none whatsoever for interest in redirecting any of the major etiological themes of the Hebrew scriptures to run in favor of the Jesus movement. There is no appeal to such important themes as the promises to the patriarchs, the priestly covenants, the Mosaic law, the land, the Davidic covenant, the Leviticus charter for the temple cult, and the prophetic visions of a return to Jerusalem. Most of the allusions to the epic of Israel, such as the references to Solomon and Jonah, are best understood as taken from popular oral lore. And there is a subversive strategy detectable in the selection of only these examples. It is almost as if, when challenged by a Jewish orthodoxy, the Galileans appealed to what they knew of the popular epic traditions of Israel generally shared by Jews, Samaritans, and Galileans. These traditions were available to all the people of Semitic extraction throughout Palestine, though in different forms. And, of course, each Palestinian province would have remembered the history in different ways. The people of Q worked these stories to their own advantage on the one hand, and to the detriment of their detractors' claims to represent the true form of Israel on the other.

We have already seen that "this generation" was linked to the fathers who killed all the prophets from Abel to Zechariah (QS 34), and that the Jesus people were encouraged to think of themselves as "fortunate" because they were treated just as the prophets had been treated (QS 8; cf QS 25). The logic was that the epic tradition supported the Jesus people because they, like the prophets, registered appropriate criticism of the status quo. The motif of the killing of the prophets could also be cited to embarrass their detractors because they, just as the fathers always had done to the prophets, were wrongfully "persecuting" and "killing" the Jesus people. But the charge was a summary fiction with respect both to the history it summarized and to its application to the Jesus people. It was based upon a familiar theme used by conservative Jews at the time to explain why history had gone wrong and to call for a return to proper observance of the Torah of Moses. The way the people of Q used the motif was not a particularly clever manipulation of the Hebrew scriptures or of the logical thrust of the biblical epic. They simply took what there was in the Jewish reservoir of stock images and turned it against their detractors. The charge could not possibly have held if the lawyers and the people of Q had been able and willing to sit down together and actually study the scriptures. So the charge was never designed to persuade the lawyers. It only sounded good to the Jesus people to think of themselves that way.

If the fathers had killed all the prophets from Abel on, what about our father Abraham, what about Isaac, and Jacob? Well, now, the people of Q had not really meant to include *those* fathers in the charge. The patriarchs were not the private property of the Jews. Samaritans, Galileans, and the Jesus people were also the children of Abraham. And when all the good people gather at the table in the kingdom of God, those who rebuked the Jesus people will have to clench their teeth when they see Abraham, Isaac, Jacob, and all the prophets in and themselves out (QS 48). So that takes care of the problem of the patriarchs and the Pharisees.

Or does the mention of Abraham really mean that the Galilean Jesus people thought it important to be children of Abraham? Did not John warn the crowd that it would do no good to count on *any* ethnic claim to be children of Abraham, because God could raise up children for Abraham even from the stones? And as for staking one's claim on belonging to "Israel," did not Jesus tell the Roman centurion that the centurion's response to Jesus' words was better than any he found in all of Israel? So what did the Q people intend by making such confusing references to the epic tradition of Israel?

What the Q people accomplished in their appeal to biblical examples was not a coherent rereading of the epic in their favor. Their achievement was a popping of pompous balloons and a freaky delight in seeing themselves reflected in the story at its most embarrassing turns. Think of Jonah. Were the Ninevites Jews? No. Did they not repent at Jonah's preaching? Yes. Now think of Jesus and the Jesus movement in the very same light, only brighter. Remember the Queen of the South (Sheba)? Was she a Jew? No. Did Solomon withhold his wisdom from her? No. See? Something greater even than Solomon is here. And the story of Noah? Be careful whose side you are on. Everyone else perished you know. It is going to be the same story when the son of man appears. And the same goes for Lot and the city of Sodom. He was called out; they were destroyed (QS 60, QS 21). So there is your epic, they seemed to be saying, if you want to know what we are about, read it.

This strategy is quite similar to that used with the apocalyptic threat. The people of Q were not particularly enamored of thinking about themselves in the idiom of apocalyptic. Their movement certainly was not generated by an apocalyptic hysteria or persuasion of imminent judgment any more than it was by a drive to reform or re-store some ethnic identity based on the promise inherent in the biblical epic of Israel. In both cases, the appeal to examples from the epic and the threat of an apocalyptic judgment, the Q people invaded the territory of their Jewish detractors and used their own idioms against them.

And yet, once involved in such an imaginative exercise, polemical as it surely was at first, a curious fascination with the broadened horizon seems to have developed. To think of the Jesus movement taking its place in the grand scheme of things, from the very "foundation of the world" (QS 34) to the "day when the son of man appears" (QS 60), was not a bad idea. No one could have started, either with the thrust of the Hebrew epic, or with the pull of an apocalyptic hope, and come up with a plan for just such a movement as the Jesus movement. But once it was there as a movement in the process of social formation, worthy of the loyalties of those within and threatened by the cuffs of those without, finding a place in the sun was exactly what the movement needed. And what a place to take, aligned with the "little ones" whose pedigree reached back to the beginning and who already knew in advance how the final judgment would go.

Thus there is more than a hint of delight in seeing the Jesus people on the right side of things as the epic history was reviewed and the apocalyptic finale imagined. The strategy of turning the history and vision this way and that to catch one's own reflection in some unexpected facet of the grand design can be seen in the selections that were made. From the epic, the authors of Q^2 had selected a few well-known stories that could work both ways, as a warning to their detractors and as a subtle suggestion that the epic of Israel championed lone figures and marginal peoples. In the case of the final judgment it wasn't as easy to picture the traditional scene working out in their favor. But by taking care with one's descriptions, the outline of an answer began to emerge. Why not think of God, whose judgment would be final, with a copy of Q in his hands as his guide?

But mythmaking demands much more. Connections need to be made among many historical moments, including the present time, and a place must be secured for the new community in relation to other peoples and their cultures. The sweep of history needs to have its rhyme and reason coursing through the present situation. And the

Archimedian point of vantage for comprehending the whole has to be located. The authors of Q² were not quite there, but they had laid some firm foundations. In order to make the connection with all that had gone before they appropriated the mythological figure of the wisdom of God. In order to make the connection with what was to come they cleverly manipulated the description of the son of man. And in order to join these two mythological figures exactly where they had to be joined, the people of Q reimagined Jesus as the child of wisdom and as the seer who knew what the son of man would say at the end of time. Each of these mythological developments deserves some discussion, for taken together they put us in touch with an amazing accomplishment. The people of Q created a myth of broad horizon by elaborating the unlikely genre of the sayings of a sage.

8

Claiming a Place

To watch a myth in the making is a rare privilege. It is especially so when the myth that emerges constitutes the core of the complex mythology foundational to one's own culture. Since that is exactly what Q² allows us to observe, the discovery of the lost gospel is a rich find indeed.

Mythmaking in the Jesus movement at the Q² stage was an act of creative borrowing and the clever rearrangement of fascinating figures from several other vibrant mythologies of the time. The two figures of primary importance for constructing the mythology of Q were the wisdom of God and the son of man. These figures, together with the concept of the spirit of God, were used to link the epic traditions of Israel with an apocalyptic finale and so create a single comprehensive vision of history that put the people of Q in the right place at the right time. The role of Jesus was appropriately reconceived, and because it now had to combine the functions of a wisdom teacher with those of an apocalyptic prophet, the figure of John was introduced. Each of these important figures, wisdom, son of man, and John, enter the Q tradition at the Q² level. Each figure is intricately related to the others and to a new significance that is given to the expanded instructions of Jesus. This chapter explains the contribution of each to the mythmaking process and shows how the myth in turn affected the community of Q.

The figure of the wisdom of God was created by Jewish scribes in the aftermath of the Babylonian exile. The destruction of Jerusalem and the exile (587–539 B.C.E.) canceled out the effectiveness of the scribal wisdom that had been generated during the kingdoms of Judah and Israel. Scribal wisdom refers both to a body of knowledge and to the idiom in which Israel and other peoples in the ancient near east thought about life, ethics, and human relations. Scribal wisdom assumed the existence of a temple-state, and intellectuals in the scribal tradition imagined the perfect society on the temple-state model. With Jerusalem in ruins and its social structures destroyed, however, Jewish intellectuals of the post-exilic period were confronted with more questions than answers. To acknowledge the crisis, some said that wisdom was no longer to be found in the world. To keep the memory of wisdom alive while the long slow process of rebuilding a safe and sane society was undertaken in the so-called restoration of Jerusalem, the scribes imagined that wisdom was now to be found only with God. Naturally, there were poems about unsuccessful attempts to find wisdom in the world (Job 28). But then, gradually, other poems began to appear about God and wisdom together creating the world as an ordered habitation (Prov. 8:22–31), about wisdom appearing incognito at the city gates and crying out to be recognized (Prov. 1:20–33), and eventually about wisdom taking up residence again in the rebuilt temple at Jerusalem (Sir. 24). Thus a mythology of wisdom emerged.

This fascinating figure enjoyed great popularity during the Greco-Roman period. A rich mythology of wisdom reflected the desire to see the world as a divine creation; the epic of Israel as a story of divine rescues; the second temple-state as the model civilization; the books of Moses as divine instruction; and the prophets, priests, and kings of the story as playing a necessary role in the divine economy for ruling a society in peace and justice. Because wisdom was personified as a woman (drawing on the mythologies of the Egyptian goddesses Maat and Isis), it was possible to imagine her actively engaged in putting the pieces of a fragmented world back together. Popular narrative themes portrayed wisdom in the act of creating, generating, building, making the rounds of heaven, seeking a people with whom to dwell, fleeing from violence, finding a house in Israel, sending messengers, rescuing, teaching, working, offering her produce, preparing meals, and, yes, even inviting her husband and her children to come and cuddle.

One can trace some very ingenious configurations of this mythology in Jewish literature of the time. The imaginary worlds created by wisdom mythology can be understood as experimental efforts in thinking about the way societies are organized, why a particular society does not always work for the well-being of the people, and how a better arrangement might be imagined. The author of the Wisdom of Solomon, a poetic treatise on kingship from the first century included in the deuterocanonical books of the Old Testament, knew that the Greco-Roman age was in the hands of godless men who had misused power and created a culture of oppression and violence. But since dwelling on this reality did not suggest a program for change, the author wrote a poem about how pleasant the world would be if only kings became enamored of wisdom and ruled their kingdoms to reflect the perfect cosmos created by her.

Philo of Alexandria used wisdom mythology to interpret the five books of Moses, or Torah, as instruction about the path that leads through this world to the house of God. The guide on the way was the *logos* (a concept that combined the ideas of "word" and "reason"), wisdom's child and the son of God. In the house at the end of the journey there would be a family reunion. Wisdom would be there to make sure that the celebration was a perfect communion.

Wisdom mythology also occurs in apocalyptic texts. In this literature, wisdom did once reside in Jerusalem, but then she fled from the evil and violence that destroyed its glory. Now she waits in heaven for the judgments that must fall, ready to return as the water of life for a parched earth in need of regeneration. In several gnostic systems, wisdom mythology was used to explore the loss of social sanity during the Roman period and the effect of this loss on the individual, who no longer knew how to master himself or his world. Wisdom's perfect world was far away. But from the beginning she had experienced the full range of psychological convolutions attendant upon the desire to create or recreate a perfect world. And so this poetry of the gnostics was actually a meditation on the psychology of ignorance, fear, powerlessness, desire, error, shame, and the quest for salvation in the midst of a fallen world. Sometimes hidden, sometimes revealed, to know wisdom was to comprehend the world as it should be.

The mythology of wisdom was made to order for the people of Q. If Jesus was a sage and his instructions were wise, it was not a far leap to think of him as a child or envoy of the wisdom of God. This thought did not occur immediately, for a Cynic sage hardly needed the help of divine attestation, and the wisdom of God was not particularly partial to Cynic-style instruction. But at the Q^1 stage the Jesus people had already entertained a natural theology, worked out an ethical code, and innocently used the figure of Solomon, legendary patron of Jewish wisdom, as an apt example of royal glory hoping to match the attire of the world as God cares for it. So it is clear that they were already thinking of Jesus as a teacher of wisdom when the time came to take their place in the larger scheme of human histories in a divinely governed world.

The trick was to think of Jesus as knowing what wisdom surely must know. But what a fund of knowledge. Jesus was imagined to have overheard what wisdom said at the very beginning of the epic history about planning to send prophets and messengers to Israel. From her vantage point she knew already that they would all be killed and that "this generation," the generation to which Jesus was speaking, would have to pay (QS 34). He consoles his followers by telling them that the knowledge he dispensed to them is the wisdom others have sought and not found. His followers were seeing what "many prophets and kings longed to see" and did not see (QS 25). He warns them to be careful about their eyes lest "the light in you is darkness" (QS 33). He tells them that everything they have heard from him in secret will be made public (QS 35), and he knows exactly what will happen when the final judgments fall (QS 37). So Jesus was now imagined to be privy to knowledge that only the wisdom of God could have from her vantage point above and beyond the entire sweep of human history.

Unfortunately, having reimagined Jesus along these lines, the authors of Q^2 were confronted with a conceptual problem. It was one thing to think of their teacher as the child of the wisdom of God, consoling and warning the children of God about the meaning of their times. It was quite another to hear that same voice thundering out the judgments of God on a world doomed to exclusion from his kingdom. The problem was how to merge the image of the teacher of wisdom, with which they had long been familiar, with the image of the apocalyptic prophet whose voice was now ringing in their ears. How to reconcile wisdom and apocalyptic teachings, how to recharacterize Jesus' role, and how to rethink the kingdom of God in terms of epic-apocalyptic history were the challenges now confronting them.

The authors solved this problem at the beginning of their book of instructions by introducing the figure of a prophet of doom and letting this prophet and Jesus exchange views about each other. By carefully constructing that exchange, the authors prepared their readers for the complex role Jesus would later have to assume. John must have been a known personage, or the stories about Jesus and John would not have worked their magic. But since this is the earliest mention of John on record (later to be called John "the baptizer"), and since the other stories about him in the narrative gospels are further embellishments of the role assigned to him here in Q^2, we cannot be sure about the real John. The main problem is that what Q^2 reports about John is more reminiscent of the prophets of doom that Josephus says stepped forth during the Roman-Jewish war in the 60s than of anyone or anything we know about during the time of Jesus. This implies that the authors created this story about John and Jesus in the light of their experiences in the 60s, not with any interest in accurately describing circumstances appropriate to the late 20s.

The authors said three things about John. He appeared in the Jordan countryside. He called the people the "offspring of vipers" and warned them to flee from some fury about to break forth. And he said that someone else was coming to execute the judgment he was announcing. This is clearly a setup for Jesus who will take up the matter in QS 16–18. The strategy is clever, for it introduces the reader to the theme of judgment by hearing it first from John, not Jesus. Moreover, the message is exceptionally harsh and seems to predict a catastrophe of apocalyptic proportions. Fire will burn the trees, which will be cut down, and the chaff, which will be separated out at the harvest. The reader is not addressed directly, for the narrative locates John (and Jesus) in the past addressing some other audience. This means that the authors of Q^2 have started down the road toward a narrative myth of origin. The approach is unsettling, however, especially since the reader does not know what circumstance called for such a preachment. And the predicted event itself is not clear even as an apocalyptic vision. At first the fire and the fury seem to refer to some future event. But as metaphors, each could easily be applied as well to the appearance of both John and Jesus and the effect of their preaching and teaching. Let John give them hell, so the strategy seems to be, so that Jesus' later warnings will sound like pleasant instructions. What the fire and the spirit might mean in reference to Jesus and his activity is not explained. But, as we shall see, this is an intentional vagueness designed to create questions in the reader's mind that will be answered later on.

After this fiery preaching, Jesus appears in the voice of the Q^1 teacher. QS 8–14 was familiar, reassuring stuff and quite a contrast: "How fortunate are the poor." "Love your enemies." This hardly sounds like the grim reaper who burns the chaff with unquenchable fire, so the contrast between John's prediction and Jesus' teaching heightens the reader's sense of uncertainty. But then there is another novelty for the reader accustomed to thinking of Jesus only in Q^1 terms. What is this? A Roman centurion comes to Jesus asking that he heal his son. Is Jesus performing miracles of healing? Well, yes and no. The story does tell of a healing, but it is clear that the miracle per se was not the point. It was told in order to make two other points. One point was that a gentile, representing the mixed constituency of the people of Q, had less trouble with Jesus than those who belonged to Israel. The other was that John, who heard about the healing, had to send his disciples to ask what it meant. The process of reimagining Jesus demanded some such ploy, some way to help the reader move by degrees from the familiar image of Jesus as a sage to his new role as an apocalyptic prophet. At first the story does not seem to move Jesus' role in that direction, but it does set things up for building that bridge in the next segment. There the reader discovers that the purpose of the story was to start thinking about Jesus in relation to the prophets.

The Q^2 authors could find no better catchall role for recasting the character of Jesus than that of a prophet. If Jesus could be recast as a kind of prophet, connections could be made with (1) the theme of the rejection of the prophets, (2) the sweep of epic history as the repeated sending of wisdom's envoys, and (3) the authority to pronounce judgment in apocalyptic idiom. But there were two problems with the profile of the prophet. One was that Jesus was already being thought of as wisdom's child, not as a prophet. And the other was that the wisdom of God was a bit cool toward the prophets, preferring kings, priests, and teachers as her envoys. To address the second problem, QS 34 expanded wisdom's role by saying that her plan was to send wise men *and* prophets. Wisdom might then be imagined as having always been concerned over the fate of the prophets. The other problem was more serious. Prophets and sages were often distinguished from one another. Prophets as a class were better known for their predictions of judgment while sages were known for their constructive proposals for social health and healing. However, some of the prophets, such as Isaiah, were known for their predictions of hope and the restoration of Israel. If Jesus could be associated with this constructive side of the prophetic tradition, readers might eventually let him step forth in full judgmental regalia.

The story of the healing of the centurion's son was designed to lead the reader to just such a conclusion. It depicts Jesus as a humanitarian whose deed triggers John's curiosity and lets Jesus allude to Isaiah's predictions. This in turn leads to a set of questions and explanations about the true roles of both John and Jesus.

According to the authors of Q^2, John had never met Jesus (it was Mark who invented the story about Jesus being baptized by John). Thus John does not know about Jesus until his disciples tell him about the healing. When they tell him, John wants to know whether Jesus is the one he had announced as the one to come. He sends his disciples to inquire about this, and Jesus answers the question by telling them to report what they had seen and heard: "The blind recover their sight, the lame walk, lepers are cleansed, and the deaf hear, the dead are raised, and the poor are given good news" (QS 16). This is an oblique reference to the miracles of healing predicted by Isaiah for the time of Israel's restoration. The healing story, John's query, and Jesus' allusions to a prophecy of constructive restoration made it possible to start thinking of Jesus in terms of the prophetic tradition. But he was not burning the chaff with unquenchable fire, a point the authors wanted to get across. Poor John, that wasn't exactly what he had expected. No offense though, dear John (and dear readers as well): "Fortunate is the one who is not disturbed [at hearing these things] about me" (QS 16).

At this point the reader can see that a narrative logic is at work on a plot that pivots on the question of who John and Jesus were. What Jesus says about himself in QS 16, namely that he was bringing good news to the poor and healing to the dispossessed, comes as a surprise both to John and the reader familiar only with the Jesus of Q^1. The idea that Jesus fulfilled Isaiah's vision is so novel and unexpected that the reader is at first put off. But the thought cannot immediately be rejected, because the scene plays a crucial role in the narrative sequence about John and Jesus, and the plot of that narrative has not yet been resolved. In the next two episodes the plot finds its resolution in comments Jesus makes, first about John (QS 17), and then about "this generation" (QS 18). Paraphrasing the text, Jesus tells the crowds, "You knew that John was a prophet and not to expect royal garments when you saw him. But what you did not know, and what I now tell you, is that John was more than a prophet. He was the one about whom it is written, 'Look, I am sending my messenger before you. He will prepare your path ahead of you.'" Suddenly the John-Jesus question has led to a much more complicated set of relationships than one might have expected. The first twist is that John predicted one to come and thought that it might be Jesus. But Jesus said no, at least he was not the kind of messenger John had expected. The second complication is that Jesus quotes some writing that predicted one to come and said that it referred to *John*. What a strange idea. John had not claimed that he himself had been foretold. So we have two predictions about "one to come" and it is not clear what either of them means. In order to see the point of the authors' playfulness, which turns out to be quite important, we need to pause for a moment and unravel their logic.

The allusion to a written text shows that the authors of Q² had engaged in a bit of literary activity. They apparently conflated (or merged) God's words to Moses in Exodus 23:20 ("Look, I am sending my messenger before you") with God's words in Malachi 3:1 ("See, I am sending my messenger to prepare the path before me"). In Exodus, the messenger will lead Moses and the people to the promised land. In Malachi, the messenger would execute a judgment in preparation for God's arrival. Malachi emphasizes the term coming in his predictions: the messenger will come, the lord will come, and the day will come. And Malachi says that the sudden appearance of the messenger would be like a refiner's fire, that the day would be like a burning furnace to consume all the arrogant and evildoers. Supposing one were acquainted with Malachi's prophecy, one could hardly miss the connection with John's preaching about the coming one, the coming judgment, and the fire.

But now the fun begins. The question is, Who will do the burning of the chaff, John or Jesus? John thought it was Jesus. Jesus seems to say that it might be John. So the reader is now confronted with a puzzle. Could it be that the authors introduced John to "prepare the way" for Jesus to appear *in their book* about Jesus? Could it be that "burning the trees," "burning the chaff," and "overwhelming the people with fire" were all intended as metaphors of speech, applicable to John's fiery preaching as well as to Jesus' announcement of judgment (yet to come)?

As if on target, and probably smiling all the while, the authors now had Jesus turn to the crowds and explain what to make of it all. At first Jesus pays tribute to John as the greatest among those born of a woman, yet lower than the least in the kingdom of God. This puts John in his place, for it is a backhanded compliment. It does honor John as the last of the line of old-style prophets, and it does serve quite well as a grand farewell to John on the part of the authors. But he has done his job and belongs to the past. The future and the rest of Q belong to Jesus and what he will say about God's kingdom. In any case, John, having introduced the theme of judgment and raised the question of Jesus' identity, can now drop from sight as the teachings of Jesus unfold. But before that happens, the question of John and Jesus comes to a striking climax when Jesus tells the crowd that both John and Jesus should be seen as the children of wisdom.

This point is made in the next segment about the children in the marketplace. QS 18 takes up the question of how "this generation" responded to both John and Jesus. This segment must have been a priceless respite for the reader, for it backs away from the theme of prophets and their preachments, switches to the theme of wisdom and her children, and holds up a mirror for the Q^1 readers to see themselves reflected in the picture.

The picture is lovely, in the sense that a Fellini movie can be lovely. There are children making music in the marketplace, inviting each other to join the chorus. Some are playing the pipes and calling for a festive dance. Some are singing a dirge expecting the rest to weep as befitting a funeral. No one responds. So it is with "this generation."

Rejection is exactly what the people of Q had experienced. Rejection was the reason for taking up their discourse of judgment on "this generation," a theme that will course through the sayings of Jesus in Q^2. To catch sight of "this generation" looking like children refusing to play in the marketplace would have toned down the picture John had painted of the "offspring of vipers." It might even have been worth a reader's chuckle. But as Jesus continues to talk to the crowd, the refusal of the children to play is not applied to the rejection experienced by the Q community, but to the rejection of John and Jesus. Do the authors want their readers to think of the difference between the tone of John's preaching about judgment (the dirge) and Jesus' instruction in wisdom (the piping)? No doubt. And while this thought is allowed to simmer in the background, yet another shift in imagery focuses on their distinctive life-styles. This generation thinks that John, who appears as an austere ascetic, is crazy. And they say that the son of man (Jesus), whose style is convivial, is a glutton and a drunk. But what does Jesus say should be made of this difference? Despite the rebuffs, he says, both are children of wisdom, and both show how right the way of wisdom is. As Ron Cameron (1990) has shown, the authors used a common distinction between two types of Cynics to characterize both John and Jesus. They described John as a Cynic of the ascetic variety and Jesus as a Cynic of the libertine type. The point was that both were legitimate children of wisdom if one thought of them as Cynic philosophers.

This means that the well-known image of the Cynic philosopher, one who could perform both a "prophetic" and a "healing" role in society, was offered as the best way to overcome the contrast between John and Jesus. This point having been made, Jesus could now step forth as one who both played the pipes and sang a dirge, or offered instruction in wisdom and announced judgment at the same time.

This saying about wisdom's children concludes the narrative introduction to Q at the Q^2 level and prepares the reader for accepting the full range of sayings and preachments in Q (Q^1 plus Q^2) as coming from Jesus. It states that both John and Jesus were children of wisdom. Wisdom sends both kinds of messenger, and one should therefore not be surprised to learn that Jesus, who is also "more than a prophet," bears both kinds of message. As we shall see, the arrangement of material at the Q^2 level reveals how serious the authors were about merging the two kinds of discourse to create a common voice for Jesus. There are also indications that individual units of material were crafted with such a two-pronged discourse in mind. A clear example of this is the segment on the sign of Jonah in QS 32. Earlier it was indicated that one purpose of the stories about Jonah and Solomon was to provide unsettling examples from the epic history that "this generation" claimed as its own. Now it can be noted that, for the reader who belonged to the Jesus movement, the combination of Jonah and Solomon played an additional role. Jonah was a preacher of judgment and Solomon was a dispenser of wisdom. The selection of these two figures was surely intended as a reminder to the reader of the contrast between John and Jesus. The contrast has been overcome in the role of Jesus, according to these stories, because he was "something greater" than either Solomon or Jonah.

A final curiosity about the sayings in QS 18 is that Jesus refers to himself as the son of man: "The son of man has come eating and drinking, and they say, 'Look at him, a glutton and a drunkard.'" The modern reader may well have trouble with this strange term, but it plays a very important role in the developing mythology of Q^2. By using it here the authors tip their hand about the role they imagined for Jesus. They were interested not only in associating Jesus with the figure of wisdom, but with the mythology of the final judgment as well. Jesus' place in the grand epic-apocalyptic schema had to be clarified, not only in relation to the past, but also in relation to the future. The authors worked out Jesus' relation to the past by portraying him as wisdom's child. They decided on the designation son of man in order to link Jesus with the final judgment. They were able to use this term because it was capable of referring both to Jesus as a "child of humankind" (one of its meanings) as well as to a figure associated with apocalyptic mythologies (another of its meanings). To appreciate the skill with which the authors used this term, we need to know what the term meant in the culture of the time and how the term was put to work in the Q tradition.

The term son of man was not at all a felicitous construction in Greek, nor did it make much sense in Greek. But in Aramaic, from which the Greek translation derives, the term meant "a human being" (literally, "a child of humankind"), and it could be used as a circumlocution for self-reference, should a speaker prefer not to use the pronoun I. In the book of Daniel, however, the term was used to describe a human figure that appeared in an apocalyptic vision. The key verses are Daniel 7:13–14, which the NRSV translates as follows: "As I watched in the night visions, I saw one like a human being coming with the clouds of heaven. And he came to the Ancient One and was presented before him. To him was given dominion and glory and kingship, that all peoples, nations, and languages should serve him." As one can see, this was an innocent use of the term with the sole purpose of saying that the mysterious figure to whom God granted sovereign power looked like a human being. But that was enough to set the juices flowing as later full-blown mythologies of the son of man show, especially in early Christian texts and the Jewish apocalypses of the late first century contained in 1 Enoch and 4 Ezra. Thus the term son of man was doubly mysterious in the Q tradition. It sounded odd in Greek, and it had the capacity for ambiguous reference, either to a particular person as a human being (in this case Jesus), or to an apocalyptic figure, or both. The authors took full advantage of this referential capacity by using the term in both ways.

There is one occurrence of the term at the Q^1 layer where it is used as an innocent circumlocution. To a would-be follower Jesus said, "Foxes have dens, and birds of the sky have nests, but the son of man has nowhere to lay his head" (QS 19). This was an interesting play on the Cynic theme of homelessness. It was also a perfectly innocent play on the ambiguity between reference to any human being and to Jesus as a human being. Note that in the arrangement of materials at the Q^2 level, this saying follows the conclusion of the John-Jesus exchange in which Jesus uses the term clearly in self-reference. This sequence is part of the authors' strategy as the following survey shows.

The first use of the term at the Q^2 level is in the section on honorific pronouncements: "How fortunate you are when they reproach you . . . because of the son of man" (QS 8). This is not an innocent use of the term. It belongs to the stage in the development of the group's thinking at which loyalty to the movement could be expressed in terms of loyalty to Jesus. The saying was added to the first three pronouncements of honor in order to introduce the themes of loyalty and judgment in the first speech of Jesus, which otherwise is composed largely of Q^1 material. It was also an appropriate place to introduce the term son of man and thus prepare the reader for its use as a self-reference in QS 18 ("The son of man has come eating and drinking") and in QS 19 ("The son of man has nowhere to lay his head"). QS 19 will now be read as a circumlocution or self-reference.

The next occurrence of the term is in the section on the sign of Jonah: "For as Jonah became a sign to the Ninevites, so will the son of man be to this generation" (QS 32). This unit associates Jesus' role as the son of man with his role as the announcer of a final judgment. Thus far there has been no indication that the authors were also thinking about a figure called the son of man who would play a significant role at the final judgment. But if one knew about that figure, one might begin to wonder about the relation Jesus might have to this apocalyptic figure. The association is already close. Jesus as the son of man pronounces judgment on "this generation" and predicts the final judgment; at the final judgment the son of man will appear as the central figure in the trial. Sure enough, this question is addressed in the next use of the term.

The relationship between Jesus and the apocalyptic son of man is stated in QS 37: "Every one who admits in public that they know me, the son of man will acknowledge before the angels of God." This is an extremely important statement, for it links the earthly Jesus to the heavenly son of man in a tight formula of reciprocity even while it retains a distinction between them. With this connection made, the conceptual work of the mythmaking project is almost complete. All that remains is to make sure that the son of man figures prominently in the apocalyptic vision of the final judgment. This is achieved in QS 41 and QS 60 where the future appearance of the son of man occurs on the day of judgment that will surely come. "So it will be on the day when the son of man appears" (QS 60).

Thus the bits and pieces of several diverse mythologies converge on the figure of Jesus and position him at the decisive turn of a fantastic history. The wisdom myth, the notion of a line of prophets, the epic of Israel read inside-out, the mechanism of prediction and fulfillment, the projection of a final judgment, and the apocalyptic figure of the son of man were all linked to Jesus as the linchpin of a dynamic myth of origin for the people of Q. The ragged seams and the rough edges had not been smoothed out. It is questionable whether the authors of Q^2 could have managed a more coherent mythology at this stage, for a fully articulated mythology on the grand scale would have required much more work and a switch to genres other than that of a collection of sayings. But they were not ready for that, or in need of it. Their connection to Jesus was firmly in place by virtue of being in possession of his instructions. So the form of their mythology was perfectly appropriate for their movement. The relationships Jesus sustained to the grand sweep of epic-apocalyptic history were thought through solely in relation to the importance of Jesus for the people of Q as their founder-teacher. Thus every mythological association was formulated and expressed as a saying of Jesus. One can see that, in daring to ascribe such importance to Jesus and his sayings, the people of Q were in the process of taking themselves quite seriously.

One can only be astonished at the claims these people were making for the importance of Jesus. It is a long jump from Cynic-sage to apocalyptic visionary. And yet, by filling in the stages of their social history, we can see that each incremental shift in their reimagination of Jesus does not appear drastic. Basic to the entire enterprise was the attraction of a teacher and his teachings, teachings that generated a discourse that soon created a social movement.

The common thread from the Cynic sage to the apocalyptic visionary was an elaboration of Jesus' wisdom. The modern reader may struggle to see the connections among the many kinds of knowledge ascribed to Jesus by the Q people. But others of their time would have recognized that, throughout all of their elaborations, they continued to regard Jesus as a sage. As a matter of fact, their ascriptions of knowledge to Jesus would not have been tested on a scale of plausibility that ran from reason to special revelation, or that asked how Jesus could have known what they said he knew, as we might want to do, but rather in terms of the appropriateness of his insights with regard to their view of the world. The people of Q were very consistent in attributing knowledge to Jesus from their perspective of a countercultural assessment of the world.

The Cynic-like aphorisms counted as gifted insight into the human, social situation. The Cynic-like injunctions were crafted as sage strategies for the survival of social critics. The elaboration of the injunctions into ethical codes for the countercultural movement drew upon a knowledge that took the form of a theology of nature. No one would have thought that strange. Epic precedence was achieved by viewing its critical principle, the line of prophets, from the vantage point of a transcendent wisdom reduced to sending envoys. The current mythologies of wisdom made that possible. And the vision of a final judgment counted as wisdom because it fit the logic of the movement's need to position itself in history.

The strange aspect from the modern reader's point of view is that Jesus was eventually pictured as knowing everything from the beginning to the end of time, including how he himself fit into God's grand scheme. Some knowledge! But this was not attributed all at once. It accrued in the course of using the sayings genre to fit all the pieces of a myth of origin together. The image of Jesus as the revealer of special, esoteric, and transcendent knowledge of all the world and human history did not evolve because the people of Q had been mesmerized by a charismatic guru. It was an accidental accumulation of wisdom created by the simple device of mythmaking in the genre of instruction. By turning every bit of collective thinking into a crystallized instruction from Jesus, the people of Q overloaded their founder with wisdom. And because he became the pivotal figure in the particular mythologized history that the group worked out, the teacher's wisdom eventually included a preposterous self-understanding. The people of Q had not yet imagined that Jesus had appeared in human history as a transcendent mythological being, but that thought could easily occur now, should circumstances change. The distinctions were already very fuzzy between Jesus and the wisdom of God on the one hand, and Jesus and the son of man on the other.

This being the case, the people of Q had constructed a very dangerous world in which to live. Although it is true that they had managed to claim for themselves a place in the sun, the place they chose was risky because it took its bearings from history, and the final word on human history was still to come. They had imagined a final judgment in order to guarantee their threat against the world outside. But judgment is judgment, and the standard was set. So the threat of judgment came back to haunt the people of Q themselves. They were the ones who knew the standard, and that was their privilege. It was keeping the words of Jesus that mattered. But they really had to keep them now. Not to keep them would have grave consequences indeed.

The authors of Q^2 were well aware that the threat of a final judgment had to be taken seriously by the Q community. Two features of their composition were designed with this problem in mind. The first is that the organization of materials in Q^2 forces the reader to interpret Jesus' instructions to the community (the Q^1 sayings) in the light of the theme of judgment (the Q^2 sayings). The second is that Jesus' instructions to the community at the Q^2 level include both warnings about the final judgment and words of assurance that everything will work out all right for those who continue to keep Jesus' words. This can be shown by outlining the organization of materials as Q^2 put them together.

Table 1 shows the organization of materials in Q by calling attention to the way in which Q^2 material frames Q^1 material from beginning to end. The framing is detailed in that the blocks of Q^1 sayings are placed appropriately among Q^2 material in order to provide an interpretive context. The outline also highlights the change of address at the Q^2 level and shows how it becomes a pattern by repetition. The pattern follows a cycle that begins with an address to the world at large, takes a turn to address the community in the light of the judgment theme, and ultimately comes to focus on the Q^1 sayings of Jesus as community rules. These Q^1 instructions were not retained by copyists because they wanted to pass on "sacred" or "received traditions," as many modern scholars have thought. The Q^1 material was included because it was still valid instruction for the community. This material represented the words of Jesus that one had to keep in order to stand trial at the judgment. The codes worked out at the Q^1 level were not left behind when the people of Q started thinking about judgment. Far from being passé, the Q^1 instructions were now all the more important. One can see this by reading through the document as a whole to note just how serious the keeping of the Q^1 instructions had become. The effect on the reader familiar only with the voice of Jesus typified by Q^1 material would have been sobering.

A final observation on the text can bring this chapter to a close by demonstrating how the people of Q responded to their own mythology. In the section on anxiety and speaking out (QS 35–37), there is a subset of three small sayings clusters that form a remarkable unit of argumentation. Disclosure, fear, and trial are the topics, and the final judgment is in view. In the last cluster one learns that the people of Q are worried about what to say should they be asked to give an account of themselves before *synagogues* ("assemblies" of the people, presumably of the Jewish people in a town). The advice

TABLE 1.

AN OUTLINE OF THE CONTENTS OF Q

The outline highlights two features of the design at the Q^2 level. One is the way in which Q^2 material frames units of interspersed Q^1 material. The other is a pattern of address that shifts back and forth between the community and its public:

Q^1 = Primary instructions addressed to the community.

Q^{2a} = Judgmental sayings that address "this generation."

Q^{2b} = Instructions to the community in the light of the judgmental sayings addressed to "this generation."

Q^1	Q^{2a}	Q^{2b}	
Introduction			(QS 1–2)
	John's Preaching		(QS 3–5)
Jesus' Teaching			(QS 7–14)
	What John and Jesus Thought		(QS 15–18)
Instructions for the Movement			(QS 19–20)
	Pronouncements Against Towns		(QS 21–22)
		Congratulations to Persons	(QS 23, 25)
Confidence in the Father's Care			(QS 26–27)
	Controversies with This Generation		(QS 28)
		Caution on Taking Sides	(QS 29–30)
	Judgment on This Generation		(QS 32)
		True Enlightenment	(QS 33)
	Pronouncements Against the Pharisees		(QS 34)
On Anxiety and Speaking Out			(QS 35–36)
		On Public Confessions	(QS 37)
On Personal Goods			(QS 38–40)
	The Coming Judgment		(QS 41–45)
Parables of the Kingdom			(QS 46)
	The Two Ways		(QS 47–48)
The True Followers of Jesus			(QS 50–53)
		Community Rules	(QS 54–55, 57–59)
	The Final Judgment		(QS 60–61)

throughout the unit is that one needs to be careful what one says at all times, but especially about how one talks about Jesus. The clusters read as follows:

ON ANXIETY AND SPEAKING OUT

QS 35 *ON SPEAKING OUT*

"Nothing is hidden that will not be made known, or secret that will not come to light.

What I tell you in the dark, speak in the light. And what you hear as a whisper, proclaim on the housetops."

QS 36 *ON FEAR*

"Don't be afraid of those who can kill the body, but can't kill the soul.

Can't you buy five sparrows for two cents? Not one of them will fall to the ground without God knowing about it. Even the hairs of your head are all numbered. So don't be afraid. You are worth more than many sparrows."

QS 37 *ON PUBLIC CONFESSIONS*

"Every one who admits in public that they know me, the son of man will acknowledge before the angels of God [heavenly court]. But the one who disowns me in public, the son of man will disown before the angels of God.

Whoever makes a speech against the son of man will be forgiven. But whoever speaks against the holy spirit will not be forgiven.

When they bring you before the assemblies of the people [synagogues or town meetings], don't worry about what you are to say. When the time comes, the holy spirit will teach you what you are to say."

The first two clusters contain sayings about secrets coming to light and not being afraid of any person. The original meaning of these sayings fits well into a Q^1 context as general cautionary advice. At the Q^2 level, however, they have taken on a more somber tone. Now they seem to apply to the situation of conflict with "this generation" as well as to the final judgment. And they serve as points of departure for the section on public hearings that follows immediately in QS 37. By treating these three clusters as a set, we can see that there are two trials under consideration, (1) the final judgment and (2) questioning before the assembly. Since each has been thought of in relation to the other, it is clear that the Q community had begun to imagine their world as a huge courtroom. What one said in private would be made public. What one said in public would be questioned before the assembly. What one said before the assembly would determine one's fate in the heavenly court or final judgment. In this situation of trial, one was and would be required to give an account of oneself as a member of the Jesus movement. Of the many topics that might come up, three were critical, each for different reasons. One needed to know the consequences when speaking about Jesus, the son of man, and the holy spirit.

About Jesus there was no room for equivocation. Either one belonged or did not belong to the Jesus movement, that is, admitted that they "knew" Jesus. The consequences were clearly spelled out. At the final judgment the formula of reciprocity would be exact. Acknowledgment now would bring acknowledgment then; denial now would bring denial then.

If asked about the son of man, however, the situation was a bit different. One should not speak against the son of man, but if one did so, it was forgivable. This sounds a bit strange at first, but it can be explained. A distinction was being made between Jesus and the son of man and what one said about each of them. One admitted or denied loyalty to Jesus; one spoke for or against the son of man. To "make a speech against" was a technical description for presenting evidence and arguments in a trial setting. So, although there could be no equivocation on what the name "Jesus" meant and whether one was a Jesus person or not, it was quite possible to have some difference of opinion on the topic of the son of man. With regard to one's view of Jesus, one simply entered a "plea" of admission or denial. With regard to the son of man, there could be debate. It was forgivable if one had to disclaim the community's talk about the son of man. This means that, although the Q community agreed on the importance of saying they were loyal to Jesus, not all were clear about the idea of the son of man and his relation to Jesus. And even the authors of Q^2, who were convinced that the son of man was an important idea, were willing to keep the son of man and Jesus in separate conceptual compartments and not demand that all agree. This was quite a concession and shows that the people of Q were aware of the mythological or symbolic status of the term son of man even while they used it to picture the final judgment.

If the topic of the son of man came up at a "trial" before an assembly, this escape clause might make a significant difference in the outcome. Since the son of man belonged to the community's mythology of the final trial, and since the mythology grew out of the community's discourse of threat against "this generation," it might have been very difficult to acknowledge and explain one's view of the son of man and the final judgment to the very leaders of the assembly who were sitting in the seat of judgment. The escape clause might even be seen as a remnant of the cautionary strategies of survival typical for the Q^1 stage of discourse. The saying in QS 45 about settling with one's accuser on the way to the judge supports this suspicion. And besides, so the thought seems to be, it was Jesus and the keeping of his words that were of first importance. It would be enough not to deny that. One might be forgiven for fudging a bit, should the subject of the judgment and the son of man come up.

What then of the distinction between the son of man and the holy spirit? Why was it forgivable to speak against the son of man, but not against the holy spirit? Does that rather straightforward threat have anything to do with the following saying about not worrying because the holy spirit would teach you what to say at the trial?

These references to the holy spirit come as a surprise to the critical reader of Q. There was no mention of a holy spirit in Q^1, and the concept occurs in Q^2 only here in QS 37 and in John's prediction that the one to come (Jesus) would overwhelm the people with holy spirit (QS 5). So we have to proceed with caution, for these references hardly constitute the development of a theme and may not give us enough information to say with certainty how the term was being used or why "speaking a word against" the spirit was unforgivable. There are, however, some clues to the answer to these questions and they should be pursued.

When John predicted the one to come, the metaphors of fire and spirit seemed first to imply an apocalyptic event in which the "chaff" would be burned by fire and the "wheat" would be separated out by the action of the wind, or holy spirit, for gathering into the barns. As a prediction of what Jesus would do, however, whether at the final judgment, or in his preachments as an apocalyptic seer, John's description was found to be questionable. Jesus even suggested that John may have performed the very function he thought Jesus would perform and that both John, the preacher of judgment, and Jesus, the instructor in wisdom, were children of wisdom. This play on the metaphors of fire and spirit in the opening scene gives us our first clue. Fire and spirit seem to be working as metaphors for the effect of different kinds of speech, the announcement of judgment on the one hand, and sapiential instruction on the other. Is that possible?

Fire as a metaphor for the judgmental edge of Jesus' teachings does occur elsewhere in Q in relation to the sayings on the divisions he came to make (QS 43). If we imagine a trial as the scene for judging the effectiveness of the words of Jesus, fire would refer to his sayings as the pronouncement of judgment upon the rightly accused. If so, the metaphor of the spirit might refer to sayings in the defense of the wrongly accused. This would fit with the function of the holy spirit at the trial before the assemblies in QS 37. But what kind of speech would that be?

Spirit and prophecy go together in the traditional image of the prophet, of course, so that the relationship between spirit and predictive speech is one possibility. But there was also a long and strong tradition of thought about the "spirit of wisdom," a metaphor that combined the notion of effective speech with that of special insight into the deep structures of the world. "Spirit" captured the aspect of insight as inspiration; "wisdom" referred to the knowledge one gained by insight. Putting the two together was a way of acknowledging insight as a serendipitous experience. If one were able to put such an insight into words, that would be speech enabled by the spirit of wisdom. Naturally, the metaphor was particularly appropriate for insight into the ways of God in the world of creation, the history of humanity, the social orders, and the secrets of the heart.

It is obvious that the vision of standing trial had traumatized the Q community. It is also clear that what one said on such an occasion would be critical, because the situation was potentially divisive. Wisdom would be required even if one thought to recall something from the community's ongoing discourse about the words of Jesus. There was really nothing one could memorize in advance. How frightening to think that one might be asked what Jesus people were saying about wisdom, the prophets, a final judgment, and the son of man.

The saying of Jesus promises that help would arrive on the spot. There was no sense in worrying about it. If one's loyalty to Jesus was in place, one could be sure that one would find the right words on the occasion and that they would be effective. One may or may not divide the house with a convincing speech of judgment directed toward one's questioners, but one could be sure of defending oneself as a member of the Jesus movement. If one did do that, it would be a holy spirit speech.

So the holy spirit was a term used by the people of Q to make the connection between their mythology and their situation. As a concept it differed from Jesus, wisdom, and the son of man in that it did not have the status of a primary agent. Instead, it served as a manifestation of the primary agent wisdom. The spirit of wisdom would make it possible for the least in the kingdom of God not to lose their footing, vision, courage, or ability to speak when pressured by the real world. The people of Q had no desire or need to imagine the continuing presence of Jesus among them. But since they had positioned themselves in such an enormously fateful history, they did need access to the wisdom of God. The concept of the holy spirit of wisdom was the ready answer. When asked, one could be sure that one's speech would be intelligent if one were confident about one's loyalty to Jesus and if one felt sure about the wisdom of the community's view of the world.

9

Coming to Terms

The Roman-Jewish war brought to an end a glorious epoch in Jewish history and created consternation for Jews and Jesus people alike. The war lasted the better part of ten years, from the riots and skirmishes of 66 C.E., through the battles that raged around and within Jerusalem for four years, to the fall of Masada in 73 C.E. Reading the history of the war written by Josephus, one gets the impression that the internecine conflicts within Judea and Jerusalem were as devastating to the social order as the armies of the Romans were to the city walls and defenses. When it was over, the temple was in ruins, Jerusalem was a burned wasteland, and many of the people of Judea had been uprooted and scattered throughout Palestine, Transjordan, and the cities along the coast. It was a bloody end to the second temple-state, and there was no official leadership left to put its pieces back together. There were, as a matter of fact, hardly any pieces left. What to think and do was the question.

None of the many forms of Jewish society was unaffected by this event. The Jewish aristocracy, the priests, the Pharisees, the village councils, the scribes attached to the network of stations, the Qumran enclave, and the local leaders of diaspora synagogues had to rethink what it meant to be a Jew and how to reorganize Jewish society. Samaritans and Galileans had also been embroiled in the upheaval, caught in the middle between the Jerusalem establishment and the Romans. Erstwhile loyalties were hardly the only issue as the armies

172

came and went. Whose side to be on was a practical question that wrenched every family, village, and town. Everyone was unsettled by the confusion and violence of the times. And the Jesus movements also had to find some way to weather the storm.

Q^3 provides a little window into the Q community after the war. It is too small a window to see as much of the social landscape as one would like, and it provides only hints of what it must have been like for the people of Q during the war. During that period of their history there was apparently little time for reflection or occasion for coming to agreements on attitudes and strategies appropriate for the movement. But some of the people of Q did manage to stay in touch with one another, and Q^3 provides us with evidence that the movement survived. It also reveals that three or four shifts in attitude occurred in the period after the war, and these point to a particular path that the Q people had decided to take.

In this chapter we shall look through that window. It is our last chance to catch a glimpse of the Jesus people according to Q, for the Q^3 additions were the last embellishments on the document of which we can be certain before it was subsumed by the authors of the narrative gospels later in the century. It is, of course, possible that Q continued to be copied and consulted by Jesus people who resisted the attractions of the new myths created by the narrative gospels, and that they went their own way. It is also conceivable that the Q^3 edition was not the last change to the document within that kind of group, and that Q continued to have its own illustrious history of revision independent of the use made of it by the authors of the narrative gospels. But if so, history passed those people by, for there are no records of a Jesus movement using only a document like Q after the narrative gospels appeared.

What we do know is that the community of Q produced a very popular document that was widely read during the last quarter of the first century. It must have been copied many times and shared among several groups of Jesus people who were going separate ways. Mark, Matthew, and Luke each used a copy of Q independent of each other, and each made use of Q from a distinctly different perspective. So Q was still in circulation as a document at the end of the first century. But what that might say for the history of the Q community is very difficult to assess. The text of Q had been dislodged from the group that produced it; the period was one of vigorous social and intellectual experimentation within the Jesus movement; and the people of Q certainly were capable of shifting perspectives and entertaining new ideas. If one were to ask which of the narrative gospels most nearly represents an ethos toward which the community of Q may have tended, it would be the Gospel of Matthew. But to see that connection should not foreclose on other turns that may have been taken. Unfortunately, after Q^3 we simply lose track of the Jesus people who produced the document called Q.

What we can do is trace four fateful turns in the history of the Q document before it also slips from sight. Three of these junctures in its literary history are the ways in which it was used by each of the authors of the narrative gospels. The fourth has to do with its relation to the Gospel of Thomas. What happened to Q in relation to these other gospels needs to be kept in mind as we turn to the matter of revising the conventional picture of Christian origins in part IV of this book.

In order to trace the legacy of Q, we need to understand the change in ethos created by the Q^3 additions. The most obvious addition is the story of the temptations of Jesus at the beginning of the document in QS 6, but there are other additions inserted here and there of even greater significance. The lament over Jerusalem is one of them (QS 49), and the sayings on the law in QS 56 is another. The list also includes the secret revelation to the "babies" about the son of God (QS 24), the saying about those who listen to God's teaching (QS 31), the qualification of the charges against the Pharisees (QS 34), the saying about hell fire (QS 36), and the last saying of the document about the people of Q who will "sit on thrones judging the twelve tribes of Israel" (QS 62).

The story of the temptations of Jesus introduces three new themes characteristic of Q^3. They are (1) the mythology of Jesus as the son of God, (2) the relationship of Jesus as the son of God to the temple at Jerusalem, and (3) the authority of the scriptures.

Upgrading the mythology of Jesus from child of wisdom (Q^2) to son of God (Q^3) may seem to be a small step, but note the consequences. Jesus was no longer imagined as a sage whose knowledge was divine. He was imagined as an otherworldly being, heir of the father's kingdom (QS 24) in battle with the accuser for the authority to rule over the kingdoms of the earth, whose hour for full disclosure would come in the future (QS 49), at which time he would turn the father's kingdom over to his followers so they could rule over the twelve tribes of Israel (QS 62). This is quite a myth. It can be understood as a further development of the Q^2 mythology, for it draws on the same traditions of wisdom mythology as were operative at the Q^2 level, and it succeeds in smoothing out the connections among the various mythological figures and roles that were still quite rough in Q^2. It achieved this unified mythology by merging all of the earlier mythological concepts in the single figure of the son of God. But the change in characterization is a radical shift, and the mythic frame now gives the sayings of Jesus an ethereal cast. One has the sense that the people of Q lost their public bearings during the war and turned within to cultivate an esoteric confidence.

The entrance of the temple into Q's field of vision is particularly telling. The temple and its establishment did not occupy a significant place in Q's world for the first forty years of the movement. Now it looms large, but only as a sad symbol of misplaced loyalties or as a lesson in the misuse of power, not as an institution whose demise created an ideological crisis for the Q community. The temple figures importantly in the temptation story and in the lament. In the story of the temptation the temple is associated with the kingdoms of the world on the one hand, and with the appropriate worship of God on the other. It is an appropriate setting for the conflict over authority and sovereignty represented by the accuser and Jesus. Naturally Jesus wins, but that does not mean he takes possession of the temple. Jesus is not interested in the temple and his kingdom will not be affected by its destruction. But if there is no desire to cleanse, rescue, or take possession of the religion symbolized by the temple, there is also no animosity toward the temple, no criticism of what the temple stood for, and no ominous portents of its coming destruction. The temple serves merely as the setting for a debate about piety and power. Apparently the people of Q had given quite a bit of thought to the lesson of the war and its meaning for their own movement. The kingdom they represented was not touched by the war, but its status as a realm apart from the machinations of Jewish and Roman history was clarified.

The lament over Jerusalem (QS 49) is even more instructive. The speaker looks back on the destruction of the temple as a desolation of the house of God and mourns its tragic end. The voice is that of the wisdom of God whose longstanding desire had been to nest there, gathering her children under her protective wings. This agrees with a major theme in wisdom mythology according to which wisdom sought a place to dwell in Israel and built or took up residence in the temple (Sir. 24). In Q, she laments her loss and promises to come again. Or is it Jesus, speaking in the voice of wisdom, who promises to return in his role as the son of man and the son of God? Either way, the mythology of Jesus as a divine being is clear.

As in the temptation story, the attitude toward the temple in this lament does not reflect any ideological investment. It does not seek to account for the destruction. It does not take advantage of the event to say "I told you so." It is not gleeful as if the Jerusalem temple got its just desserts. But it does contrast with the Q^2 saying in QS 34 about wisdom sending her prophets who she knew would be killed. That saying is a composite of three distinct themes: the intention to send the prophets, the statement that "this generation" would be held accountable for the blood of all the prophets, and a reference to an unknown Zechariah "who perished between the altar and the sanctuary." One suspects that the additions were made at different times, the last one in the shadow of the war itself. The reason for this suspicion is that the saying sounds implausible until one reads Josephus' accounts of the bloodshed in the temple precincts during the war. If that is so, one can see that the people of Q used the myth of wisdom's envoys to express horror of the war (QS 34), then the myth of wisdom's quest for a home to express sorrow in its aftermath (QS 49). At the Q^3 level Jesus no longer needed to be justified as a prophetic figure, and the myth of wisdom sending her messengers and prophets to Jerusalem was now a matter of past history. She mourns, and Jesus her child, the son of God, is allowed to echo her lament. For the people of Q the destruction of the temple was a monument to the failure of second-temple Judaism to construct a society worthy of wisdom's residence. And so, although a critique of second-temple Judaism had not been a primary motivation in their movement, the Q people took advantage of its end to think of themselves as the heirs of Israel's wisdom. The destruction of the temple released the wisdom myth from its link to Jerusalem as the traditional place for its practical incarnation, and it set wisdom free to care for the kingdom of God represented by the people of Q.

The third and truly surprising novelty in Q^3 is an attitude that the people of Q took with regard to the authority of the Jewish scriptures and the relevance of the written law. In the temptation story Jesus is pictured in debate with the accuser over the requirements of the law. In the saying on hearing and keeping the teaching of God the reference appears to be to the scriptures (QS 31). The charges against the Pharisees are effectively retracted by the Q^3 addition that the codes on washings, alms, and offerings are to be kept (QS 34). And in the segment of sayings on the law, the written law stands even if heaven and earth were to pass away (QS 56). There is even a saying to the effect that remarriage after divorce counts as adultery (QS 56).

It thus appears that the people of Q made some adjustments in their self-understanding. The period of conflict with "this generation" was past. The debate over the Pharisaic standards of piety was no longer wrenching. The community was still committed to its claim to represent the kingdom of God, but it was now aware of its own dislocation from the social and political landscape of its times. A retreat from social conflict to care for its own ethical integrity had apparently found the words of Jesus insufficient as a guide. Having already used the scriptures for the purpose of laying claim to the epic tradition of Israel, they were now reconsidered as ethical guidelines appropriate to the kingdom of God. The function of the scriptures as an epic with etiological focus on Jerusalem was a thing of the past; the scriptures were now available for reappropriation. Thus a Jewish sensibility won out as the community settled in for the long run.

This move toward an accommodation of Jewish sensibility, reflected in the last layer of compositional history, is a most remarkable feature of Q. Although such a move seems surprising in light of the earlier history of the Q people, it must have been an appealing solution to the confusion created by the destruction of Jerusalem. It is, at any rate, the earliest evidence for an accommodation of the Jewish law within the Jesus movement, an accommodation that, when we meet it again in the Gospel of Matthew, can be called Jewish-Christianity. Jewish-Christianity became a very popular, widespread, influential, and long-lived legacy of the Jesus movements. The community of Q had not yet become a Christian community of this kind, however, and a move to accommodate Jewish law was not the only option taken by the followers of Jesus.

We must set the history of the Q community in the context of other groups of Jesus people who took different paths, experienced different social histories and group formations, and worked out different mythological rationales. The Christ cult, for instance, can only be understood as a Jesus movement that spread at an early period to northern Syria and Asia Minor where it quickly developed into a religious society on the model of a hellenistic mystery cult. The author of the Gospel of Mark was at home within some Jesus movement that had spread to the cities of southern Syria and tried, without success, to work out a common understanding with the local diaspora synagogues. To write his gospel, Mark used written traditions from yet another Jesus group that had experimented with a myth of origin in the genre of miracle story. And the Gospel of Thomas shows that a group very much like the people of Q, and perhaps a part of the Q movement during its very earliest phase, refused to get involved with the Q mission and then struck off on its own when the people of Q ran into opposition and began to call down judgments on "this generation." So the people of Q were only one configuration within a variety of groups that formed among the followers of Jesus. But the people of Q must have established one of the stronger traditions, because the document they produced came to be regarded by others as a very strong text.

Strong texts attract strong readers, and strong readings intentionally subvert the original meaning of a text in the interest of creating a new vision by composing a new text. In the case of Q we have clear evidence of three very strong readings of the complete text (Mark, Matthew, and Luke) and one very strong reading of a sizable selection of the sayings in Q (the Gospel of Thomas). Q was the most important text in the hands of Mark, Matthew, and Luke as they composed their narrative gospels. Without Q they would not have been able to write the stories they did. And the Gospel of Thomas stands in the tradition of Q, subverting the original intention of its sayings in the interest of creating an entirely different ethos. A brief sketch of the way in which each of these authors purposely misread Q will be a fitting conclusion to the story of the lost gospel.

Mark wrote his story of Jesus some time after the war and shortly after Q had been revised with the Q^3 additions. If we date Q^3 around 75 c.e. to give some time for the additions obviously prompted by the war, Mark can be dated between 75 and 80 C.E. Mark's community also had been confused by the war, but it drew a conclusion about the war's meaning that was quite different from the position taken by the people of Q. Mark thought that the destruction of the temple was exactly what the Jews deserved. He based this partially on an old Jewish idea that had been used to account for other disasters and was alive once more, namely that the failure of their leaders to respond correctly to God's intention for them had occasioned his wrath and resulted in the destruction of the temple. But also, Mark thought they deserved it because the Jewish synagogues with which his group had been in contact had rejected the Jesus movement. This forced his group to reconsider their identity apart from this link to Israel's heritage. He therefore wrote his story of Jesus to give the impression that all of the Jewish leaders had rejected Jesus and thus sealed the fate of second-temple Judaism.

To show this he told the story of Jesus' crucifixion as if it were a plot on the part of the Jewish leaders to get rid of Jesus because he had challenged their religion, law, and institutional authority. He was able to get by with this because the Jerusalem establishment and temple were no longer in existence. He achieved this fiction by combining (1) a few traditions from the Christ cult, such as its view of Jesus' death as a martyrdom and its practice of a memorial meal; (2) material from several Jesus movements other than Q, such as the stories in which Jesus debated with his opponents, called pronouncement stories, and two sets of miracle stories; and (3) the material that comprised Q.

For Mark, Q was extremely useful, for it had already positioned Jesus at the hinge of an epic-apocalyptic history, and it contained themes and narrative material that could easily be turned into a more eventful depiction of Jesus' public appearance. Q provided Mark with a large number of themes essential to his narrative. He was taken with the epic-apocalyptic mythology, the theme of prophetic prediction, and the announcement of judgment upon the scribes, Pharisees, and "this generation." The figure of the son of man intrigued him, as did the notion that the kingdom of God would be fully revealed only at the eschaton when the son of man (or Jesus, according to Mark) (re)appeared. Q also provided material that could easily be turned to advantage as building blocks in a coherent narrative account. The

John-Jesus material was a great opener. The figure of the holy spirit was ready-made to connect the Q material on John and Jesus with the miracle stories Mark would use. Q's characterization of Jesus as the all-knowing one could be used to enhance his authority as a self-referential speaker in the pronouncement stories Mark already had from his own community. The notion of Jesus as the son of God could be used to create mystique, divide the house on the question of Jesus' true identity, and develop narrative anticipation, the device scholars call Mark's "messianic secret." The instructions for the workers in the harvest could be turned into a mission charge, and the theme of discipleship could be combined and given narrative profile by introducing a few disciples into the story. The apocalyptic predictions at the end of Q could then become instructions to the disciples at that point in the story where Jesus turns to go to Jerusalem. And, as scholars know, there are a myriad of interesting points at which the so-called overlaps between Mark and Q show Mark's use of Q material for his own narrative designs.

Naturally, Mark had to recast everything. An obvious switch is that Mark radically changed the Q material on John and Jesus. He pictured John as knowing his role as the predicted precursor for Jesus, invented a story about John actually baptizing Jesus, and used that scene to introduce Jesus to the reader and the world as the son of God endowed with the holy spirit. A very dramatic beginning. The temptation story would not work as Q had it, but it could be used in a truncated reference to make the transition from the Jordan to Galilee and dramatize Jesus' entrance there. The conflict with the scribes and Pharisees required a narrative setting and so would take place, according to Mark, in synagogues. And the mission that failed had to be revised. This turned out to be the hard part.

To match Mark's plot, Jesus' appearance in Galilee had to be a public event in the grand style. It had to make sense as an occasion both for a successful mission and for a disturbance of sufficient gravity to launch the plot to have Jesus killed. Mark worked it out by dividing the populace into four groups. One was the people who were eager for Jesus' teachings and healings; in this sense the mission was a success. A second group, the Jewish leaders, understood enough to agree among themselves that Jesus had to be destroyed but not enough to accept his role as the king-to-be; in this sense the mission was a failure. A third group, the disciples, were given instructions about the future kingdom of God, but were too dense to get it straight; so in this sense the mission was one of failed instruction. Who then were the ones who knew for certain what was happening? According to Mark it was the fourth group, the demons, but they were forbidden to tell. What a story.

One can see why Mark left out most of the Q^1 instructions. There was no place in his story for Jesus to be instructing people in the ethics of a Jesus movement. And besides, it was the mythological Jesus that had to be killed in order for the story to work as a myth of origin for Mark's rejected community because that is the way Jesus had come to be imagined. Any other Jesus would not have been their Jesus. And as for storytelling, it was one thing to cast Jesus as a sovereign figure whose challenge to the authorities resulted in his crucifixion, but it would have been an even greater problem to have imagined the Jewish leaders killing him because of his Q^1 teachings. A plot against the teacher of Q^1 material would have been even more horrific than the plot Mark devised against the son of God. So he could not use the Q material as the public instructions of a teacher who wanted to be understood. The overlaps that do occur between Mark and the instructional sayings in Q are interpreted mainly as Jesus' private instructions to the disciples. These include the sayings on things hidden and revealed, the lamp, the grain of mustard, the measure, savorless salt, taking up one's cross, and the formula of reciprocity on confessing or denying Jesus. Mark was highly selective in his use of Q material and he knew what he was doing. He had no intention of writing a story to grace and highlight the teachings of Q. He wanted to write a story that put the test to Jesus, not at the beginning as was befitting for a sage, but at the end as was befitting for a martyr for the kingdom of God. He did it. Now there were two strong texts among the Jesus people: Q and the gospel that Mark wrote. With both Q and Mark in circulation, we are now poised to see what Matthew and Luke made of them.

In the meantime, however, yet another group of Jesus people had decided to pronounce a plague on both of these houses. The followers of Jesus responsible for the Gospel of Thomas had grown accustomed to the idea of Jesus as a sage and had given a great deal of thought to his teachings. For them, the significance of his teachings lay in their capacity to enable an individual to withstand society's pressures to conform. They had meditated deeply on his sayings and taken seriously the challenge to disassociate from society and develop self-awareness, self-confidence, and self-sufficiency. When the Q people formed groups, started their mission, and then retreated behind a smokescreen of apocalyptic pronouncements when their mission failed, the Thomas people decided to go their own way. When Mark's community tried to imagine itself as a determining factor in the course of human history, the Thomas people thought that the legacy of Jesus had been betrayed.

The Coptic Gospel of Thomas was a translation from a Greek original that scholars now date to the last quarter of the first century. It contains a truly amazing collection of the sayings of Jesus. When compared with Q, approximately one-third of the sayings in the Gospel of Thomas have parallels in Q, and about 60 percent are from the Q^1 layer. This shows that the Thomas tradition had roots in the earliest stages of the Jesus movement and that there must have been some association with the Q people during that period. From that point on, however, the Thomas tradition is marked by a strong sense of independence. Three features of the text reveal just how independent the Thomas people were.

The first noteworthy feature of the text is the use of dialogue in order to present the sayings of Jesus as answers to a number of questions his disciples ask. The reference to his disciples is, for the most part, collective. But Peter, Matthew, and James are mentioned, as are Thomas, Salome, and Mary. Thomas, Salome, and Mary say the right things, ask the right questions, and so are privileged to be part of an inner circle, as is James who is spoken of in his absence. These figures obviously represent the true followers of Jesus and thus reflect the Thomas group in the text. But Peter, Matthew, and "the disciples" usually ask the wrong questions and repeatedly and brusquely have to be corrected. Thus the dialogue format works both ways. It allows Jesus to instruct the inner circle in the true meaning of his teachings while also allowing the other disciples to represent views the Thomas people have rejected as wrong. A look at these other views is most instructive.

The questions that Jesus consistently rejects as gross misunderstandings of what he represents can easily be classified in two categories. One is that concerns about the future are all misplaced. Over and over again the disciples ask when the kingdom will come, how it will be, and whether they will be able to enter. In every case Jesus tells them that they have completely misunderstood his teachings about the kingdom. The kingdom, Jesus explains, is already present, and if they knew who they were, namely the true disciples of Jesus, they would know not to ask. The other set of questions has to do with ritual behavior. The disciples want to know whether and how they should fast, pray, give to charity, wash, diet, and whether circumcision is required. In every case Jesus treats their questions as silly, but takes the occasion to turn the ritual reference into a metaphor of the contemplative self-awareness characteristic for his true disciples. Thus the ruse of dialogue is used to clarify the position of the Thomas people on two fronts: Jesus people who became apocalyptic, and Jesus people who worked out an accommodation with the Pharisaic codes of ritual purity. Neither the Markan community nor the people of Q would have measured up as the true disciples of Jesus according to the Gospel of Thomas.

The second noteworthy feature of the Gospel of Thomas is the content of the teachings that have no parallel in Q. All of them are what might be called second-level elaborations on those sayings that do have a parallel in Q. In Q the compositional history reveals identifiable strata. This is not the case with Thomas. But just as there was a shift in Q from aphoristic instruction to prophetic and apocalyptic discourse, so there was a shift in the Thomas tradition from aphoristic injunctions to another distinctive style of instruction. Highly metaphoric and largely enigmatic, the teachings of Jesus to his disciples tell them that true knowledge is self-knowledge, and that true self-knowledge is a state of being untouched by the world of human affairs, a state of being in touch with a noetic world of divine light and stability.

In relation to the world of human affairs Jesus' true disciples are to "become passersby" (Saying 42). As those who know themselves they are the "solitary ones" (Saying 49). As those in touch with the noetic world they are "from the light" (Saying 50), "sons of the living Father" (Saying 50), those who "stand at the beginning and know the end" (Saying 18), who encompass male and female in "a single one" (Saying 22), who "know the kingdom" (Saying 46), and who are "the same" (Saying 61). Jesus refers to himself as the "light from above"

(Saying 77) who represents all that the disciples are to become. Once they see it, however, they won't need Jesus anymore: "Whoever drinks from my mouth shall become as I am and I myself will become he, and the hidden things shall be revealed to him" (Saying 108).

It is this level of elaboration that qualifies the Gospel of Thomas as a proto-Gnostic treatise. The mythology is that of the incarnation of wisdom in the midst of a dark and senseless world. From the options available in Q and Mark, the Thomas people rejected the mythology of the apocalyptic son of man and the notion of the prophets as the envoys of wisdom or as those who predicted Jesus. They took, instead, the mythology of Jesus as the child of wisdom and son of God, detached it from its epic-apocalyptic frame, and cultivated his teachings as signatures of his self-knowledge as the incarnation of divine wisdom.

The third feature of the text is the riddle-like feature of the sayings. According to the introduction, "These are the secret words which the living Jesus spoke and Didymos Judas Thomas wrote. And he said: 'Whoever finds the explanation of these words will not taste death'" (Saying 1). With such an introduction, the author compounds the mysterious quality of the already enigmatic sayings. Not only are these secret sayings in the private property of the Thomas people, but when one gets to read them one finds riddles in need of the correct answers.

So the text was written as a revelation document available to and understandable only by those who were privileged to be included in the Thomas community. As such a text makes apparent, the Thomas disciples were living in an imaginary world far removed from the people of Q or the Markan community. Their response to the troubled times was one of detachment. "Whoever finds himself," they heard Jesus saying, "of him the world is not worthy" (Saying 111).

About this time (ca 85–90 c.e.), Matthew found a way to put Mark and Q together in a single account. Matthew's sympathies were with Q and it is quite possible that he belonged to a community in the tradition of Q. If so, the people of Q had continued to work on their problem of self-identification, for Matthew represents several solutions to issues still unresolved for the people of Q at the Q^3 stage. It would also mean, as difficult as this is to imagine, that Matthew's branch of the people of Q had taken note of the Gospel of Mark and found it interesting. Matthew, in any case, did find Mark acceptable reading, and created from the two strong texts an even more impressive story.

Although Matthew accepted the basic plot of Mark's story, and used it as the narrative outline for his own account, he had little interest in the logic of vicarious martyrdom that underlay Mark's account of the crucifixion. Thus he worked hard to tone down those aspects of Mark's gospel that accented violence, self-sacrifice, and social and political conflict. He appended some birth narratives and a genealogy to soften the beginning and link Jesus up with the epic of Israel in a totally different way. He shifted the characterization of Jesus away from Mark's man of power toward that of the patient teacher. The highly charged mythological identifications in Mark, such as son of man, son of God, messiah, and wisdom, are all treated matter-of-factly as titles befitting a superior sage. And the disciples were not bumblers, according to Matthew. They understood, responded properly, and were blessed with the "keys to the kingdom." Thus Jesus' teachings were of primary importance for Matthew, not Jesus' social critique, political agenda, apocalyptic vision, or martyrdom for the cause of founding a new religion. According to Matthew, Jesus' teachings captured the best intentions of the Jewish ethical codes based on the Torah and made them available even for gentiles.

Matthew inserted Q into Mark's narrative by dividing it up into five blocks of instruction. These blocks were organized by theme and situated throughout the narrative as speeches Jesus gave on different occasions. The most familiar to modern readers of the New Testament is the so-called sermon on the mount (Matthew 5–7). To the Q material in these speeches Matthew added some instructions of his own. He was not bashful about doing so for, from his point of view, what he added was exactly what Jesus must have intended. The most obvious and significant Matthean additions are the so-called antitheses in the sermon on the mount. They take the form: "You have heard it said . . . , but I say unto you . . . " Antithesis is not the right word, however, for the point was not that Moses' law and Jesus' teachings were antithetical. Matthew made his point quite clear in his introduction to the section which the NRSV translates as follows:

> Do not think that I have come to abolish the law or the prophets; I have come not to abolish but to fulfill. For truly I tell you, until heaven and earth

pass away, not one letter, not one stroke of a letter, will pass from the law until all is accomplished.

The point of the comparison between the law and Jesus' teaching is that Jesus' teaching gets to the heart of what the law of Moses intended. For Matthew, appropriate piety was a matter of attitude, perfection of spirit, and the control of desire. Matthew read Q and wanted his readers to understand the sayings in Q as instruction in the ethical intentions of Jewish law. Matthew thought Jesus' teachings functioned to stabilize the confusion created by the end of the second temple-state and to validate the law of Moses as that which remained constant when all else crumbled. Matthew said that Jesus "fulfilled" the promises and predictions of the epic of Israel. As for the destruction of the temple, it signaled only that an epoch was ended. The new congregation of Christians, which Matthew called the *ekklesia* ("assembly"), would take up the Jewish legacy quite nicely.

When one turns to the Christian literature written during the second and third centuries, one can see that Matthew's achievement carried the day for the emerging institution of the church. His became the preferred gospel and it was the one primarily cited as the source for the teachings of Jesus. But the citations are frequently ad hoc, out of context, and highly selective. One notices that the aphorisms of Q^1, although they had lost all their bite by landing in the Gospel of Matthew, were scarcely able to carry the weight assigned them. And so, just as Matthew had found, the teachers of the church had to spell things out more clearly. Jesus was always acknowledged as the founder-teacher and thus the great shepherd of the church. But as the churches settled down to codify their teachings, they looked to the apostles, bishops, and theologians for guidance, not just to the teachings of Jesus. An early Jewish-Christian handbook of instructions called the Didache ("Teaching of the Lord to the Nations by the Twelve Apostles") does not even make the attempt to distinguish among sayings of Jesus cited from Matthew, maxims taken from the Jewish scriptures, ethical wisdom sayings taken from hellenistic philosophy, and instruction for prayers to be said when the community gathered for worship. So Matthew actually buried Q in the fiction of Jesus as a Jewish sage.

Luckily for the modern scholar, Luke also found Q attractive for his project in early Christian historiography. Luke wrote sometime early in the second century and thought it good to trace the beginnings of the Christian movement from the time of Jesus through the period in which the apostles were actively founding churches. His plan was to show that the church, as he knew it, was true to its founders and their teachings. For Luke, being a Christian meant joining a Christian congregation. In order to do that one received a rite of baptism (now understood as a "washing"), acknowledged a "change of mind" (later to be called repentance), received the spirit of God (at work in the congregation), and accepted the ethical standards and codes of the new community as one's own. And that was about it.

One would not have joined without giving assent to what Christians believed, of course, but even that was not a very difficult thing to do. The beliefs that mattered, according to Luke, were simply that God had always wanted people to be good and had always made sure that he had a spokesman to help the people do that. For the epoch of Israel there were the prophets. Then Jesus came and surprised the world by making it possible for gentiles also to belong to the people of God. The apostles spread this good news, preaching by the same spirit of God that had always called the people to goodness. Some said yes, some said no. And that was that.

So Luke did not have to struggle with apocalyptic issues, messianic questions, political confusion, or resentment toward the Pharisees. Luke's problem was to claim for the church its rightful place in the Roman world, demonstrate that it was no threat to the Roman order, and make a case for its positive contributions to society. He accomplished these goals by lining up three illustrious epochs of the people of God, an epic history that now included the Christian church. Luke used the notion of the line of prophets in every generation in order to align (1) the epoch of Israel with that of (2) the life of Jesus (history's illustration of the ideal, how it might be if every prophet-teacher were perfect and everyone listened and behaved) and (3) that of the apostolic period (or the first chapter of the history of the church). He devised a profile of the prophet-teacher to illustrate the point that the spirit of God had functioned similarly in every epoch. The spokesmen for God warned the people about the consequences of not doing good and taught the people what it meant to do good. In every case the main illustrations in their teaching were taken from the preceding epoch and, curiously, had to do with the fate of the true prophet-teacher. Some said yes. Some said no. Those that said no persecuted the prophet-teacher.

This plan turned the notion of a line of prophets into a chain that used Jesus as a link to connect the history of the church with the epic of Israel, but it left open the question of what it meant to be good. Luke may have purposely left this question open. As a highly educated Hellene, he certainly would have been aware that categories such as the good, the beautiful, and the true were blanks that every cultural tradition filled in differently. Luke, at any rate, refrained from spelling out the details of what it meant to be good in each of the different epochs. He did not try to equate the details of the Jewish law with the teachings of Jesus, nor the teachings of Jesus with the teachings of the apostles and whatever the codes were in his own Christian congregation. For Luke it was enough to imagine that the people of God were the leaven of morality in any society and that their effect on the society was constructive.

Luke was certainly indebted to both Q and Mark for his conception of the line of prophets as the way to link up Jesus and the apostles with the epic history of Israel. He was also indebted to Q and Mark for the notion of the spirit of God that provided the mythological principle of continuity from prophet to prophet and epoch to epoch. His remarkable astuteness lay in the fact that he was able to use the notion of the spirit to merge the several functions of the spokesperson for God. Wise instruction, prophetic pronouncement, and miraculous effect were combined in the ideal speech of the prophet-teacher. When compared with the extravagant mythologies of earlier traditions (Jesus as the messiah, vindicated martyr, wisdom of God, son of God, eschatological prophet, son of man, and so forth), Luke's mythology is rather tame, if not banal. He used it to great advantage, however, for with it he was able to read Mark and Q together as saying essentially the same thing. Thus he wrote his gospel in such a way as not to trouble his readers with the themes of conflict, judgment, apocalyptic reversal, and vindication that determined the tenor of Mark and Q. All were toned down, made to appear appropriate to earlier times, and countered by the addition of other material, such as stories about good Pharisees and parables of reconciliation. Jesus, for Luke, was a man who "went about doing good" because the spirit of God was upon him.

So Luke incorporated Q into his gospel, but he was not overly interested in using its contents as instruction applicable in his own day. He treated Q as a period piece, one resource among many for the historian interested in developing a picture of Jesus, the prophet-teacher. This is why Luke did not fuss with Q as did Matthew, either by systematically rearranging the sayings by theme, or by making sure that the reader got the full import of the teachings of Jesus as Christian law. Luke saw the connections between Q and Mark in the stories about John and Jesus, and so took that part of Q and merged it with Mark at the appropriate place. He also followed the Q sequence by inserting the first block of Q^1 material into the story as the "sermon on the plain" before introducing the dialogue between John and Jesus. But from that point on, Luke turned Mark's march toward Jerusalem into a long and leisurely journey during which Jesus walked and talked with his disciples, sent them on their mission and received their reports, had dinner with a Pharisee, performed a few healings, instructed the crowds, received a group of Galileans, and so forth. And Q was simply interspersed as the instructions Jesus gave on the way. The historian's sense of distance put Q in its place, albeit as a historian's fiction. The reader was no longer addressed directly, as in Q, by a voice speaking with immediate authority. Neither was the reader addressed indirectly, as in Matthew, by a founder-teacher laying down the law for all time. In Luke's account, the reader is allowed to imagine Jesus talking to those of Jesus' own time. It was a glorious time, but it was past and the times had changed. The importance of the teachings of Jesus for Luke was not their relevance for all time, but the record they left of a marvelous teacher and prophet whose effectiveness was only that he enlarged the congregation of the people of God to include gentiles. Thus the church was born.

The irony is noteworthy. Luke's treatment of Q as a document not worth saving as a handbook of instructions relevant for his own time was the very feature of his composition that made its recovery possible in modern times.

PART IV

THE RECONCEPTION OF CHRISTIAN ORIGINS

10

Jesus and Authority

The discovery of Q has forced a revision of the history of Christian beginnings. It has also demanded a shift in the way we understand early Christian mythmaking. Q documents a Jesus movement that produced a myth of origin simply by adding new sayings to a growing collection of the instructions of a founder-teacher. Such a mode of mythmaking has been difficult for modern scholars to accept. Early Christian myths of origin have usually been classified as kerygmatic or narrative. Q has expanded the options and thus invites a special consideration. What we need to understand is the process by which sayings continued to be ascribed to Jesus long after he lived.

The traditional criteria for determining the "authentic" words of the historical Jesus are no longer valid. The question must now focus on the "inauthentic" teachings. New Testament scholars know that Jesus could not have said everything ascribed to him in the vast literature produced during the first three or four centuries. A recent collection of the sayings of Jesus from early Christian literature numbers 503 items (Crossan, 1986). Of these, less than 10 percent are considered candidates for authenticity by scholars working on this question.

The traditional quest for the authentic words of Jesus focused primarily on the criteria for determining which sayings are authentic. Sayings that occur in gnostic treatises, or in the popular literature traditionally called pseudepigraphical, or "falsely written and signed," have easily been set aside. No critical scholar thinks that Jesus said,

"Cleave wood, I am there; lift a stone, you will find me there," as found in the Gospel of Thomas (Saying 77). No one doubts that the author of the gnostic treatise called *Pistis Sophia* invented Jesus' instructions to his disciples about the fall, repentance, and salvation of Pistis Sophia: "And the time came that she should be saved from the chaos and brought forth from all the darkness. . . . And the [first] mystery sent me a great light-power from the height, so that I should help the Pistis Sophia and bring her up from the chaos" (*Pistis Sophia* I, 60). And there is absolute embarrassment about the words of the child Jesus found in the infancy gospels. When slapped on the face by another child, for instance, Jesus, the six-year-old, told him to "finish his course," so that he died forthwith (*Infancy Gospel of Thomas* 5:1).

The sayings that occur in the canonical gospels are a bit more tricky. Scholars have no trouble thinking that the words of Jesus in the Gospel of John were invented in the course of the community's meditations. Sayings such as "I am the living bread which came down from heaven; if anyone eats of this bread, he will live for ever" or "He who eats my flesh and drinks my blood has eternal life" are simply dismissed as "Johannine." But the sayings ascribed to Jesus in the synoptic gospels have proven to be very difficult to assign. That is because New Testament scholars have assumed the image of Jesus created by the narrative gospels and thus have found it hard to discount self-referential sayings that in any other mouth would be found highly inappropriate.

The criteria for judging authenticity have all been forms of a single persuasion, namely, that since Jesus was a unique individual, his teachings must have been novel. The difference between the sayings of Jesus and what others might have said has therefore been the major consideration for determining authenticity. A saying with parallels from Jewish or Greek traditions of proverbs and maxims would therefore be discounted. Sayings that address the theological or ethical concerns of the emerging "church" have likewise been considered inauthentic. Studies based on such criteria have not been without value, for they have situated many of the teachings of Jesus in appropriate traditions of discourse and demonstrated the inauthenticity of the majority of sayings ascribed to Jesus. But the short lists of "authentic" words that result from such an endeavor lack coherence, fail to enhance the picture of Jesus scholars have had in mind, and do nothing to help explain the practice of ascribing the sayings to Jesus that scholars have called inauthentic.

Meanwhile, consternation reigns outside of scholarly circles when people are told that Jesus did not say what Mark or Matthew or Luke said he said. Such consternation has been documented time after time in letters to the editors of newspapers in response to the published judgments of the Jesus Seminar. This group of New Testament scholars has been at work for several years preparing "the scholars' red letter edition" of the gospels (Funk, 1992), with the aim of summing up the best judgments of critical scholars in the quest for the authentic teachings of Jesus. Preliminary results of the voting with red, pink, gray, and black beads have regularly been published in the media. And then indignation is expressed by Christians who have always imagined that Jesus said what the scholars now say he did not.

Part of the problem is that the Jesus Seminar has not been able to explain to the public how it arrives at its conclusions. When it has tried, the frightful lack of basic knowledge about the formation of the New Testament among average Christians has blocked the conversation. But even so, the explanations that are given fail to convince because the criteria for authenticity are still beholden to the notion of a unique Jesus. With such a Jesus in mind there is really no way of deciding which saying is authentic and which is not. "Authentic" turns out to be a theological category, not a helpful term for understanding Christian origins.

The consternation of average Christians needs to be taken more seriously. What they are troubled about has to do with the reverse side of the notion of authenticity, namely with the notion of inauthenticity. What they are saying is that, if Matthew said Jesus said it, and Jesus did not say it, then Matthew was lying. Or he was mistaken. Or he invented it and did not tell his readers. Their question, then, is how could he have done that?

It is very easy to explain how Matthew or the people of Q could have done it. The explanation may not be comfortable for some Christians, but it is eminently understandable, given some historical background on teachers, teachings, and their followers in the Greco-Roman age. Historians of the period have this information and it is fully apropos in a book about Q. Thus this chapter is devoted to Greco-Roman attitudes and practices with regard to the sayings or maxims of a teacher. We shall see that these attitudes were different from our modern sensibilities about the authenticity of sayings attributed to a certain author.

It has already been shown that the authors of early Christian texts felt free to attribute new sayings to Jesus. The point has been made that these sayings were appropriate to the views of Jesus current in an author's tradition and to the social circumstances under which an author wrote. This means that attribution was acceptable if judged appropriate. What we need to understand is the criterion by which people in antiquity measured appropriateness when ascribing a given saying to a known figure.

In the cultures of antiquity, proverbs, maxims, and pithy formulations were an extremely important form of discourse at all levels of society. Bright sayings crystallized the insights of a people in memorable form and became commonplace theorems that everyone used to interpret and master the common events of the daily round. A bit of skill, and perhaps a wink, would be required to put a certain construction upon some action in wont of explanation, but that was fully understood by everyone as part of the challenge of living, and a clever application of an old adage was considered a mark of wisdom. "See a pin and pick it up, all the day you will have good luck" might apply in some ways, not in others, to an occasion of picayune behavior, but saying it would nevertheless acknowledge the moment and might be quite enlightening.

Proverbs were generated among the people, but collected by scribes at temple schools, the courts of the kings, and the centers where schools of philosophy flourished. Collecting proverbs was a scholarly enterprise, and a collection of a certain kind of proverb would normally be attributed to a figure of the past renowned for his wisdom. Thus we have the Proverbs and Wisdom of Solomon as books in the Bible. In the wisdom literatures of Egypt and the ancient near east, there is also a large number of collections of various kinds of wise sayings attributed to some courtier or sage.

During the Greco-Roman age, collecting sayings flourished at centers of learning. Attributing them to a legendary sage, poet, or the founder of a Greek school was the major method of classification. The *gnomologium,* or sayings collection, was looked on as an important way to conserve the wisdom of the past in a time of change. Thus we have the *Maxims* of Theognis, the *Gnomology to Cyrus*, the *Monostichoi* (or "One Liners") of Menander, the *Kyriai Doxai* (or "Principal Teachings") of Epicurus, the *Sentences of Sextus*, and so on. In the case of authors whose written works were available, a collection might begin by excerpting quotations, but it would soon become a repository for other sayings in kind. A coherent collection of sayings was highly regarded as a distillation of a particular wise man's wisdom and would attract other sayings in kind to the collection in his name.

Preoccupation with the sayings of the sages was not merely an expression of antiquarian interest, and collecting them was not done just to conserve the truisms of the past. Working with the sayings of the wise was driven by an interest in what the Greeks called *ethos*, or what we would call character. Character for the Greeks was not a matter of personality or a matter of what we would call ethics. The modern notion of ethics is moralistic and assumes generally agreed upon standards of virtue. The Greek notion of character had to do with an individual's distinctive life-style. It was closer to what we moderns mean when we say that a person is "a character."

A character for the Greeks had a profile created by a consistent pattern of behavior and a corresponding mode of speech. The Greeks understood how important words were and that what one said on a given occasion made a difference. What one said revealed one's stance toward another as well as one's view of the world. Speech was also a behavioral mode, but one that was capable of manipulating deception. Characters were therefore judged by the correspondence between what they said and what they did, or how they usually behaved. If a person was a teacher, one's character was judged by whether one lived according to the teachings one espoused. If the character of a teacher had been determined, the sayings of the teacher could be used to represent that character. Founders of the various schools of philosophy were regarded as characters that embodied the teachings of their schools. Thus the sayings of a sage or a teacher were understood to be an expression of their character.

Since sayings were assessed as the expression of a particular view of life, and since word and deed were understood to match in the ideal character, the ascription of sayings to ideal figures was a matter of appropriateness. Thus even the truisms coined and in circulation during a later time could be culled for appropriate attribution to the collections of this or that philosopher or sage from a previous period. Founders of schools regularly got credit for the philosophies that developed in the school tradition in their name.

Because character was defined by the correspondence of espousal, mode of speech, and life-style, profiles of an individual in action were also of great interest. Thus biographical literature burgeoned during the Greco-Roman period. The problem, of course, was that most of the figures thought to be worthy of a biography were dead and gone, and, lacking documentation, it was impossible to trace the course of a person's life. There were, however, lore and other forms of legacy about public figures. If an important individual had left a written legacy, it could be used to infer the kind of person he had been and the way of life he had espoused and followed. So even the scripts of the tragic and comic poets were pored over centuries later for clues as to which sayings, perspectives, and speeches expressed the author's own views, and from them biographies could be written. In the case of kings, commanders, and statesmen, there were histories, eulogies, family lore, and letters that could be used. And circulating among the adherents of the various schools of philosophy were countless anecdotes about founders and their disciples. All of this material could be used in composing a biography, or as the Greeks called it, a *bios,* or "life."

We have a remarkable collection of anecdotal material about the founders of philosophical schools in *The Lives of Eminent Philosophers* written by Diogenes Laertius around 200 C.E. He mentions numerous collections of memorabilia, anecdotes, maxims, and biographies that he used as the sources for his own compendium. His overall plan was to trace the sequence of the Greek school traditions by writing a life of each founder and successive head of a school, beginning with the seven sages and working through the classical period to about the first century B.C.E. The typical life begins with the mention of what was known about a person's family, home town, teachers, and star pupils. It then turns to a registry of the philosopher's teachings. A list of the philosopher's known works is included by title, but instead of summarizing his philosophy in treatise form, Diogenes usually used the format of memorable sayings. Included are *apophthegms* (terse formulations of the "know thyself" variety), maxims, precepts (advice in imperative formulation), *doxai* (succinct summary statements of the teacher's opinions on a particular philosophical or ethical issue), and *dogmata* (the philosophical principles of the school). But what about character? Lacking the kind of information modern biographers use to trace the course of a person's life, Diogenes provided his readers with numerous pictures of the person on this or that occasion. These he referred to as lore (*to legomenon*), reminiscence (*apomnemoneuma*), and anecdote (*chreia*). Reading through the eighty-two lives in Diogenes' history, it is remarkable how different the character profiles become simply by comparing these snapshot-like images and sayings.

The *chreia*, or anecdote, is a particularly interesting building block of the Greek biography. It consisted of a brief hint or description of a typical situation plus a succinct formulation of a person's response. It could be reduced to the form "When asked . . . , So-and-so said . . ." or "On seeing . . . , So-and-so said or did . . ." As one can see, what a philosopher might have said or done on a given occasion counted as a test of character. Sayings in this form did double duty. One could check to see if they fit the teacher's espoused philosophy, and one could also assess their appropriateness as a response to a situation.

Anecdotes were used in the schools of rhetoric as examples of effective speech. Since they contained the basic ingredients of a rhetorical situation (speaker, speech, and audience), anecdotes could be analyzed for their appropriateness to the character of the speaker to which they were attributed (*ethos*), their fit with the espousals or teachings of the speaker (*logos*), and their rhetorical effectiveness as an address to the listeners (known as *pathos*). Anecdotes could also be memorized, restylized, coined, paraphrased, and embellished into scenarios with full-blown speeches.

Finding the right words when composing a speech for a certain character was considered a skill. To compose a speech, even for oneself, one needed to find the right words. The Greeks called this *heuresis,* or "discovery." The Romans, who learned their rhetoric from the Greeks, translated *heuresis* as *inventio,* or "invention." Either way, finding the right words or making them up, rhetoric was understood as a bricolage approach to composition, putting together materials already at hand in novel combinations. That is because a speech, to be effective, had to draw upon common language, stock figures, telling metaphors, interesting analogies, and well-known examples from popular and literate discourse. The trick was to find the right phrase or appropriate image to make the point.

The real test, however, was to write a speech for someone else. This was called "speech-in-character." Lawyers were trained to write speeches-in-character for their clients. Teachers were trained to write and perform speeches-in-character for public officials and ceremonial occasions that hearkened back to hoary times. Biographers, historians, and playwrights were trained to compose speeches-in-character for every turn in the lives of their characters. Making a speech was how the Greeks described human encounter, and hearing a speech was how the Greeks registered the import of a given exchange. Hellenism was a culture of rhetoric. The literature of the time is chock-full of sayings and speeches. Speechmaking was the order of the public day. One got high marks for composing a fine speech and higher marks still for composing a speech-in-character.

Students learned to compose speeches-in-character in school. Quintilian, a teacher of rhetoric who lived during the first century, explained that, to write a good speech one needed to imagine oneself in the situation and character of the speaker. If one chose to do so, one could even create a character by composing a persuasive speech appropriate to such a character. Students were asked to learn this skill by inventing speeches for imaginary situations, such as, "What would a monkey say if he wanted to be the leader of the pack?" Students were also asked to invent speeches for historical personages on specific, memorable occasions, such as, "What would Theseus have said when he learned that his father had committed suicide because Theseus had forgotten to change the color of the sails on his return to Athens?" So the standards for judging the appropriateness of a speech attributed to a particular person had little to do with modern notions of historical truth, but much to do with ethos, or the correspondence of a person's speech and character.

But now, a shift in sensibility took place during the early Roman period that needs a bit of explication before we return to the sayings of Jesus in Q. The point has been made that character, or ethos, was a neutral concept without moralistic connotation. This insight remains valid for the period and needs to be kept firmly in mind. Characterization had to do with the correspondence of speech, espousal, and life-style, no matter what kind of life-style was projected. This does not mean, however, that the Greeks were incapable of rendering judgment about the way to live. They simply tackled this question in ways other than those to which we are accustomed. The important factor was the philosophy one followed as a guide for living one's life. Thus the question of the best way to live was a matter of espousal, of alignment with some philosophical school. Each of the many philosophical schools had its own ideas about what was "good," "right," "noble," and so forth. These values were debatable in antiquity, and a given character would be discussed, not in personal terms but in relation to issues under debate among the philosophical schools. The shift that took place during the early Roman period was that a largely Stoic popular philosophy became the generally preferred standard for a lifestyle of independence and personal integrity appropriate to the times, and this in turn affected the ranking of ideal character types.

There are hints in the educational literature of the first century that this shift in sensibility was widespread and had pushed educators into serious reflection about the role of classical education in a period of cultural transition. One begins to read cautionary advice to teachers about using only "approved" speeches from the canons of classical literature for lesson material and about using only "approved" sayings and maxims when learning to elaborate a thesis. There is also advice about using only the judgments, maxims, and sayings of "approved sages" in arguments for a thesis. If we were to ask *what* the standards for approval were, we would probably encounter a popular Stoic philosophy that encouraged individual integrity without rocking the social boat. If, however, we were to ask *why* the concern focused on the selection and ranking of speech material, we would stumble upon a very interesting social psychology of the time.

A friend of Seneca, the Stoic philosopher and adviser to Nero, asked him for a copy of a certain collection of sayings. In a letter, Seneca said that he would comply with the request but wondered why his friend wanted them. He went on to advise his friend about the selection and use of sayings, indicating that one should be extremely careful because not every collection was worth having. Choose wisely and knowingly, Seneca said, because *conversatio* ("frequent use," "intimate contact") with the sayings of a philosopher would have the effect of reproducing the character of the author in the reader. He did not know how this happened, he said, but he was sure that it did happen. One should therefore take care, knowing that the kinds of sayings one found interesting would have their effect.

Conversatio was Seneca's term for describing the way in which literate persons in late antiquity read and treated their texts. Learning to read and write in antiquity was a laborious process governed at every level by copying, called *mimesis* (in Latin, *imitatio*, from which we get "imitating"), and memorization. From learning letters to composition, the procedure was the same. The student was presented with paradigms, sayings, and model compositions to be mastered by careful repetition. This fixed the patterns in one's mind. Then there was rehearsal, reading aloud, and a presentation of the material from memory. Only then would slight elaborations be countenanced such as experimenting with changes in the tone of voice and paraphrase (giving the meaning in other words). Imitation aimed at what we would call the internalization of a model composition by making the model one's own and being able to present it as if it were one's own composition. The skilled and the gifted were expected eventually to compose what we would call original and creative pieces, but this was reserved for the few and was still understood as a process of bricolage, "finding" the right figure for making a point from the vast reservoir of already well-formulated sayings and figures in the literary and cultural tradition.

Seneca knew that conversatio with a collection of sayings would have its influence on the reader. His concern was that the sayings one selected represent the kind of character one would be happy or willing to become. The assumption underlying the concern was that the sayings of an author were a sufficient vehicle of ethos, and that by making them one's own a person would take on that ethos.

We need not delve into the correctness of Seneca's social psychology or discourse theory before returning to the question of attribution in Q. We need only see that the sayings of a sage had become a most significant genre for the transmission of what the Greeks called ethos, and that ethos was a fundamental notion in the definition of culture and enculturation. In the mentality of the Greco-Roman age, the sayings of an author were an expression of a particular ethos, other sayings that corresponded to that ethos could easily be attributed to that author, and by cultivating those sayings one could imitate and internalize that ethos. Ethos, not personality, was the important thing.

This mentality was taken for granted throughout the hellenistic world, and it gives us the proper cultural context for understanding the way in which the Jesus movements treated Jesus' sayings. Jesus was regarded as a wise teacher whose sayings were a sufficient index to the ethos he represented. The metaphor used by the people of Q that corresponds to Seneca's *conversatio* was to "keep" or to "hear and do" Jesus' sayings. This indicates not only the importance that was placed on Jesus' sayings, but also that they were the object of cultivation in the discourse of the movement. Loyalty to the movement was registered in terms of "hearing and doing" these words. And because of the tight relation between word and deed and the notion of ethos, one's loyalty to the movement was the same as one's loyalty to Jesus whose image idealized the ethos of his school. Thus the genre of a collection of sayings was not a weak or insufficient foundation for a movement of followers in Jesus' name. It was a powerful and fully sufficient vehicle for a movement engaged in the formation of a group with a particular ethos.

The question of attribution should now be capable of resolution but for the fact that the types of sayings attributed to Jesus changed in the course of Q's history and the history of other Jesus movements during the early period. We have been able to account for new sayings by referring to shifts in the discourse of the movement. Such shifts can be related to changes in the movement's social circumstance, experience, and formation. These changes are clearly reflected in the layering and reworking of the Q tradition. Now we need to ask how the people of Q managed to attribute sayings to Jesus that expressed an ethos different from the image and voice of the Jesus to which they had been accustomed.

Several observations will help. One would be that these shifts in characterization did not occur precipitously but took place incrementally over time. The strata we have used to chart the history of the movement's development are literary moments accidentally available to us because of compositional features of the text. In actuality, one needs to imagine a vigorous give and take as groups discussed their options, shared insights, and voiced frustrations. By slowing down the experimental process, one can easily imagine a normal process of attribution.

At any given point in the process the group must have been familiar with a particular image of Jesus. At this point, attribution of sayings in kind was possible by any of the usual means customary for the times. We might note, for instance, that much of the material added to the collection in the course of elaboration and growth was proverbial, already at hand in the cultures of context. Adding such material would not have required great ingenuity. Slight shifts in characterization would also have been possible as long as they were felt to be elaborations or embellishments appropriate to the image already in place. If one could imagine that the Jesus of the familiar sayings could also have said such and such, that would be enough to allow consideration of the comment. At some later point, supposing that the accumulation of sayings contained an intolerable ethical tension, it might be necessary to recast the character of Jesus by speech attribution and other narrative devices. As we have seen, that is exactly what the people of Q had to do, and did do.

The most important observation, however, is that the image of Jesus shifted in tandem to changes in the sayings attributed to him. There is no indication that the people of Q were interested in or worried about the personality of Jesus. Jesus was important as the founder-teacher of the movement but only in relation to the function of his teachings within the movement. The attributed teachings were the expression of the group's ethos and behavior. They were also the standard by which the voice and image of Jesus were continually recast. His character and role were enhanced in keeping with the expansion of the community's discourse. When the discourse shifted to include an epic-apocalyptic perspective, for instance, authorization was achieved by imagining Jesus as wisdom's child. The authority of Jesus was firmly attached to the authorship of his instructions to the community, but authorship was not understood as we moderns understand it. In the modern sense of the term, the Jesus people were the authors of the sayings they attributed to Jesus. But as they understood what they were doing, it was a matter of inventing appropriate speech-in-character. They did this in order to authorize the agreements they reached on the ethos of a discourse appropriate to their times.

Thus the history of the Q community can be traced by noting the shifts in its discourse documented in its collection of the sayings of Jesus. A first stage comes to light with the aphorisms of Q^1. Noting that Q^1 is composed of blocks of material that elaborate aphoristic material into rationalized codes, the aphorisms must reflect the discourse of the preceding period. Judging from these aphorisms, the discourse of the first stage was playful and the behavior public. Individuals were challenging one another to behave with integrity despite the social consequences. A shift toward imperative forms of address indicates that some kind of association was practiced by these people. Another indication of this interest in association is the way in which the terminology of the rule of God is used. There are also a few hints that moments of encounter were used to construct human relationships, not merely to display individual virtue. If we ask about the character of the speaker of this kind of material, it has its nearest analogy in contemporary profiles of the Cynic-sage. This is as close to the historical Jesus as Q allows us to get, but it is close enough for us to reconstruct a beginning of the movement that is both plausible and understandable. One should not underestimate the attraction of a Cynic-like sagery capable of enticing individuals into forming a discursive association.

The blocks of material in Q^1 represent a second stage. The aphoristic discourse of stage 1 was codified. Selected imperatives were elaborated as community rules by formulating argumentations to support their importance and reveal their appropriateness. Much of the material attributed to Jesus at this stage was proverbial wisdom taking the form of stock figures and comparisons. The public arena was still the setting for this kind of behavior, but there is also evidence that a network of small groups must have formed. There are signs of recognition and instructions concerning "reception" at a house that offers hospitality. A sense of expansion and growth is obvious, although there is no indication of a program to reform society or a demand for the conversion of would-be members of the movement. This shift in discourse was easily attributed to Jesus. No attempt was made to recast his profile by narrative or descriptive means. And yet the voice of Jesus was quite different from the speaker of the aphorisms. Jesus' voice was now that of a founder-teacher giving instructions for the manner of life that should characterize his school. In the parlance of the Greek school traditions, Q^1 represents Jesus' principal teachings or doctrines (*doxai, dogmata*).

A third stage must be imagined for the period between Q^1 and Q^2. Such a shift in mood could not have happened overnight. The social distress registered in Q^2 has to be considered. It cannot be explained as a weariness with reproach or a discouragement born of dashed expectations. It gives every evidence of social conflict within close circles of acquaintance. Such an experience of conflict, occasioned by one's association with the Jesus movement, must have evolved gradually and resulted in painful separations. It would have been during this period that the language of judgment used by those involved in this conflict eventually settled into place as Jesus' own. The expansion of Jesus' repertoire from the instructions of a teacher to include prophetic pronouncements would have made it necessary to address the problem of redefining his character or role.

Q^2 gives evidence of a fourth stage, a period in which the group's investment in a movement with recognizable borders triggered reflection on its social place and purpose. Q^2 is actually a myth of origin for the movement, although it would not have been thought of as such by the group and certainly was not imagined all at one time. Jesus had to authorize several kinds of pronouncements, and the process of attribution would have been ad hoc and experimental, moving from provisional allusions, through the give and take of repeated expression and refinement, to a situation in which some brave soul dared to insert a saying or two when making a copy of Q for a friend. By degrees, the voice of Jesus was heard uttering things that only the wisdom of God could have known. The whole sweep of history was now in review, but of course the instruction Jesus had to offer from that grand perspective was not for the public ear. And so the voice of wisdom's child took on a tinge of revelation discourse, private knowledge for in-house use as the community came to terms with its subcultural assignment.

A fifth stage, documented in Q^3, was distinctly different from all that had gone before. One wonders what happened to the people of Q during the Roman-Jewish war. A retreat took place from the vigor with which these people had engaged their social environment to a kind of resignation, an acceptance of the fact that the rule of God was a matter of personal and ethical integrity. An amazing accommodation seems to have been made with a Jewish piety against which earlier battles had been fought. And Jesus was heard quoting the scriptures even though he now was imagined as the son of God whose kingdom would only be revealed at the end of time. These fuzzy profiles at the Q^3 level, both of Jesus and of the community, give one the impression that the cost of surviving the war must have been very high.

Q^3 is not the only evidence we have for Jesus movements generated by the cultivation of a collection of sayings, but it is the last bit of evidence for the people whose history we have followed. When next we catch sight of the document Q, it had been merged with narrative accounts that created their characterizations of Jesus quite differently. The marvel of the Q tradition is that characterization was achieved, not by narration, but by artful ascription in the genre of a collection of sayings or instructions. The measure of their accomplishment is that this authorization of Jesus created a mythic figure with which each of the authors of the narrative gospels had to contend in order to appropriate Jesus in the composition of their stories.

11

Mythmaking and the Christ

An explosion of the collective imagination signals change, and the first Christian century experienced just such an explosion. It marks the time as uncertain and it registers an outpouring of human energy and intellectual activity in the production of myths. Christians were not the only people creating new myths. The literature of the time is famous for its fantastic worlds and imaginary explorations of legendary figures. But Christians were the ones who managed the mythology that western culture eventually accepted as its own.

Christians have never been comfortable with the notion of myth or willing to see their own myths as the product of human imagination and intellectual labor. This strong resistance is not due to a perversity peculiar to Christians but is a peculiarity integral to the Christian myth itself. The Christian myth was generated in a social experiment aware of its recent beginnings, and because the myth was about those beginnings, early Christians imagined their myth as history. The myth focused on the importance of Jesus as the founder figure of the movements, congregations, and institutions Christians were forming. Thus history and myth were fused into a single characterization, and the myths of origin were written and imagined as having happened at a recent time and in a specific place. Christians of the second, third, and fourth centuries found themselves troubled by the resemblance of their myths to both Greek and Jewish mythologies.

They could distance themselves from these other cultures and distinguish their myths from the others only by emphasizing the recent historical setting of their myths and the impression given by the narrative gospels that the myths really happened.

So they carried on a running debate among themselves about what to call their stories of Jesus. There were two terms in Greek that constantly came to mind as the appropriate descriptions for such stories, namely *mythos* and *logos*. These were considered dangerous, mythos because it was commonly used for imaginary inventions, not histories, and logos because it was the common term for a story about the Greek and pagan gods. Christians consistently eschewed the term mythos and they used the term logos only in a specific connotation. Logos was used in the sense hellenistic Jews had given the term when referring to the way in which wisdom was present in the written and remembered epic of Israel. Instead, by clever linguistic finesse, the historical development of which we do not have the leisure to follow in this book, Christians used the Greek term *pistis*, which means both "faith" and "faithfulness" as well as "trust" and "trustworthiness," in ways that eventually made it possible to use the Latin term *credo* ("believe") for a succinct summary of the main events in narrative gospels. Credo first was used as a verb, since those who would be Christians were asked to say that they "believed" the gospel story in its shorthand version as a "statement of faith." But soon the statement of faith itself was called credo, or the creed basic to the Christian faith.

No other religion demands that its adherents say they believe in their myth. And, as a matter of fact, it is not necessary to believe in a myth or a story for it to have its affect upon the imagination. As with any story, myths project an imaginary world in which a people see themselves reflected at a distance. Idealization and the abstraction of values create images that take on objective status, but they actually function as concentrated symbols of the forces at play in a people's social experience. These forces need to be acknowledged, managed, and shared with the next generation of its members. It takes a lot of living together and talking to achieve a common mythology and use it for cultural inculcation.

A myth projects the agreements that have been reached about the proper way to do things and what to value in human relationships. By a marvelous use of metaphor, dislocation, and visual transformation, myth combines these agreements with a people's memory traditions and recasts its history as a storied world. The world it describes functions to remind a people that they are not the first to have lived where they do and the way they do. Although a myth is the product of a people's social experience and best judgments, it tells a people that the world they live in is *not* their creation but has already been inhabited. The codes, arrangements, and patterns of authority are already set. Myths frequently tell about the time when those arrangements first were made.

Once a myth is in place and the social world is stable, it is possible to take the myth for granted and depend upon it being there in everyone's mind. One can then tell other stories that play upon the larger frame of reference. The mythic world can become a field of play for further imaginative elaboration, reflecting upon the relationships it proposes among the agents of its story. Other stories set in current time and place can then be used to explore the details, complexities, and limitations of a significant human relationship or exchange by assuming the larger mythic world as backdrop without ever having to mention it. Think of the cinema and the way in which it satisfies or tweaks us by telling a story that works out right, or one that presses the limits of our sensibilities about human and social relationships. The standard for a story to be good, or to engage us fully in the exploration of some human relationship, is always some myth we hold in common, such as the American dream, or the taking of the West, or the mountain man's quest.

But when the patterns of a society change and cultures collide, a myth already in place comes under considerable pressure. Because myth is an imaginary construct, and because it is dense in symbolism and peopled by extravagantly ideal figures, the mythic world itself can be explored and rearranged in the hopes of finding some new perspective that can clarify the times.

In the course of Christian history, to take one example of a series of social and cultural shifts, the Christ has been refigured many times over. In the period before Constantine, when bishops were taking their place as the leaders of the churches, the Christ was commonly depicted as the good shepherd who could guide the flock to its heavenly home. After Constantine, the Christ was pictured as the victor over death and the ruler of the world. During the medieval period, when the church was the primary vehicle of both social and cultural tradition, the story of Christ's ascent from the cross (or the tomb) to the seat of sovereignty, judgment, and salvation in heaven focused the Christian imagination on a Christ of a truly comprehensive, three-decker world. Somewhat later we see the Gothic Christ appear, and then the Christ of the crucifix, the man of Galilee, the cosmic Christ, the feminine Christ, and so on. In every case, the rearrangements were necessary in order to adjust the mythic world to new social constraints and cultural systems of knowledge.

Myths can be rearranged because they project a narrative universe. The edges of a mythic world are always vague and vulnerable to the intrusion of alien figures. Myths are set in the past and many tell of the time when the world as presently experienced came into being. All peoples are aware of the time between the mythic events and their own time, and there are many ways of recognizing and accounting for what we in western culture have called tradition or history. Any and all of these relations between a myth and some actual social situation are subject to resignification and rearrangement.

When a social history introduces changes in the structure of a society and its patterns of activity, the function of a myth is challenged because it no longer depicts how the present state of affairs came to be. Such a challenge demands that both the myth and the new social configuration be rethought. In western tradition and in antiquity, where myth is linked primarily to an epic history, a particular method of rearranging symbols or mythmaking has been the rule. The epic is reviewed in relation to the current situation, and depending on one's sense of the tension between them, particular events from the epic are chosen as paradigms for reflecting upon the present. A golden age, for instance, may be revised and then held up as a contrast to the present situation as critique, program, or utopian ideal.

In the case of social fragmentation and the collision of many cultures, such as that experienced by all peoples during the Greco-Roman age, no single epic tradition becomes a model for new patterns of social activity. And yet these patterns must be linked up with the past. Some measure of novelty is allowed because of obvious changes in circumstance, but the new pattern cannot be seen as brand new without violating a group's awareness of being in a world long since inhabited. And so the process of social formation includes working out agreements, settling on symbols, and projecting a mythic time frame. A group needs to do this in order to identify its place vis-à-vis the surrounding cultures and to claim legitimacy as an appropriate response to the times. This response will be judged in relation to the best traditions of the previous histories of the peoples and cultures that have converged.

We have traced one tradition of social experimentation and mythmaking among the followers of Jesus. The Jesus people first imagined the society to be structured on the hellenic model of a school in the tradition of a teacher. At every turn in social experience and its accompanying shift in discourse, Jesus was reimagined. But revising and compounding the roles of their teacher was not the only factor at work in this process. The group was also at work on the question of the ideal social order they wanted to represent. They noted how they differed from other groups and social configurations and where they overlapped with the ideals of cultural traditions that were no longer locatable as dominant in the social histories of their times, and they wondered how they might lay claim to those ideals as their heritage. Working with a minimal set of symbols, Jesus as their founder-teacher had to represent the link with and the present incarnation of all the valuable symbols they had gleaned while sorting through what was remembered and valued from the past.

Others naturally read those same or similar histories in ways that supported their own experimentations with social formations. Thus all of the epics, Greek, Syrian, Egyptian, Roman, and a myriad of illustrious local traditions, as well as the Jewish, Samaritan, and northern Israel traditions, became prizes over which ideological battles raged. As with the recent debates in America about the "original intention of the constitution," different groups laying claim to the same epic traditions were thrust into ideological competition. Those with the least claim on an epic tradition would naturally be the most threatened and the most likely to engage in hostile polemics against those whose positions of privilege argued for another interpretation. It is primarily for this reason that early Christians developed such a strong polemic against their Jewish competitors for claims upon the epic of Israel.

The discovery of Q has made it possible to identify several first-century junctures in the social and ideological histories of closely related groups of Jesus people. At the beginning, as we have seen, there was no need and therefore little interest in sorting through any epic tradition in order to claim legitimacy for the groups that formed. Jesus was remembered as a Cynic-sage whose insights were immediately accepted and whose importance lay in the obvious success of his type of discourse that challenged others to consider a change of lifestyle. The first attempt to borrow from an epic tradition was occasioned by internal and local social stress and was performed in a thoroughly defensive fashion. There was no need to enhance Jesus' importance by portraying him as a prophet on the model of the prophets of Israel. The people of Q simply usurped the epic of their detractors and read it against them. "Get off our backs. Your own history should tell you that what we represent is a critical voice in unhealthy times and has always been needed. See, we are OK even on your own terms." But of course, having found a way to see the movement reflected in the epic traditions, this mythmaking strategy was in place when loyalty to the group became an issue and its borders had to be marked.

We have followed the development of a Jesus mythology that drew upon the popular figure of personified wisdom. Wisdom mythology was used to shift from a characterization of Jesus as a teacher to one that imagined Jesus first as an envoy of the divine agent in Israel's history and then as a kind of prophet. In this characterization, the notion of a line of prophets could work both ways, polemically and constructively. It could serve as a polemic both against an establishment Judaism that read the epic as an etiology for the second temple-state, the advantage Mark took, and against a Pharisaic definition of Judaism that read the epic as a charter for the ethical and ritual laws of purity, the advantage that Q^2, the Thomas people, and Luke took. On the constructive side, imagining Jesus as an envoy of wisdom in the role of a prophet-teacher enhanced his importance and thus the importance of his teachings for Q^2, the Thomas people, and Luke. It even made it possible for Q^3 and Matthew to fudge on the earlier polemic against the Pharisees, use the prophet motif merely as a predictive device, and reinterpret the teachings of Jesus as thoroughly compatible with Pharisaic law.

The conclusions to be drawn from the story of Q are therefore obvious. The followers of Jesus were normal human beings, responding to their times in understandable ways, investing intellectual energy in their evolving social experiments, and developing mythologies just as any society-in-the-making does. As for methods and means toward the creation of a mythic universe, the Jesus people also performed according to normal patterns. They assessed their social and cultural context with critical care, laid claim to the cultural traditions most relevant and ready at hand, sorted out the combinations most appropriate to their movement, and borrowed creatively from the mythologies current at the time.

The importance of these conclusions for a revision of Christian origins is enormous. Q's story puts the Jesus movements in the center of the picture as the dominant form of early group formations in the wake of Jesus, and it forces the modern historian to have another look at the congregations of the Christ. The congregations of the Christ will now have to be accounted for as a particular development within the Jesus movements, not as the earliest form of Christian persuasion and standard against which the Jesus movements have appeared as diluted accommodations to banal mentalities.

The history of the Q movement demonstrates that several mythologies of Jesus as a divine agent were possible without any recourse to martyrological notions. The mythology of Jesus as an envoy of wisdom, or even as the manifest incarnation of wisdom's child, was not generated by any experience or notion of Jesus' resurrection from the dead. It was, as we have seen, generated in the course of mythmaking in the genre of the teachings of a teacher.

The discovery of Q also cautions us about the traditional view that Christianity emerged as a reformation of the religion of Judaism. Even the appeal to the epic of Israel was an ad hoc strategy that was not integral to the primary motivations of the Jesus movement. Other ideological resources were as much in play, including popular forms of hellenistic philosophy and the mythology of wisdom. The attraction of the new community was not rooted in a plan to reform a religious tradition that had missed its calling, or in a clarion call to start a new world religion based on a recent revelation, but in the enhancement of human values experienced in the process of social formation itself.

In the midst of the large, unmanageable world of confusing cultures and social histories, a small group of like-minded individuals would have been its own attraction. Such a group would have provided a forum for new ideas. A sense of critical distance from the world would not have meant that positive attractions within the group were lacking or that constructive proposals for ordering their social relationships would not have been forthcoming. Heady thoughts such as representing the rule of God as an alternative to the kingdoms of the world were possible. But at the core of this attraction was the idea that a mixed group of people could represent the best of the heritage of several ethnically exclusive cultural traditions and claim to be a new kind of community.

The evidence for a multiethnic constituency in the Q traditions is sparse, mainly because the Jewish-Galilean issue dominated the terms of the group's response to social rejection, not because the Q communities were closed to persons who were not of Jewish ethnic extraction. The mood of the group was not generated by ethnic loyalties, and evidence of a multiethnic, multicultural mix, prepares us for understanding the spread of the Jesus movement to settings where the mix of peoples surfaced for celebration and then became an issue, as well as for the eventual formation of a network of Jesus-Christian groups as a new hellenistic religion. Mark, Thomas, Luke, and even Matthew provide strong evidence for the mix of peoples characteristic of the Jesus movements, and the mythology of the Christ cult is understandable only on the basis of a multiethnic, cross-cultural movement.

The Q people were not the only group that formed within the Jesus movement. To take five additional groups as an example of the experimental nature of the Jesus movement, there is some evidence for (1) a group of Jesus people distinguished by its allegiance to Jesus' family, (2) Jewish followers who took up residence in Jerusalem for a time, (3) the people who designed sets of (five) miracle stories as their myth of origin, (4) the Jesus movement in which Mark was at home and in which the pronouncement story genre was highly developed, and (5) the tradition within which Luke was at home, a tradition with a sketchy history but one in which a distinctively human view of Jesus prevailed. All of these groups, with the exception of Luke's, are discussed in my book, *A Myth of Innocence* (1988), from which the following brief descriptions are taken.

The sets of five miracle stories for which we have evidence in the gospels of both Mark and John are particularly interesting as an example of mythmaking in the Jesus movement. The sets include a sea-crossing miracle at the beginning and a feeding miracle story at the end. In between are three miracles of healing focusing on socially marginal people in impossible circumstances and including at least one gentile. Scholars have traced the design of these sets of five miracle stories to motifs from the miracles of the Exodus tradition and the healings of the Elijah-Elisha cycle. Thus we have another example of Jesus people thinking of themselves on the model of an epic precedent. It is important to see that there is not the slightest hint of any polemic against Jewish claims to these traditions. There is instead a sense of delight in imagining that a mixed constituency of Jesus people could be thought of as a group constituted on the Exodus model. "Look. That's us. It's great," seems to be the message.

The pre-Markan pronouncement stories, on the other hand, show that Mark's group of Jesus people somehow became fixated with the issue of whether the Pharisaic codes of purity applied to the Jesus movement. Their answer clearly was no, but the extravagant arguments against the Pharisees in these stories show that the debate had been carried on for some time and was taken quite seriously. The pronouncement stories contain numerous hints that during the first phase of this tradition, Jesus was remembered for an aphoristic wisdom much like that reflected in Q^1. And in the course of this group's history, the voice of Jesus eventually took on absolute authority just as it did in Q^2. However, the issues underlying the debate called for arguments and pronouncements that were quite different from the simple charges against the Pharisees in Q^2. In Mark's group Jesus' authority was not derived from a wisdom mythology but attributed to his skill in argumentation. Thus they did not picture Jesus as wisdom's child but as an accomplished rhetor, a lawyer for the defense of the Jesus people who knew the law but outfoxed the Pharisees in argument at every turn. He did this as the champion for the legitimacy of a group composed of people who, by Pharisaic standards, were ritually impure.

An altogether different mythology developed in the congregations of the Christ known to us from the letters of Paul. This mythology is the one most familiar to modern Christians, for it focuses on Jesus' death as a saving event and includes the notion of his resurrection to cosmic lordship. New Testament scholars call this mythology the kerygma for short, for that is what Paul said Christians preached. (*Kerygma* means "proclamation.") The kerygma developed in the congregations of Jesus people in northern Syria (Antioch and beyond) and appears to have overshadowed, if not erased, the memories and importance of Jesus as a teacher. Only the faintest suggestion of having started as a Jesus movement can be discerned in the thought and practice of these congregations, even though it must have been from the Jesus people who spread to northern Syria that the Christ cults emerged.

The transformation of a Jesus movement into a Christ congregation is signaled with the term christ. Christ, not Jesus, was the name that came to be used for the one who was crucified and raised. But why? In Greek the term was a common adjective that meant "smeared" or "anointed" (as with oil or ointment). It was never used as a name and had no special significance in that culture. So the term christ must have been used in the sense of messiah, the Hebrew term for "anointed." In Jewish tradition, "anointed" had the additional connotation of installation to royal or priestly office. Why would the Christ congregations have used it if, as we have seen, the Jesus movement had not thought of Jesus as a messiah?

The term christ came into use during the mythmaking process that resulted in the kerygma. It was a concept that could relate both to the idea of the kingdom of God, common to the Jesus movement, as well as to the idea of Jesus as the king of the kingdom of God as represented by the congregations of the Christ. As understood in the Jesus movements, the kingdom of God did not call for a messiah. In the Christ cults, however, the congregations thought of themselves as a realm over which Jesus as the Christ presently ruled. Thus the term christ soon became only another name for their God. If we are able to reconstruct the logic by which Jesus came to be thought of as a god with a right to rule over these communities, we may be able to understand why christ was chosen for his new name.

The clue to the logic of the kerygma lies in the phrase that christ died "for us," namely the congregation of Christians. Such a notion cannot be traced to old Jewish and/or Israelite traditions, for the very idea of a vicarious human sacrifice was anathema in these cultures. But it can easily be traced to a strong Greek tradition of extolling a noble death. The tradition has its roots in the idea that a warrior "dies for" his country, its laws, or his people. In the case of Socrates, the noble death notion was applied to a philosopher-teacher who died for the truth of his vision for the very city that condemned him to death. During the hellenistic and Roman periods, the Socratic ideal became the prime model for ethical integrity, and facing death, especially at the hands of a tyrant, was considered the ultimate test of one's philosophical and ethical commitment. When leading teachers and court counselors suffered banishment or execution, the notion of the noble death immediately came to mind as the standard that was used to assess and eulogize the mettle of all martyrs.

The notion of a resurrection from the dead, on the other hand, offended hellenic sensibility. It was a new notion, entertained in desperation by Jewish authors who were struggling with the question of theodicy, or the problem of justice in the case of the righteous being killed by those in power who had no right to rule. As an idea it was born in the fusion of an apocalyptic imagination with an age-old narrative plot sometimes called a wisdom tale. This tale turned on the reversal of two trial scenes. An innocent Jewish victim was charged with disloyalty to a foreign king and condemned to prison or death but was later rescued and vindicated when it was discovered that his wisdom and Jewish loyalties were not seditious but greatly beneficial to the king and his people. Familiar examples are the Joseph story, Esther, and the Daniel tales. When a realistic assessment of the times forbade a naive telling of this story, and the apocalyptic projection of a future vindication for the righteous was imagined, the wisdom tale was given a new twist. Even if the innocent victim was killed, there would still be a retrial and a thorough vindication, together with a reversal of circumstance, after death. Various views of transformation were possible at this point, including immediate ascension and/or an eventual resurrection from the dead. The wisdom story and the model of the noble martyr merged in a martyrological literature that memorialized the history of the Maccabees (2 and 4 Macc.) and fascinated other authors such as Philo and the author of the Wisdom of Solomon. This happened in hellenistic-Jewish circles from northern Syria to Alexandria.

The Jesus people in northern Syria embraced this mythology and applied it to their own situation. They were aware that their association, a mix of peoples from disparate cultures, which Paul reduced to the two categories of Jew and gentile, was without precedent. For those who had responded to Jesus' vision of living by the rule of God, the thought that he died as a martyr for their cause would not have been an impossible first step. But as with other Jesus movements, born in the crosscurrents of Palestinian traditions and hellenistic culture, and repeatedly bumping up against the strong presence and articulate intellectual force of Jewish involvement from within and Jewish critique from without, the Jewish question of gentile participation in a mixed congregation was raised. Could the notion of Jesus as a martyr answer such a question?

This martyrology was enhanced with three additional notions. One was that the God whose kingdom they represented was the God storied in the epic of Israel. If Jesus had died for the cause of *that* God's rule, the congregation could think of itself as a new configuration of "Israel," the people of God, fully "justified" though including gentiles. Another notion was that God raised Jesus from the dead as a vindication for his faithfulness to the cause for which he had died. It might be considered an audacious presumption for Christians to have imagined that a certain god was intentionally involved in the destiny of Jesus and to have assumed to know what that god thought about Jesus' crucifixion and resurrection. And yet, that is what mythic thinking allows. Creating such a martyrology was actually no different than creating a mythology of Jesus as the child of divine wisdom. Both mythologies dared to gain the Archimedian point of view necessary for the placement of Jesus (Christ) at the center of a world with horizons vast enough to be considered universal.

The third addition followed from this theological twist on the martyrology, namely that Jesus was recognized by God as the rightful heir to his kingdom. The idea of the son of god as heir to his father's kingdom was available in many hellenistic mythologies. Thus the enhancement of Jesus' mythological role can be understood as a shift from Jesus as the child of wisdom, or the righteous one whom wisdom rescued, to the son of God whom God designated as king. The shift can be thought of as a simple move if one sees it at the formal level of rearranging related symbols in a system. However, the consequences at the level of the recharacterization of Jesus' mythological role were stupendous. The move turned a prophet-teacher into a divine sovereign. No longer would Jesus' authority be experienced as a voice of instruction and judgment from the past. He would now be a king who would execute his authority over the congregation in the present, and since resurrection meant ascending into heaven, the Jesus people came to think of Jesus as a god. The Christ was installed as ruler of God's world and lord of God's people. With such a dramatic mythology focused on the death and resurrection of Jesus as the Christ, the congregations of the Christ no longer needed to cultivate the memories of Jesus as a teacher.

The Christ myth created a much more fantastic imaginary universe than anything encountered in the Jesus traditions. The myth is also curious and ironic from a modern historian's point of view. A Jewish question about the social constitution of the Jesus movement was answered by a combination of Greek and Jewish narrative logics, neither of which would have been attractive to the other culture's traditional mentality. That irony is strong evidence for the multiethnic mix and multicultural ethos of the new congregations. Note that the God in question need not be thought of as the private property of the Jews, although Paul as a Jew thought of God that way. Christians probably thought of Jesus' father as the God of overlapping epic traditions common to Jews, Samaritans, and Galileans alike. There is also no indication that the Christ people thought of Jesus as having been killed by the Jewish establishment or that God's vindication of his martyrdom therefore intended a judgment on the Jews. In distinction from the narrative gospels, the kerygma did not situate the death and resurrection of Jesus in a specific time and place. The kerygma was simply "that" Christ died (for the kingdom) and was raised (as its king). The logic would not have worked equally for all parties of the mixed congregation if the tyrants who killed Jesus had been named and blamed. Thus the "event" of the cross and resurrection was dislodged from social circumstance and placed in a thoroughly mythological once upon a time. Hellenized Jews could think of the myth in terms of the wisdom tale; Greeks could imagine the resurrection on the model of apotheosis or of the translation and transformation of a hero into a god.

The evidence from Paul's letters is that the congregations of the Christ were attractive associations and that their emerging mythology was found to be exciting. A spirited cult formed on the model of the mystery religions, complete with entrance baptisms, rites of recognition (the holy kiss), ritualized meals (the lord's supper), the notion of the spiritual presence of the lord, and the creation of liturgical materials such as acclamations, doxologies, confessions of faith, and Christ hymns. It was a new religious society celebrating freedom from cultural traditions and the personal experience of transcending social constraints by means of induction into a mythic world centered in a symbol of transcendence and transformation.

It was in the Christ cult, not in the Jesus movement, that the Christian notion of conversion as a personal transformation emerged. The notion seems simple, but it depends on a highly developed collective imagination that sharply distinguishes the ethos of a community from its larger social world. In the case of the congregations of the Christ, a spirited ethos and its mythic world were joined and conceptualized on the Greek model of a sphere of being, most often called a *cosmos* (ordered "world"), sometimes an *aeon* (vast, all-encompassing "age"). Christians imagined that their ethos was a cosmic order of existence created by the Christ and that therefore there were two aeons available for human habitation. The difference between these aeons was variously described as new/old, heavenly/worldly, spiritual/fleshly, or even divine/demonic. It was this conceptuality that allowed Paul to develop the notion of the church as the body of (the cosmic) Christ, and describe the experience of joining a Christian congregation in terms of conversion, forgiveness, freedom, transference, transformation, and new creation. Such a conceptuality is further evidence of the strong sense of identity achieved in these groups. But of course, inhabiting such a mythic world, even as an ethos that required social congregation, was dangerously close to living in a bubble world whose only attachment to social reality was a flotation on the surface of its currents.

One might think that such an extravagant mythology would surely mark the outside limits of early Christian imagination. Not so. The stakes were apparently felt to be high, the rewards of the new religion worthy of further intellectual investment, and the cross-cultural mix of mythologies heady. One could write a poem to celebrate the cosmic event and have it sung by the congregation. One could declaim on the benefits released by the spiritual presence of the congregation's lord. Social intercourse in a world governed only by the spirit of freedom must have been enticing to say the least. There was still much to experience, think about, and do. The Christ myth was an extremely complex symbol capable of further elaboration.

The New Testament letter to the Ephesians is a meditation on the cosmic order created by the Christ, a poetry of praise, wonderment, and thanksgiving, and a prayer for an increase of the wisdom and insight required to understand its "heights and depths" of mystery. The letter to the Hebrews is an even more preposterous elaboration of the Christ myth. The vicarious aspect of the martyr's death ("for" some cause) invited elaboration as a "sacrifice," and the author of the letter to the Hebrews did not hesitate to interpret Jesus' death as "better" even than the sacrifice of the erstwhile Jewish high priests on the Day of Atonement. It was "better" because Jesus was the son of God, not a human high priest, who performed the sacrifice once for all, not repeatedly, and offered himself as the sacrifice, not some other sacrificial victim. This thought, the author of Hebrews said, should help Christians take comfort during their trials and think of themselves as living within the forecourt of the great cosmic temple of God with all eyes on the veil behind which the timeless self-sacrifice of the son of God was being performed on their behalf. Modern sensibility may not find this image as helpful as the author of Hebrews thought it would be.

The difference between the Jesus movements and their mythologies and the congregations of the Christ and their mythologies should now be clear. One important contrast is that between a focus on the instructions of a teacher and the dramatic event of a martyr's death and resurrection. Another is that the mythic worlds of the Jesus movements placed Jesus in epic and historical time and place. In the Christ cults the founding event resisted location in historical time and place and was imagined to have created a spiritual or noetic world detached from the social and environmental orders. With such a difference in social sensibilities and mythologies, one would hardly imagine that Jesus people and Christ people would ever be able to recognize one another, much less find a way to accommodate both types of social experimentation and mythology in a single configuration. And yet they tried.

Mark's merger of the kerygma with the Jesus traditions has already been mentioned. Mark was able to merge the two distinctly different traditions by identifying a conceptual bond common to both and use it to structure his composite account. The common concept was the relation of Jesus to the wisdom of God. Mark's genius was to use a form of wisdom mythology that could relate both to the Jesus traditions and to the Christ myth and so mediate between them. The particular form of wisdom mythology he used was the wisdom tale of trial and vindication. The Jesus people had not made use of it, for they had no need or desire to reflect on questions pertaining to theodicy and vindication. But they would certainly be familiar with the plot and were capable of seeing the connection to their own myths of Jesus as wisdom's child. For the Christ people, the logic of the wisdom tale was fundamental to their kerygma, but they had not needed or dared to use it as a script for thinking about the historical circumstances of Jesus' death. Mark dared to use it and thus drew the Jesus traditions and the Christ traditions together at the point of the passion narrative.

We have already noted the reasons Mark had for thinking of Jesus' death in terms of judgment and vindication. Now we need to underscore the point that Mark's sympathies were still with the Jesus people, not with the Christ cult. He took from the Christ myth only what he needed in order to jockey his apocalyptic Jesus mythology into a dramatic and visual "historical" account of judgment against those who had rejected his Jesus group. He was not interested in the notion of a sacrificial death celebrated by means of a ritual meal in a cult of spiritual presence. He used the term christ in its messianic connotation, not to refer to a cultic divinity. The "lord's supper" in Mark is simply the last supper of Jesus with his disciples, a time for disclosures, fond farewells, and predictions. It was not intended as an etiological script for ritual reenactment by the Jesus people. The message of the empty tomb was not that Jesus was alive and available as a spiritual presence, but that Jesus was absent until the eschaton and that one should not go looking for him. So Mark walked a narrow line between the two types of mythology and apparently succeeded in persuading people in the Jesus traditions to consider Jesus as having been the christ-messiah and to think of his death as a martyrdom for their cause.

Mark's reduction of the Christ myth to terms compatible with the Jesus myths was an intellectual and literary accomplishment of truly historic proportions. It was not, however, the most imaginative combination of the two traditions possible. That achievement took place in yet another Jesus tradition, one that I have not mentioned until now. The author of the Gospel of John wrote his novel account of Christian origins toward the end of the first century. He was solidly at home in a movement that had cultivated a peculiar style of discourse and created a most distinctive ethos. This movement started at an early time and appears to have had connections with the people who composed the miracle story sets. But in the course of a long and vigorous history, a community formed that found it possible to appropriate the views from many Jesus groups and turn them all into food for its own kind of thought. The community turned a set of miracle stories into "signs" that signified the Jesus movement as the replacement for the Jewish religion. Much like the Thomas people, this community turned the sayings of Jesus into a highly developed discourse of encoded meanings of self-reference both to Jesus and to themselves. They embellished the pronouncement story genre to create extended dialogues and monologues for Jesus who spoke of himself as the son of God in rhythmic and mesmerizing patterns of self-revelation. And they had no trouble accepting the Gospel of Mark, the story of Jesus' death and resurrection with its themes of judgment and vindication.

The way in which the John people handled the Christ myth provides a distinctive twist of the gospel genre. Instead of downplaying the death and resurrection of the Christ as the moment when a new world of spiritual presence came into being, as Mark had done, the crucifixion was fixed upon as a moment in "history" that revealed a divine world of life and light that had always been present but never clearly seen until Jesus as the son of God made it known. The crucifixion was the son's hour of glory, a (con)descension to the darkened world of humankind and a reascension of the son to the father. The distinction between Jesus teachings and Christ event coalesced in the Gospel of John, as did timeless presence and its location in history. The spiral-like rhythms of the endless monologues of the self-revealing son of God, the logos of God or wisdom's child, purposely benumb the reader. The whole point, according to the author of the gospel who expressly developed the theme of Jesus' self-revelation as an offense to normal reasoning, was to cease making judgments and go with the flow. Hearing and rehearsing the words of this Jesus would conjure up the imaginary world he created.

Like the Gospel of Thomas, the Gospel of John represents a community that was very close to becoming a gnostic sect. The difference between the Gospel of Thomas and the Gospel of John is that by cultivating only the sayings of Jesus, Thomas created a noetic world of self-referential presence that was detached from the social world. John developed a mythology that combined the time frame characteristic of the narrative gospels with the spiritual order created by the Christ myth. This was an auspicious stroke of imaginative genius. As any church historian knows, the Johannine image of Jesus at the center of a universe pulsating with the powers of light and darkness, the miraculous and the banal, is a very early projection of the mythic mentality that became characteristic of medieval Christianity.

John pictured Jesus as the manifestation of God's son from the realm of light, the very expression of God that created the world but which repeatedly failed to find recognition until Jesus appeared. According to John, who used Mark's narrative to define the time and place of Jesus' appearance, the revealer was in the world from John the Baptist until the crucifixion. This attachment of the mythic world to human history in the story of Jesus has been a very important feature of Christian imagination and thought. This connection becomes tenuous, however, when Jesus' mythic role is primarily that of the revealer of spiritual enlightenment. Whenever a Christian congregation of the Johannine variety loses its own sense of attachment to the world at large, the attachment of the revealer to the time and place of the narrative gospel also can easily be severed. This is what happened in gnostic circles where the Gospel of John became the favorite narrative gospel. Not only was the Gospel of John read in these circles as if its setting were merely a "once upon a time," the narrative frame was dropped as other accounts of Jesus' conversations with his disciples were written. One gnostic ploy was to discount the narrative as history by placing the conversations in some ethereal setting at a time after Jesus' resurrection. But other gnostic treatises imagined the revealer appearing in dreams or visions at any time and thus completely detached from any epic or historical frame of reference.

From Q^1 to the Gospel of John is a long, long way for the imagination of any movement to journey in such a short period of time.

The myths that these people produced can only be called fantastic. But they settled in to play the dominant role in the shaping of the worldview basic to western culture. A culture grows accustomed to its mythic universe. Attention is drawn to it only on certain occasions when the etiquettes of pious reverence and attention prohibit critical expression, if not thinking. But now, observing this explosion of fantasy from a distance, and as historians interested in understanding the forces that generated such a mythology, we see that the times were right, the mythic resources ready, and that human ingenuity was fully capable of such novel creations.

This account of early Christian mythmaking has revised the traditional picture puzzle of Christian origins by making three moves. One has been to underscore the many forms of early Christian mythology. The second has been to take multiformation as evidence of intellectual labor. And the third is to see the variations in myths or "christologies" as evidence for vigorous social experimentation. The attraction of the social formations in the early Jesus movements and congregations of the Christ has largely been left out of account in previous descriptions of early Christianity. But as it turns out, it was hardly the myth or the message that generated Christianity. It was the attraction of participating in a group experimenting with a new social vision.

12

Bishops and the Bible

Q's fate was sealed when Mark wrote his story and Matthew and Luke merged Q with Mark's account. Mark's story was attractive for several reasons. It created a character for Jesus strong enough to integrate images of Jesus within the Jesus movement with the Christ myth. It also settled on a single narrative logic to link Jesus up with an epic past and render a full account of the way in which this Jesus related to well-known historical events of the time. Despite the fact that Mark's Jesus was overloaded with fantastic mythological roles, Mark succeeded in creating the picture of a person who took his place in full public view and engaged the full spectrum of the people and powers of his time. It was this historical placement, achieved by the narrative device of the incognito son of God, that fascinated readers of all persuasions and laid the foundation for the Christian epic, the biblical account of human history that eventually became the charter for the Christian church. Because of Mark's accomplishment, Q's mythology became obsolete.

Q as a book of instruction was another matter. Mark did not relegate Q to the sidelines as a source for the teachings of Jesus. Q continued to be read along with Mark until at least the turn of the century and apparently enjoyed a wide reading in various circles, as both Matthew and Luke attest. When Matthew and Luke each found a way to work Q into their expanded versions of Mark, however, Q as a separate document may have lost some of its attraction.

The merger of Mark and Q was possible because of the view, common within the Jesus movement, that Jesus had been a teacher. Because of Mark's plot and its motif of secrecy, Mark was not able to incorporate instructions of the Q^1 type, but he did not reject the image of Jesus as a teacher. Mark's Jesus was a teacher whose instructions consisted of private, esoteric knowledge. So the later insertion of Q into the narrative framework of Mark was just another elaboration on the theme of Jesus the teacher, another reconfiguration in a series of profiles that stretched back to the picture of the teacher created by Q^1. Matthew and Luke were able to merge Mark and Q because of this fundamental persuasion.

It does seem strange, however, that Q became the lost gospel merely by absorption into the gospels of Matthew and Luke. That has been the customary scholarly view. But if Jesus continued to be honored as a teacher, and if Q was a standard collection of his teachings, why didn't Q continue to be used as a handbook of instructions alongside the narrative gospels? Why was Q not included among the texts that eventually became canonized as the New Testament? Duplication of material was not a problem in the formation of the New Testament. If four narrative gospels were not too much, a separate collection of the teachings of Jesus surely would not have overloaded the collection. And Q was a strong text, much stronger than others that were included, such as the so-called letter of James, that one wonders how Q could have been overlooked. The contents of Q were obviously acceptable to authors whose gospels were included.

Thus the question of Q's omission from the selection of texts that compose the New Testament needs to be addressed. This is because, as the reader is now aware, the consequences of its loss were enormous. By excluding Q, the process of canonization effectively erased direct access to the genre of instruction forged during the first chapters of Christian history. Thus the reasons why Q dropped from sight need to be understood. Only then will our story of Q as the lost gospel come to an end and the stage be set for a concluding reflection on the significance of its recent discovery.

We can gain a bit of leverage on the question by turning it around. What was the purpose of collecting the writings in the New Testament in the first place, and what were the principles of their selection? We begin by noting that the question of Christian texts appropriate for use in the Christian church became an issue around the middle of the second century and continued to be debated until sometime during the fourth century. At that point, when the Christian church was recognized as an institution of the state, the texts regularly in use became the "norm," or what we have called the biblical *canon* of the church. The canon of the Bible was never an issue taken up for official action by any church council, however, so there is no statement even from the fourth-century church of the reasons for its formation. Canon is our word for the end result of a long history of practice.

To get at this history we must survey the literary production of Christians during the first two centuries and compare it to lists of early Christian writings recommended for use in the churches. Such lists began to appear at the end of the second century, and the writings included in these lists are essentially those we recognize as the New Testament. What is striking about the comparison is the severe reduction of a large, spirited literature to a very small set of gospels and letters. Q is not the only document from the early period of Christian history that does not appear on these lists.

Much of the literature from the first century has not survived in its original form. But judging from the Jesus traditions that were brought together in the gospels, from the editions of Q and the Gospel of Thomas, the Christ cult materials reflected in the letters of Paul, books included in the New Testament such as the letter to the Hebrews, lore in the Acts of the Apostles, the mention by later authors of works now lost, and the highly developed treatises of the second century that presuppose earlier efforts, what we have in the New Testament is only a small portion of what must have been a very rich and sizable production. If we include the literature we know about from the second century, a period during which some of the New Testament writings (such as Luke-Acts, Jude, and 2 Peter) derive as well, the body of literature for comparison with the New Testament is immense.

The range by type of literature is also impressive. We have miracle story sets, pronouncement story sets, various collections of the sayings of Jesus, narrative gospels, infancy gospels, hymn books, instructions for community practice, liturgical prayers, devotional prayers, sermons, meditational treatises, ethical treatises, theological treatises, philosophical treatises, commentaries on the Old Testament, apocalyptic allegories, gnostic treatises of many kinds, letters, exchanges of correspondence, acts of the apostles, martyrologies, and polemical writings against the Greeks, the Jews, the Romans, the Gnostics, the Marcionites, and other Christian persuasions. So we dare not assume that the writings in the New Testament are a sufficient documentation of Christian beginnings.

Why gospels and letters? There are only two exceptions to this twofold classification for inclusion in the New Testament. The two exceptions are the Acts of the Apostles and the Apocalypse of John. These exceptions can be explained when the logic of the gospels and letters is clear.

Why the gospels? Why were the gospels preferred instead of any number of other myths of origin, such as the Jesus of Q, the Christ of the kerygma, the wisdom of the Gospel of Thomas, the revealer of the gnostic gospels, and other characterizations? The reason is that the gospels provided a historical point of origin that supported the institutional claims of Christianity as the church. The gospels were read as accounts of Jesus' life written by the apostles. They were important for three reasons. First, without sacrificing the mythic role of Jesus as the son of God, the narrative gospels portrayed Jesus as a personage who appeared at a specific time in human history. Second, the meaning of Jesus' appearance was clearly derived from its relationship to the epic history of Israel. And third, the gospels pictured Jesus preparing his disciples for leadership in the church he came to inaugurate. This means that their primary function as narratives was to create the illusion of a chain of tradition that not only linked Jesus with the epic traditions of Israel but also with the disciples as the apostles of the church. The purpose of the gospels as instructional literature was less important than their authorization of the disciples as those who knew Jesus personally and whose own teachings and writings were therefore trustworthy records of what Jesus had said the church should be. The notion that was crucial for this new epic mythology was that of the disciples as apostles. The term apostle meant one who was "sent" or commissioned to represent the sender. The idea that the disciples were apostles, commissioned to represent Jesus in the missions that established churches in various regions, became an integral part of the church's mythology early in the second century. According to this myth, the apostles served as guarantors that the teachings of the church were derived from Jesus.

From the second century there is evidence that, in order to make this schema work, Mark was thought to have gotten his information from Peter, and Luke was thought to have gotten his information from Paul. As for Paul, though not numbered among the disciples, he was regarded as an "apostle" whose claim to authority was based on revelatory experience of the risen Jesus instead of actual experience with the historical Jesus. With the two other gospels according to Matthew and John, the problem of authorship by a disciple-apostle was solved by the fiction of direct attribution.

As for the letters, one can see that they were understood to be the writings of the apostles. They are the letters of Paul, Peter, John, James, and Jude. But, with the exception of the seven authentic letters of Paul, apostolic authorship of the letters is as much a fiction as the apostolic authorship of the gospels. So a better question is, Why so much interest in the letter as a genre? The answer is that the encyclical letter was the major medium for disseminating a bishop's instruction to the churches. In the course of the second century the leaders of local Christian congregations in important cities came to be known as bishops (from *episkopos,* "overseer"). Bishops presided over a network of congregations in their region, and the letter was used as a way to address issues of governance, ethic, and instruction in the faith. By the end of the second century there were bishoprics with strong central authority in the larger cities of political importance, such as Antioch, Smyrna, Jerusalem, Rome, and Alexandria. Bishops at these centers of Christian power were to battle one another for ideological and practical leadership of the church, as the church councils of the fourth and fifth centuries show, and as the subsequent regional fragmentations of Christendom attest. During the earlier period of the second century, the literature shows that an appeal to apostolic tradition became the major device for giving a bishop's instructions legitimate authority.

Early examples of the bishop's letter reveal the most amazing sense of authority for the oversight of the churches. Already at the beginning of the second century, Ignatius, bishop of Antioch, was writing letters to churches in Asia Minor to prepare the way for his reception on the way to Rome where he expected to be martyred. He urged Christians to be obedient to their bishops, propounded and elaborated the essentials of the Christian faith, and put himself forward as a living example of what a Christian should be. There is also a long instructional treatise from the early second century, dressed up at some point as a letter to the Corinthians by Clement the First of Rome, that addresses Christians in general about the virtuous life. According to First Clement, Christian virtue consists of obedience to the illustrious examples of obedience for the sake of "faith, fear, peace, patience, long-suffering, self-control, purity, and sobriety" (1 Clement 64). Jesus was the prime exemplar, but the list of examples ran through the epic of Israel, included a few "heathens," emphasized the apostles, especially Peter and Paul, and of course ended by enjoining Christians to be obedient to the bishops as the guardians of Christian piety.

There can be no doubt that this kind of instruction was the order of the day during the formative period of the church. When Christians congregated, sermons of this kind would be heard and letters of this type would be read. If so, one wonders why letters like those of Ignatius and Clement were not included in the canon. The answer is that letters related to this kind of instruction were included, but only those that could be fit into the apostolic myth. As First Clement put it, "The apostles received the gospel for us from the lord Jesus Christ, Jesus the Christ was sent from God. The Christ therefore is from God and the apostles from the Christ." As for the apostles, "They preached from district to district, and from city to city, and they appointed their first converts, testing them by the spirit, to be bishops and deacons of the future believers" (1 Clement 42). So the letters of Ignatius and Clement were from "third-generation" bishops, not from apostles, and therefore were not candidates for inclusion in the New Testament.

The authors of the letters attributed to Peter, and the so-called pastoral letters of Paul (1 and 2 Timothy, Titus), paid the price of anonymity by writing pseudonymously but did achieve renown for their compositions by means of their inclusion in the New Testament. Note, however, that the subject matter of 1 Peter and Paul's pastorals has to do with the qualifications for the offices of elder and bishop, and that the concern addressed in 2 Peter (dated ca 150 C.E.) has to do with rejecting the false teachers of heresy and staying true to the "commandment of the lord and savior through your apostles" (2 Pet.

2:1, 3:2). These letters, then, are not intended to be read as the instructions from a bishop to his flock but instead as the instructions from the apostles about the importance of the bishops. A most coincidental buttress to the apostolic myth right there in the canonical corpus, wouldn't one have to say?

This myth of a chain of tradition from Jesus through the apostles and on to the bishops is similar to the Greek notion of the succession of teachers in the tradition of a philosophic school. It therefore developed quite naturally among Christians and granted legitimacy and authority to the office of the bishop and to his instructions to the churches. As a result of this mythology, however, the importance of the teachings of Jesus, whether in the form of a document like Q or as contained in the narrative gospels, became merely symbolic. Jesus was still the guarantor for the truth of the church's instruction, but the sharp edge given to his own sayings as the sole source for Christian instruction was dulled. It was no longer necessary to attribute every instruction to the founder-teacher. Instruction *about* Jesus was now just as important as instruction *from* Jesus, and the instructions from Jesus needed a great deal of interpretation in order to clarify their import for Christian faith, piety, and virtue.

The letter of First Clement is an excellent example of this shift in the content of instruction for the church. It documents the attrition of the authority of Jesus' teachings and the rise of the authority of the bishops' instructions. The bishops' authority was derived from Jesus the founder-teacher, but the bishops' instruction could now draw upon the Jewish scriptures, the writings of Paul, Greek philosophy, hellenistic wisdom, and the bishops' own teachings. The same is true of the Didache, a book of instructions supposedly from the twelve apostles. It begins by citing some teachings of Jesus from Matthew's gospel on "the [Christian] way of life" but quickly moves to the ten commandments; then to general ethical proscriptions given in the genre of wisdom instruction, then to instructions about obedience to church leaders, household duties, the performance of baptism, proper days for fasting, prayers for the meal of thanksgiving, how to treat apostles and prophets, how to select bishops and deacons; and finally to an apocalyptic warning. The voice of the author does not change from beginning to end. It is the voice of one who knows the tradition and speaks with authority as exegete of many scriptures, guardian of the teachings of the church, and shepherd over the piety of his flock. It is clearly the voice of a bishop, not that of the apostles, and thus for that reason alone may have been excluded from the New Testament canon.

Thus Q vanished from sight, not only because the narrative gospels told a better story, one that positioned Jesus at the hinge of epic history, but also because the instructions it contained were no longer sufficient for the teaching that had to be done. It is not enough to say that Q was no longer needed when Matthew and Luke incorporated its contents into their gospels. Rather, Q was superseded by later mythologies that had no room for its singular focus on the authority of Jesus.

Q lacked any mention of the disciples named in Paul and Mark. The disciples had to be mentioned in the story of Jesus in order to serve as guarantors of the apostolic tradition. The two authors of greatest importance to the church's myth of succession were Peter, the founder of the first church in Jerusalem who then moved to Rome, and Paul, the apostle to the gentiles associated with Antioch who also, according to Luke, ended his mission in Rome. This explains the inclusion of Luke's Acts of the Apostles in the canon of New Testament writings. By writing the history he did, Luke actually contributed to the making of the myth that later determined a favored position for his writings.

Luke was a daring genius for his time. He saw the significance of major centers of Christian instruction; imagined that the church could be an institution united under a single authority at Rome; sensed the danger of the difference between Jewish Christianity, with its roots in the Jesus traditions, and gentile Christianity, with its roots in the Christ cult; and wrote his two-volume history to suggest that the two traditions had merged into one. He chose Peter and Paul as representatives of the two types of Christianity and so constructed their sermons and their missions to illustrate the agreements. In doing so, Luke purposefully left out of account the many different varieties of Christian experimentation that were still accumulating during his time. But his monolinear history could be used to great advantage as the bishops of the church worked out their own ideological and institutional arrangement. Luke's history became the official account precisely because of its apostolic mythology. Thus the Acts of the Apostles was given its place in the canon between the gospels and the letters. From the church's point of view, Acts positioned the apostles correctly as those whose connections with Jesus gave them authority to establish Christian congregations by preaching about Jesus.

Briefly, in order to trace the logic of the canon to its fitting conclusion with the apocalypse of John, two additional considerations need to be mentioned. Given the two rubrics of (1) apostolic authorship of (2) gospels and letters, questions remain as to the reasons for the selection of just these writings. Why four gospels and why the letters from just five apostles?

As we have seen, the second century produced a variety of literature, much of which reflected local traditions having little interest in the notion of a common standard for a universal, or catholic, church. Some writings were signed, such as the letters of Paul and Ignatius, some were already written pseudonymously for apostolic founders of a particular tradition, such as the letters written in Paul's name (Ephesians, 1 and 2 Timothy, Titus), and some were written anonymously and thus available for attribution, such as Hebrews (later attributed to Paul) and Didache (attributed to the "twelve apostles"). So the process of selection was actually the work of bringing together what was available, representative, and already being used in the various regions. Since there is no evidence that any of the apostles actually wrote any of the writings attributed to them, except for Paul, one sees that those who were interested in collecting apostolic writings had to make do with what they could find.

Nevertheless, more can be said about the principle of selection than this. Reading the New Testament against the background of the institutional and theological history of Christianity from the second to the fourth centuries, one senses a very strong flavor of accommodation. Several strong traditions of diverse persuasions are represented in this corpus. Taking this sense of the selection as a clue, it is possible to chart the range of tolerance represented by the canon. It runs from James and Matthew on the Jewish-Christian end of a spectrum; is strongly mainstream by means of the Lukan material, the letters of Peter, and the Pseudo-Pauline letters; includes the letters of Paul on what might be called the kerygmatic flank; and doffs its hat to the gnostic forms of Christianity by encompassing the Gospel and Letters of John in the collection. That, to be sure, is as far as the church was willing to go in its accommodation of gnostic forms of Christianity. John, not Thomas, would be the acceptable patron of these traditions. And, wonder of wonders, included among the writings attributed to John one finds an apocalyptic vision born of the most orthodox piety. What a fitting conclusion to the epic rationale of the church's apostolic mythology.

With this selection of texts in place, it is no wonder that Christians have always imagined the birthday of the church on the Lukan model. It is therefore also no wonder that the discovery of Q in modern times has created some confusion. According to the myth of apostolic tradition underlying the canon of the New Testament, there is simply no place for Q and the first followers of Jesus who were not Christians.

13

Christians and Their Myth

The discovery of Q may create some consternation for Christians because accepting Q's challenge is not merely a matter of revising a familiar chapter of history. It is a matter of being forced to acknowledge an affair with one's own mythology. The disclosure of a myth is deemed academic as long as the myth belongs to somebody else. Recognizing one's own myth is always much more difficult, if not downright dangerous.

The reason for this is the way myths work their magic. Myths are guardians of cultural identity and work best when taken for granted. Left undisturbed, a myth makes it possible to assume that others agree in advance on the rules that govern the daily round. Should a myth ever be named and questioned, the collective agreements basic to a society's well-being come unglued and people feel unsettled.

The Christian myth is particularly vulnerable to unsettling questions. Most myths take place once upon a time in an irreal world. Like all stories, they allow the listener to suspend judgment while watching the story unfold. Christian myth claims to be history and asks its adherents to believe that it is true. As long as there is no other data from which to construct a different account of the same chapter of history, the Christian myth can work much the same way as other myths. Christians can simply bracket the story of Jesus from the rest of human history and treat it as an exceptional moment, realizing that the events recorded are fantastic but allowing the story to stand. If, however, the history yields to other explanations and the fantastic features of the gospels are explained as mythic, the Christian gospel will be in very deep trouble, and Christian mentality will have to renegotiate both its real and imaginary worlds. That is exactly where Q enters the picture.

Q challenges the New Testament account of Christian origins by offering another, more plausible account of the first forty years. The Jesus movement is a more believable group of people than the disciples and first Christians who are depicted in the narrative gospels. Q provides a documentation for the Jesus movement that the narrative gospels cannot provide for the congregational fiction they project. This is serious business, because the gospel story is the cornerstone of the Christian's mythic world. Christians understand the gospel as the story of events that generated the Christian church and invite personal imitation. The gospel functions as the source for the special knowledge Christians claim, as the cluster of symbols that focus Christian meditation, and as the script for ritual reenactment in both individual experience and congregational liturgy. The gospel is firmly in mind in western culture. It is the story that has determined the shape of Christian mentality.

When Christians recall the gospel story, they do not think of four distinct narrative accounts, but of an amalgam of the four stories. For nearly two thousand years, these stories have been merged in the iconography and liturgical rehearsals of the church. The church has never been bothered by having four different accounts of the same story. Each account has been regarded merely as another telling "according to" a different witness, or apostle.

The invitation to merge the four gospels into one gospel story is integral to the design of the New Testament. When, during the fourth century, the writings to be used in Christian congregations became widely available in a single codex or manuscript, a conceptual fusion took place that effectively effaced the huge ideological differences among the various writings. From that time on the four gospels collapsed into a single narrative world of the life of Christ according to the bishops' myth. The letters took their subsequent place as the apostolic interpretation of that single gospel story. It is this coalescence of disparate writings that justifies speaking in the singular about "the gospel" as Christians imagine it.

Thus the New Testament was not put together as an ad hoc collection of writings for the purpose of conserving the earliest records of Christian beginnings. It consisted of a highly select set of writings, carefully arranged. The criteria for selection and arrangement were discussed in the preceding chapter, including the observation that the selection represented several streams of Christian persuasion and reveals the bishops' desire to fashion from them a universal church. We can now ask about the consequences of that strategy for the Christian imagination. What the bishops achieved in putting together that unlikely collection of writings, whether it worked for them according to their institutional plans or not, was an astounding literary success. Their selection became the New Testament, and the New Testament became the textual foundation for Christian myth and ritual in all of its many manifestations.

Notice how the apostolic myth supports the merger of all the writings into one account of Christian origins. If the four narrative gospels differ merely because they are the accounts of four different disciples, and if the letters were all written by disciples who became apostles, the various preachments throughout the New Testament are bound to have weight as formulations made during the apostolic period. This really means, mythically, that "witnesses" to Jesus recorded their experiences soon after his death and resurrection. It works. The selection and arrangement of writings in the New Testament project a single history and make of the several writings one book.

Given this arrangement, it is all but impossible to read the narrative gospels in any other light than that provided by the apostolic interpretations of the significant events. Even Mark would be read now through the eyes of Peter and Paul. What irony. We have seen that Mark combined martyrological motifs from Paul's Christ myth with various traditions about Jesus from the Jesus movement in order to write his gospel. This combination produced the passion narrative, a novel interpretation of Jesus' death that did not agree with the views of either tradition he used. But now, included as one of the gospels in the New Testament, the differences between Mark and his sources could no longer be seen. Mark would be read as a witness to the synoptic story on a par with the other three evangelists, even though each of the other three had gotten their start from Mark and had changed his story to agree with their own views. Mark's passion narrative would be interpreted in agreement with Paul's kerygma, not as a correction of it. Both Paul and Mark would be read as witnesses to the same Christ event, and both of their interpretations would coalesce in its layered meaning.

The effect of this phenomenon has been deep, lasting, and profound. All the writings in the New Testament have been read as witnesses to the story of Christian beginnings that was created from the merger of these very same writings. The result has been that each writing has been read as one interpretation of the common underlying story and that the many interpretations have turned the story into a richly nuanced, multilayered symbol. Two events are especially important for the Christian imagination, and these have become places in the story where the fusion of multiple and conflictual meanings is most dense. A brief description of how these two events were overlaid with connotation will prepare us for a final meditation on the radical nature of Q's challenge to the Christian mind.

The first event is the death of Jesus. Two enrichments of its significance occurred that are absolutely fundamental for Christian myth and ritual. One is that, by reading the story of Jesus' death in light of the Pauline kerygma, the "passion" of Jesus became the sign of his willingness to "sacrifice" himself for the "salvation" of the world. This meaning was not a part of Mark's story.

The other event of significance is the last supper of Jesus with his disciples. Overlaid with kerygmatic and sacrificial theology drawn from the reinterpretation of the passion narrative, the last supper became the Lord's supper, an act charged with symbolic significance by pointing to Jesus' self-sacrifice on the cross. The supper story could now be read as Jesus' acknowledgment of the deep meaning of his death (the Christian myth) and used as a script for ritual reenactment (the Christian liturgy). At some point not earlier than the third or fourth century, a priest actually stepped in to take Jesus' place at the table and the Christian mass or eucharist was created. Mark had not told the story of the supper in order to institute the Christian eucharist.

That does not mean that meeting together for meals was not the normal practice for Christian congregations from the earliest times. Meals were certainly the occasion for gathering in the Jesus movements and congregations in the Christ cults. But not all meals were memorials of Jesus' death, and none were ritual occasions on the model of the later eucharist. The tradition Paul cites in 1 Corinthians 11:23–26 was not a script for reenactment but an etiological legend with pedagogic intent. The instructions for a meal in the Didache, a meal of thanksgiving for the knowledge Jesus had given the community about their belonging to the people of God, does not refer to the death and resurrection of Jesus at all. And Mark's last supper was not yet the Lord's supper. So the eucharist as a reenactment of the sacrificial death of Jesus evolved later, slowly, and by degrees.

The Christian eucharist created a mimetic imagination capable of marvelous mental gymnastics. Christians could now experience the "first time" at other times. Christians could now be present at the "sacred place" in other places. Christians could participate in the drama of the sacred event by participation in its symbolic reenactment. And so the stories recorded in the New Testament turned into icons for the visual representation of the sacred drama within the precincts of the medieval church. As objects of meditation, these narrative images became the occasion for mimetic transformation into the imaginary world over which the church presided. The New Testament became the myth and ritual text for a world religion.

The Jesus movement represented by Q is hardly a match for Christianity as a world religion. Even after the development of an essentially timeless imaginary universe, best expressed in the visual form of triptychs, the Bible still functioned as the textual record and authorization of the events to be memorialized and reenacted on liturgical occasions. With the Bible repositioned by the reformers, and the notion of history given privilege in the enlightenment academy, the claim of the church on the gospel as history finally surfaced as an important question. It is in this arena, the arena for understanding the relation between myth and history, that Q registers its challenge.

The challenge will have to be taken seriously because Q is integral to the history of the formation of the gospels. Had Q been discovered as an independent text extraneous to the New Testament, such as the Gospel of Thomas, or as a separate writing within the New Testament, such as the letter of James, it might be discounted as a document from some mistaken, heretical side branch of the "true" Christian tradition. But Q is foundational to the very composition of the narrative gospels. Take Q away and they fall into fragments without narrative or instructional significance.

A remarkable irony can serve as a final observation on the nature of Q's challenge from within the New Testament. Q was not only essential to the gospels as a source for the teachings of Jesus, or as a precursor mythology upon which the narrative gospels were built. In the course of developing their mythology at the Q^2 level, the authors of Q used a clever intertextual reference that caught the attention of the authors of the gospels and eventually determined the logic by which not only the gospels but also the New Testament canon were linked to the Hebrew scriptures to form the Christian Bible. This textual reference was the use of the Malachi citation to predict the appearances of John and Jesus. It has been mentioned that Mark made programmatic use of the John-Jesus story to introduce his gospel and that Matthew and Luke followed Mark and embellished his account. Mark used the Malachi citation (Mal. 3:1) in combination with a forceful prediction from Isaiah about a voice crying in the wilderness (Isa. 40:3) to introduce John at the very beginning of his story. Matthew and Luke undid this combination, using the Isaianic prediction to introduce John at the appropriate point toward the beginning of their stories, while reserving the Malachi prediction for its proper annunciation by Jesus, just as Q had it (Matt. 11:10; Luke 7:27). We can now make the observation that these references to Malachi helped determine the structure of the Christian Bible.

During the period of canon formation, the early Christian writings were not the only scriptures of importance to the church. The epic literature of Israel was also under constant discussion as a record of the history of divine intention that Jesus and the church "fulfilled." The Christian claim to novelty could only be forceful if its recent origin could be seen as the perfection of ancient ideas. But, of course, the Hebrew scriptures belonged to the Jews, not to the Christians. Thus the Christian appropriation of the epic of Israel became an issue of fundamental significance for the church. It had to be read as a story that somehow anticipated the Christ, and it had to be arranged to interlock with the New Testament.

In the process of making the Hebrew epic one's own, Christians rearranged the order in which the Hebrew scriptures occurred in the Jewish Bible. The Jewish order was, first the law (or Torah, the five books of Moses), then the prophets (including the "early prophets" from Joshua through the histories of Samuel and the Kings), and

finally the writings (including the Psalms, the so-called wisdom literature, Esther, and Daniel). Of great significance is that the postexilic
histories of Ezra-Nehemiah and the Chronicles were placed among
the writings at the very end of the collection. Thus the Jewish epic
ends with the edict of Cyrus about building a house for the Lord in
Jerusalem and the call to "all the (Lord's) people" to "go up." Christians reversed the order of the prophets and the writings in order to
end with Malachi. Eureka! One reads the Hebrew epic to the end,
reads about the messenger to come, turns the page, and hears the
voice of John (or Jesus) saying that Malachi's prophecy is coming to
pass. What a neat connection between the "Old Testament" and the
"New Testament."

In the arrangement of the writings in the New Testament, any of
the three synoptic gospels could have been placed first to gain this
same effect. But Luke and Matthew would have been the most likely
candidates for first position, because they were more compatible with
the church's instructions than Mark. Matthew's gospel was, in any
case, the preferred gospel for citations of the teachings of Jesus, and
Luke's gospel properly belonged closer to its sequel, the Acts of the
Apostles. (John's gospel did not fit well into the epic-apostolic logic of
the arrangement and so was placed last of the four, even though this
separated Luke's gospel from his Acts.) And so the story of Q's legacy
reaches beyond the appropriation of Q by Matthew to end with
Matthew's favored status as the first book in the New Testament. Q
had provided the very logic by which the Old and New Testaments
were linked together in the making of the Christian Bible.

What a legacy! And what a discovery! We are now ready to ask
about Q's chances for making a difference in the modern world.

The Consequences

Q's challenge strikes to the heart of the traditional understanding of Christian origins. Lying at the bedrock of the earliest traditions about Jesus and his first followers, Q documents a Jesus movement that was not Christian. The Jesus movement that produced Q cannot be shunted aside as a group of people who missed the dramatic events portrayed in the narrative gospels. They cannot be dismissed as those who mistook Jesus, failed to understand his message, or misunderstood their mission to found the church. The reason they cannot be dismissed is because they were there at the beginning. Q reveals what Jesus people thought about Jesus before there was a Christian congregation of the type reflected in the letters of Paul, and before the idea of a narrative gospel was even dared. When that thought did occur, it was Q that the authors of the narrative gospels used as a foundation upon which to build their own novel myths of origin.

Q is the best record we have for the first forty years of the Jesus movements. There are other snippets of early tradition about Jesus, but they all generally agree with the evidence from Q. As remembered by the Jesus people, Jesus was much more like a Cynic-teacher than either a Christ-savior or a messiah with a program for the reformation of second-temple Jewish society and religion. In addition to Q we have evidence for the early Jesus movements in the pre-Markan pronouncement stories, the pre-Markan miracle story sets, the Gospel of

Thomas, and the parables. All of these traditions about Jesus demonstrate a remarkable independence from the congregations of the Christ and provide evidence for a revised history of Christian beginnings that does not agree with the traditional Christian imagination based on the gospels.

As we have seen, the narrative gospels can be described both as a further development of the Jesus traditions and as a reserved acknowledgment and cautious appropriation of the Christ myth that first emerged in northern Syria and the Pauline churches. The underlying logic of the Christ myth was a martyrology. A martyrology was fastened on for reasons specific to the congregations of the Christ in which a most unlikely mix of Jesus people was in need of "justification," or rationalization by means of a myth of origin. How the Christ myth answered that problem has been discussed in chapter 11. Once it was in place for that purpose, the myth of the death and resurrection of Jesus as the Christ was then further embellished as a symbol of a personal transformation and spiritual presence. The genius of the narrative gospels was their appropriation of the martyrology of the Christ that did not require an acceptance of the cultic implications of the Christ myth.

In the light of Q, the congregations of the Christ now have to be explained as emerging from the Jesus movements. The direction of development cannot be the other way around. Q reveals a vigorous movement that was not generated by a belief in Jesus as the Christ whose death and resurrection dramatically changed the course of history. There is no indication that any of the Jesus movements were interested in salvation by personal, spiritual transformation on the model of the Christ event.

As for the narrative gospels, they were composed much later at crossroads in the history of the Jesus movements where various social and ideological issues of self-definition and external challenge influenced the way in which Jesus was reimagined. Despite their appropriation of the Christ martyrology to compose a passion narrative as the climax for their story of Jesus, the narrative gospels take their place in the rich history of mythmaking characteristic of the Jesus movements. Mythmaking was already far advanced in the Q tradition, as we have seen, and this had been achieved without any recourse to the Christ myth. The narrative gospels developed that tradition and continued the process of mythmaking along essentially the same lines. Jesus' importance for the Jesus traditions was that of a founder-teacher, not that of the Christ who died and was raised. The fantastic portrayal of Jesus in the narrative gospels was the result of a layered history of imaginative embellishments of a founder figure, not historical reminiscence, not a meditation on the way in which spiritual life was generated from a crucifixion.

Merely readjusting the conventional picture of Christian origins will not suffice to meet Q's challenge. Q's challenge is not a matter of shifting emphases within the Christian imagination as if, for instance, it would be better to think of Jesus as more of a teacher than a messiah. Q's challenge is absolute and critical. It drives a wedge between the story as told in the narrative gospels and the history they are thought to record. The narrative gospels can no longer be read as the records of historical events that generated Christianity. Q puts us in touch with the earlier history of the Jesus movements, and their recollections of Jesus are altogether different. The first followers of Jesus did not know about or imagine any of the dramatic events upon which the narrative gospels hinge. These include the baptism of Jesus; his conflict with the Jewish authorities and their plot to kill him; Jesus' instruction to the disciples; Jesus' transfiguration, march to Jerusalem, last supper, trial, and crucifixion as king of the Jews; and finally, his resurrection from the dead and the stories of an empty tomb. All of these events must and can be accounted for as mythmaking in the Jesus movements, with a little help from the martyrology of the Christ, in the period after the Roman-Jewish war.

Thus the story of Q demonstrates that the narrative gospels have no claim as historical accounts. The gospels are imaginative creations whose textual resources and social occasions can be identified. The reasons for their compositions can be explained. They are documents of intellectual labor normal for people in the process of experimental group formation. Q positions the gospels as period pieces from the later phases of the Jesus movements and thus challenges the traditional imagination of Christian origins as portrayed in the narrative gospels.

The question now is whether the discovery of Q has any chance of making a difference in the way in which Christianity and its gospel are viewed in modern times. The question is quite serious, because neither in the university, nor among knowledgeable people in our society, nor among the Christian churches have the results of biblical scholarship ever made much of a difference. One reason is that critical biblical scholarship is pursued as a classical discipline that generates its own discourse within a narrowly prescribed field of study. But the main reason is that, as we have seen, New Testament scholars have traditionally seen their role as contributing to a theological enterprise, a clarification of Christian origins that supports Christian belief. New Testament scholars still regularly refer to the first church in Jerusalem forming shortly after the resurrection of Jesus as the Christ. That is the reason why the discovery of Q's significance took so long to be realized and why the traditional view of Christian origins has prevailed even in scholarly circles. As a result, biblical scholarship has been read mainly by theologians and Christian ministers, not by scholars in the humanistic disciplines, and seldom with interest and understanding by the literate public. Nevertheless, the discovery of Q might be an exception to the rule. Q is hard evidence from the earliest period of Christian beginnings, a new text that has recently come to light, one that tells a different story. And Q can now be read by anyone interested in the question of Christian origins.

Historians of religion, dependent on the gospels and their scholarly interpreters, have always fumbled when trying to understand early Christianity. In comparison with other religions, early Christianity has indeed appeared to be exceptional, a novel persuasion based on a unique and incomparable set of events. So most historians of religion have treated it gingerly or turned instead to study later forms of Christian myth and ritual that bear more resemblance to other ancient and living religions. The discovery of Q makes it possible to have another look at Christian origins, recognize common human strategies in the construction of myths and rituals, and study the process by which an attractive alternative to traditional social identities produced a new religion based on a new social anthropology. We might even learn something about the conditions and processes by which new religions form, now that early Christianity can serve as another example of such a phenomenon. Historians of religion should be delighted with the discovery of Q.

The media may also be enlightened, in so far as the question of the historical Jesus occasionally surfaces for public discussion. The reason the Jesus question captures attention, of course, is because the figure of Jesus looms so large in American forms of Christianity. The Christians' Jesus is therefore the Jesus that is in everyone's mind, whether Christian by confession or not. Western culture has a long tradition of writers and artists who have found themselves interested in the figure of Jesus. Any contemporary artist, filmmaker, writer, essayist, or sociologist can count on everyone knowing the Jesus of the gospels and what he represents. Filmmakers, for instance, have retold the gospel story many times, playing on its fantastic features to create both sensational and sentimental portrayals. A measure of license is accorded the cinema and stage as these portrayals unfold. But scriptwriters can tweak Christian sensibility as well, and then the hue and cry revolves around the question of truth. The standard used for the true picture of Jesus is invariably the narrative gospels. How could it be otherwise, when that is the only history we have had in hand? The embarrassment for critics in such a situation is that the gospel portrait often appears as fantastic as any modern cinematic depiction.

A recent article on the Jesus of history by the editors of *Time* magazine can serve as an example of this problem. The occasion for the article was a public outcry in conservative Christian circles about the movie *The Last Temptation of Christ.* In response, the editors of *Time* produced an article on the various views of Jesus held by modern scholars in relation to other views projected throughout the history of Christianity. The startling aspect of the article was not that the editors brought to light a number of different images of the Christ, but that as critics they thought of them all as variations on a single theme. All of these views were assessed against the standard of the figure portrayed in the narrative gospels. Among the experts they consulted were historians, biblical scholars, theologians, and clergy. They handled them all on the common par of opinion. The editors of *Time* magazine simply could not tell the differences among a historian's judgment, a theologian's dogma, and a clergy's pronouncements. They thought the current scholarly portrayal of Jesus as a Cynic-like sage "odd." And so the editors offered their own conclusion, namely that Jesus must have been a "robust" reformer because that fit most easily with the gospel accounts.

Critics will now have to be more cautious. And they will have to be more knowledgeable about the question of the historical Jesus and early Christianity. The discovery of Q effectively challenges the privilege granted the narrative gospels as depictions of the historical Jesus. The difference between the narrative gospels and modern retellings of the story can no longer lie in the distinction between history and fiction. The narrative gospels are also products of mythic imagination. The difference lies in the status of the gospels as foundation stories for a religion in distinction from interpretations of that story in genres of a surrounding secular culture. So the modern critic who seeks to understand a public outcry over Jesus is now confronted not only with the question of modern myth and ancient history, but also with the more interesting question of the reasons why the gospels are so hard for moderns to recognize as myth. If the media want to do a responsible job when the question of Jesus surfaces as news, they will now have to do much more than getting a bit of history straight. The Jesus question is really about religion, culture, and contemporary social institutions. Critics will have to consider whether they are able and willing to engage in social and cultural critique.

For Christians the challenge is even more serious. That is because the gospels have functioned for the Christian imagination not only as a faithful account of Christian origins but as a mandala-like cluster of symbols for Christian meditation. This narrative collage has been the Christians' window that opens to the world of divine intention, the Christians' mirror used to reflect upon their patterns of Christian piety, and the lens through which Christians look upon the world. For each of these symbolic functions understanding the sense of the narrative is very important, namely that the depicted events happened in human history. The result has been the creation of a Christian mentality that finds meaning in only certain kinds of events. Events capable of Christian nuance are therefore given privilege as the Christian evaluates any period of social history. Q challenges the authority Christians assume when making judgments about their world.

Christians seldom assess their world by making a direct comparison with the gospel story. Instead, as with all cultures and their myths, coded formulations reduce the mythic mode to attitudes, gestures, and clichés for negotiating the everyday world. A partial list of adjectives that express Christian mentality can illustrate the point. Christians grant privilege to personal performances and events that are unique, dramatic, original, charismatic, miraculous, radical, transformational, and apocalyptic. All else is often considered banal by comparison. The daily round, repetitious labor, customary chitchat, negotiations, compromises, folk wisdom, and ordinary humor all fail to create sensations. What counts as significant are crises, break-throughs, victories, and transformations. With the gospels in place, one might note, the symbols for solving critical problems are a vicari-ous crucifixion at the beginning and an apocalyptic destruction at the end. Both coalesce in a meditation on destructive violence and cre-ative transformation. The Jesus of Q hardly stands a chance of being recognized within this symbolic world.

Myths, mentalities, and cultures go together. Myths are cele-brated publicly in story and song. Mentalities are nurtured just be-neath the surface of social conventions by means of unexpressed agreements. Myths, mentalities, and cultural agreements function at a level of acceptance that might be called sanctioned and therefore re-stricted from critical thought. Myths are difficult to criticize because mentalities turn them into truths held to be self-evident, and the analysis of such cultural assumptions is seldom heard as good news.

Christian myth and western culture go together. This is true whether we imagine a long, continuous history of Christian influence on western forms of art, literature, thought, and politics, or whether we imagine a series of missions to expand the borders of western Christian empires. For example, one might call to mind the spread of early Christianity, the crusades, the age of discovery, colonial expan-sion during the eighteenth and nineteenth centuries, and the envel-opment of the world in modern times by western armies, ideologies, and corporations. In every case, Christianity and empire have taken possession of the territory hand in hand. Christian missionaries have gone along to bless the conquests and spread the good news. Since we have never questioned where this sense of mission comes from, we have never been quite sure of the reasons for all of these expansions and who should get the credit for them, the kings and commanders, the spirit of western culture, or the church.

The Christian gospel and American culture also go together, ex-cept that, in this case, the pairing is harder for us to see. One reason it is harder to see is that Americans have frequently felt uncomfortable with the very notion of a culture. We prefer to think of ourselves as a democracy dedicated to the pursuit of individual freedoms, not a social system that governs on the basis of a set of shared values. Another reason for not wanting to recognize the Christian influence in American culture is that we are dedicated to the principle of the separation of church and state. We pride ourselves on being tolerant of all religious persuasions, with the result that religious persuasion is understood by us to be a matter of personal preference and opinion, not a factor that makes a difference in the way we negotiate our lives together. Religious persuasions are not to be subjected to embarrassing questions. They are never to be seen as the reason why people act the way they do, or as the basis for our society's values, motivations, and prejudices. A third reason for resisting the comparison of American culture with Christian mythology is that, if pressed to recognize a set of common values, we prefer to talk instead about the American dream. The American dream is an acceptable way to acknowledge our ideals of progress, privacy, free enterprise, and expansion. To acknowledge publicly that our dream may owe something to the legacy of western Christian culture is, on the other hand, taboo.

The exception to this general rule occurs, interestingly enough, when pressure on public policy and patriotism results in exaggerated expressions of those values for which our nation stands. We have a history of such platitudes: new world, new land, new people, righteous nation, manifest destiny, city set on a hill, liberty enlightening the world, a beacon for the homeless, one nation under God, moral majority, defenders of the free world, and new world order. These truisms signal a messianic mentality. When times are not perceived to be critical, it is easy to discount these expressions as the harmless formulations of a well-meaning people. Then we are willing to recognize the influence of Christian symbols on our self-understanding. But in periods of critical decision, when the rhetoric is used by our leaders in support of some national interest, few find it easy to blow the whistle and ask for debate on the reasonableness of attitudes rooted in religious convictions. Why? Is it because we do not dare, or because we do not know how to criticize our myths?

Christian mythology is not the only source of the distinctive set of attitudes that make up American culture. And yet, even though the Christian legacy of the western cultural and religious traditions has been greatly modified by the social histories we have experienced, Christian mentality in its secular dress is certainly one of the more important ingredients in the magical mix of American self-definition. Many scholars in the burgeoning field of American studies and many intellectuals currently engaged in American cultural critique have made this observation. The question is whether anything more can be said.

Social issues within the American context have raised questions about the many ways in which identities, loyalties, and motivations are generated in subcultural groups or classes. We know that there are many factors in human association, collective recognition, and social behavior. These include gender, ethnicity, social position, economic status, national loyalty, cultural tradition, religion, ideology, and lifestyle. What we do not know or talk about is the mythic equation, how these factors are rooted in mythologies, how myths surface to inform new patterns of motivation and association, how they impinge upon the creation of new mythologies, and how a mythology works in return to inform and support a particular social configuration. We do not know how to talk about the mentalities that underlie a culture's system of meanings, values, and attitudes. Some cultural critics are saying that it is time we set to work at cracking that equation.

I also think that the time is right. Americans have lost their sense of our nation's innocence, though the rhetoric of the righteous nation continues to be heard from our leaders. The recent history of what we have done with our technology and power throughout the world is troubling, as are the human cries for help from around a world grown small and yet too large to handle. The list of concerns has run off the page, and we seem to be overloaded with unsolvable problems and unanswerable questions about social and cultural conflict, ethnic strife, and ecological responsibility. For thoughtful people, the issues have to do with assessing the chances for constructing sane and safe societies in a multicultural world while understanding the conditions for predation and prejudice, power abuse, and violence. In either case, it is irresponsible not to engage in public discussion of our own system of cultural values.

Social historians, historians of religion, and cultural anthropologists have provided us with an immense accumulation of knowledge about the many skills humans have for constructing societies and developing richly nuanced cultures to inculcate rewarding patterns of behavior. This knowledge can be used as data as we engage in the analysis of our own culture and ask what makes our society pulse. But in order to get to the heart of the matter, we need to break the taboo against talking about our myths. Cultural critique without exposing the myths that support the truths held to be self-evident is merely interesting, not telling. Recognizing myths without being able to compare one with another might be titillating, but hardly worthwhile. In order to understand ourselves and register reasons for our social options, cultural analysis will have to include a comparative evaluation of mythologies. And that means having a close look at our own mythology.

Q should help with this analysis by breaking the taboo that now grants privilege to the Christian myth. That is because the story of Q gives us an account of Christian origins that is not dependent upon the narrative gospels. That is a great advantage. Christian mythology can now be placed among the many mythologies and ideologies of the religions and cultures of the world. The Christian myth can be studied as any other myth is studied. It can be evaluated for its proposal of ways to solve social problems, construct sane societies, and symbolize human values. The gospel can be discussed as an enculturating mythology, and the question of its influence in American culture can be pursued without the constant interruption of questions and claims about the historical truth of unique events.

Some may find such a conversation difficult, but others may well find it exhilarating to accept Q's challenge. Q enters the arena of public discourse at a time when all Christians are engaged in a turbulent quest to redefine commitments and rearrange traditional Christian values. Christians are actively engaged in sorting through the rich archives of myths, teachings, and attitudes that have defined their religion, trying to locate the symbols that may constructively address the problems of our time. The quest is turbulent because the world has come alive with problems for which traditional clichés no longer work.

Christians have been known for their global visions and their concern for other peoples. They have also been known for taking a critical stance, often called "prophetic," over against political and social systems seen as unjust and oppressive. Christians do this best while standing within some Christian community. But Christians enjoy this privilege because Christian communities do not have to produce a fully fledged working society. The church as a social institution has only to produce other Christians and inculcate Christian ideals. So Christians invariably end up living in two social worlds, the community of Christian values and the work-a-day world of the society in which they actually live.

In our time, Christians of all persuasions have been forced to think about the tensions created by this strange division of identities and loyalties. Reactions range from the political action committees of the moral majority and their attempt to make society conform to Christian standards, to retreat into therapeutic enclaves and/or the washing of one's hands characteristic of privatistic and apocalyptic views of personal salvation. Neither extreme commends itself to Christians caught in the middle who worry about the effective difference they had hoped Christianity might make in the world.

So the times are troubled for thinking Christians who wonder about the social and political consequences of Christian mythology in its secular dress. The effect of Christian mythology has not always been humanizing. *The Captain America Complex*, a book by Robert Jewett (1973), has traced our zealous nationalism to its biblical roots. Others have reflected deeply on the Christian persuasions that have undergirded colonial imperialism, the taking of the West, the Indian wars, and the slave trade. Still others have studied the relationship of the gospel story to the profile of the American hero, the American dream, and the destructive politics of righteousness wherever we have intervened in the affairs of peoples around the world. The conclusion seems to be that the Christian gospel, focusing as it does on crucifixion as the guarantee for apocalyptic salvation, has somehow given its blessing to patterns of personal and political behavior that often have had disastrous consequences.

Two major issues have surfaced for those concerned about the effective difference Christianity might make in a world where nations and cultures are struggling to find ways to work together. One is the long-standing practice of Christian mission with its implicit claim to know what is best for other people. This claim came about at a very early time in Christian history, when the ideal of an inclusive community, open to any and all people, turned into a mandate to convert the world exclusively to Christianity. Christians are now in the process of vociferous debate about the need to continue such a persuasion. It is certainly time to reconsider.

The other major issue for traditional Christian mentality has to do with problems concerning the use and abuse of power. Everyone knows that the exercise of power is part and parcel of the human enterprise. Critique is regularly leveled at those who have power by those who seek empowerment. But we have not been able to imagine a social system capable of adequate constraints on the abuse of power, much less a society in which the exercise of power is rewarded for its programs in support of human well-being. Unfortunately, the Christian gospel does not seem to help, generating as it has the messianic vision of a powerful superhero to right the world's wrongs. With such a hero in mind it is difficult to think clearly about issues of power and the need for constraints when the use of power gets out of hand. We are horrified, to be sure, by the many strong men who have slaughtered the innocents in our time. But as for an alternative, we still delight in the image of the Lone Ranger with his silver bullet. This thinly veiled Christ figure, who brings salvation from elsewhere to a society incapable of solving its own problems, is not a helpful image to have in mind when selecting our presidents, for analyzing social systems that empower some and victimize others, or for trying to think clearly about better ways to structure our societies.

Q should help, not in the sense of providing ready-made answers, or highlighting the essential teachings of Christianity, for this would overlook Q's challenge to the Christian penchant for locating authority in the words and deeds of an incomparable person at the beginning of Christian history. Instead, Q shows us that the notion of a pure origin is mythic and that the process of endowing Jesus with superlative wisdom and divinity was and is a mode of mythmaking. Q shifts the focus of conversation about Christian origins away from fascination with the many myths condensed in the New Testament and onto the people who produced them.

Q lets us catch sight of real people struggling with a social vision. They were sustained in their efforts to actualize their vision by a small selection of aphorisms, maxims, and images garnered from a profuse field of thought, lore, and mythology swirling around them in the many cultures of the time. At first that might seem strange to us, as if these people achieved so much when they had so little with which to work. And yet, on second thought, that is the way most people live, making sense of their lives by drawing upon a limited number of truths and symbols. A few proverbs, maxims, and memorable figures can offer guidance even in the midst of confusing times. The people of Q coined a few injunctions that still work as golden rules for many Christians: "Love your enemies" and "Turn the other cheek."

But the story of Q tells us more. It reminds us that golden rules are effective not because of some external authority, but by virtue of the agreements a community reaches in choosing to be guided by them. The agreements are reached in the process of living together and struggling with a social vision. The voice of authority from the distant past is a mythic mode of ratifying the agreements of a present community and its recent past in the hopes of inculcating a next generation in the society's image and ethos. The tenets that guide modern Christians, including the golden rules from Q, are selections made from rich reservoirs of Christian wisdom and the American cultural heritage. They are only facets cut on dense and convoluted symbols that have been turned many times, like objects in the hand, until a people catch a reflection of themselves that illuminates their situation. Q tells us that it has always been so.

Q's story shows us that it was no different for any of the other Jesus movements, Christ congregations, or Christian churches at the beginning of the Christian tradition. Each took what they had in hand and coined new myths for new circumstances in the interest of compelling social visions. The people of Q did it, the Pauline churches did it, Jewish Christians did it, and so did the bishops, the church councils, Augustine, the medieval churches, Aquinas and the reformers, as well as every generation since those times. In every case Christianity has been redefined by social forces and rethinking that changed the picture, not only of the Christ, but also of the church and its world. It has not been different for any other people.

Q's challenge to Christians is therefore an invitation to join the human race, to see ourselves with our myths on our hands and myth-making as our task. The question before us is what the Christian religion might have to offer as we rethink how to live in a multicultural world. Who knows? If Christians acknowledged their gospel as myth, others might find it possible to talk with us about it. And we Christians might even find it possible to make some contribution to the urgent task of cultural critique where it seems to matter most—understanding the social consequences of Christian mythology.

So goodbye Q. You might be taken up by many different hands. Do take care. You are no longer as strong and illustrious a text as once you were. Christians may think you embarrassing, and critics may find you trite. So much has changed since first you were read. But my, what a difference you could make if read anew and seriously questioned. Who knows? The story of things lost and found may never sound the same. Godspeed.

EARLY CHRISTIAN LITERATURE

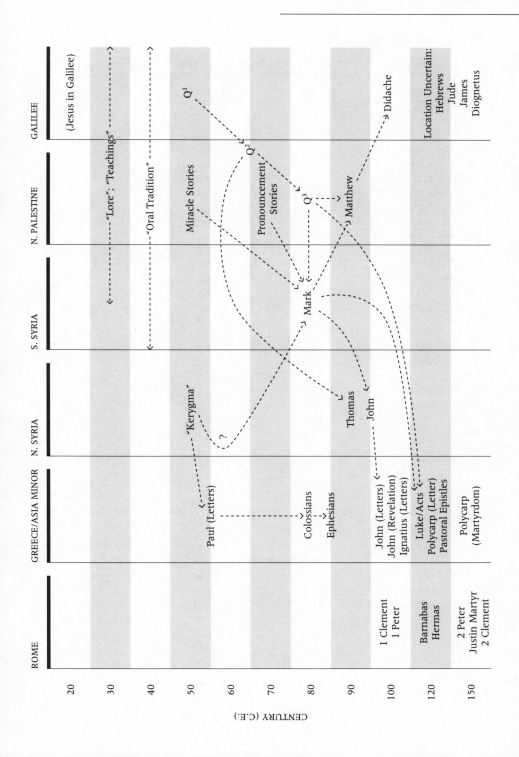

Q SEGMENTS

The Lukan Text and Parallels

Q	LUKE	GOSPEL OF THOMAS	Q PARALLELS (Kloppenborg)
QS 1	—		S 1
QS 2	—		—
QS 3	3:1-6		S 2
QS 4	3:7-9		S 3
QS 5	3:16-17		S 4
QS 6	4:1-13		S 6
QS 7	6:20		S 7
QS 8	6:20-23	54; 68; 69	S 8
QS 9	6:27-35	95; 6:2	S 9
QS 10	6:36-38		S 10
QS 11	6:39-40	34	S 11
QS 12	6:41-42	26	S 12
QS 13	6:43-45	45	S 13
QS 14	6:46-49		S 14
QS 15	7:1-10		S 15
QS 16	7:18-23		S 16
QS 17	7:24-28	78; 46	S 17
QS 18	7:31-35		S 20
QS 19	9:57-62	86	S 21
QS 20	10:1-11	73; 14:2	S 22
QS 21	10:12		—
QS 22	10:13-15		S 23
QS 23	10:16		S 24
QS 24	10:21-22	61?	S 25
QS 25	10:23-24		S 26
QS 26	11:1-4		S 27
QS 27	11:9-13	2; 92; 94	S 28
QS 28	11:14-23	35	S 29
QS 29	11:23		—
QS 30	11:24-26		S 30
QS 31	11:27-28		S 31
QS 32	11:16, 29-32		S 32
QS 33	11:33-35	33:2	S 33
QS 34	11:39-52	39:1; 89; 102	S 34
QS 35	12:2-3	5:2; 6:3; 33:1	S 35
QS 36	12:4-7		S 36
QS 37	12:8-12	44	S 37, 38, 39
QS 38	12:13-21		S 40
QS 39	12:22-31	36	S 41
QS 40	12:33-34	76:2	S 42
QS 41	12:39-40	21:3; 103	S 44

The Lukan Text and Parallels

Q	LUKE	GOSPEL OF THOMAS	Q PARALLELS (Kloppenborg)
QS 42	12:42-46		S 45
QS 43	12:49-53	16	S 46
QS 44	12:54-56	91	S 47
QS 45	12:57-59		S 48
QS 46	13:18-21	20, 96	S 49
QS 47	13:24-27		S 50
QS 48	13:28-30		S 51
QS 49	13:34-35		S 52
QS 50	14:11; 18:14		S 54
QS 51	14:16-24	64	S 55
QS 52	14:26-27;17:33	55; 101	S 56
QS 53	14:34-35		S 57
QS 54	15:4-10	107	S 58, 59
QS 55	16:13	47:2	S 60
QS 56	16:16-18		S 61
QS 57	17:1-2		S 62
QS 58	17:3-4		S 63
QS 59	17:6		S 64
QS 60	17:23-37	3; 51; 61; 113	S 66
QS 61	19:11-27	41	S 67
QS 62	22:28-30		S 68

SELECT BIBLIOGRAPHY

Boring, M. Eugene. *Sayings of the Risen Jesus: Christian Prophecy in the Synoptic Tradition*. Society for New Testament Studies Monograph Series 46. New York: Cambridge University Press, 1982.

Bultmann, Rudolf. *Die Geschichte der synoptischen Tradition* [*History of the Synoptic Tradition*]. Göttingen: Vandenhoeck & Ruprecht, 1921. English translation by John Marsh. Harper & Row, 1958, 1963.

———. *Jesus*. Berlin: Deutsche Bibliothek, 1926. English translation by Louise Pettibone Smith and Erminie Huntress Lantero. New York: Scribner's, 1934.

Cameron, Ron. "'What Have You Come Out to See?': Characterizations of John and Jesus in the Gospels." In R. Cameron (Ed.), *Semeia 49: The Apocryphal Jesus and Christian Origins*. Atlanta, GA: Scholars Press, 1990. Pp. 35–69.

Clement of Rome. "1 Clement," *The Apostolic Fathers*. Vol 1. English translation by Kirsopp Lake. The Loeb Classical Library. Cambridge, MA: Harvard University Press; London: William Heinemann, 1965.

Crossan, John Dominic. *Sayings Parallels: A Workbook for the Jesus Tradition*. Philadelphia: Fortress Press, 1986.

Dibelius, Martin. *Die Formgeschichte des Evangeliums* [*Form Criticism of the Gospel*]. Tübingen: J. C. B. Mohr, 1919. English translation by Bertram Lee Woolf. *From Tradition to Gospel*. New York: Scribner's, 1934.

Didache, or Teachings of the Twelve Apostles, *The Apostolic Fathers*. Vol. 1. English translation by Kirsopp Lake. The Loeb Classical Library. Cambridge, MA: Harvard University Press; London: William Heinemann, 1965.

Diogenes Laertius. *Lives of Eminent Philosophers*. 2 vols. English translation by R. D. Hicks. The Loeb Classical Library. Cambridge, MA: Harvard University Press; London: William Heinemann, 1931–38.

Dodd, C. H. *The Parables of the Kingdom*. Rev. ed. London: Nisbet, 1961 (Originally published 1935).

Edwards, Richard A. *A Theology of Q: Eschatology, Prophecy, and Wisdom*. Philadelphia: Fortress Press, 1976.

Epictetus. *The Discourses as Reported by Arrian*. 2 vols. English translation by W. A. Oldfather. The Loeb Classical Library. Cambridge, MA: Harvard University Press; London: William Heinemann, 1941.

Funk, Robert W., and Roy W. Hoover. *Five Gospels, One Jesus: What Did Jesus Really Say?* The Scholars Red Letter Edition. Sonoma, CA: Polebridge Press, 1992.

Griesbach, Johann J. *Synopsis Evangeliorum Matthaei, Marci et Lucae. Textum Graecum* [*A Synopsis of the Gospels of Matthew, Mark and Luke. In Greek*]. Halle: Curtius, 1774–76.

Harnack, Adolf. *The Sayings of Jesus: The Second Source of St. Matthew and St. Luke.* Translated by J. R. Wilkinson. London: Williams & Norgate; New York: Putnam's, 1908.

Havener, Ivan. *Q: The Sayings of Jesus.* With a Reconstruction of Q by Athanasius Polag. Wilmington, DE: Glazier, 1987.

Holtzmann, H. J. *Die synoptischen Evangelien: Ihr Ursprung und geschichticher Charakter* [*The Synoptic Gospels: Their Origin and Historical Character*]. Leipzig: Wilhelm Engelmann, 1863.

Infancy Gospel of Thomas. In *New Testament Apocrypha.* Vol. 1. Edited by Edgar Hennecke and Wilhelm Schneemelcher. Translated by R. McL. Wilson. Philadelphia: Westminster, 1963 (German original: Tübingen: Mohr, 1959). Pp. 388–400.

Jacobson, Arland D. *Wisdom Christology in Q.* Doctoral dissertation, Claremont Graduate School, Claremont, CA, 1978.

Jewett, Robert. *The Captain America Complex: The Dilemma of Zealous Nationalism.* Philadelphia: Westminster Press, 1973.

King, Karen. "Kingdom in the Gospel of Thomas." *Foundations and Facets Forum* 3/1 (1987): 48–97.

Kloppenborg, John. *The Formation of Q: Trajectories in Ancient Wisdom Collections.* Studies in Antiquity and Christianity. Philadelphia: Fortress Press, 1987.

———. *Q Parallels: Synopsis, Critical Notes, and Concordance.* Sonoma, CA: Polebridge Press, 1988.

———. "Redactional Strata and Social History in the Sayings Gospel Q." Paper presented to the Society of Biblical Literature Q Seminar, Chicago, November 1988.

———. "The Sayings Gospel Q: Translation and Notes." In John S. Kloppenborg, Marvin W. Meyer, Stephen J. Patterson, and Michael G. Steinhauser (Eds.), *Q Thomas Reader.* Sonoma, CA: Polebridge Press, 1990.

Lachmann, Karl. "De Ordine narrationum in evangeliis synopticis" ["Narrative Sequence in the Synoptic Gospels"]. *Theologische Studien und Kritiken* 8 (1835): 570–90.

Locke, John. *The Reasonableness of Christianity with a Discourse on Miracles and Part of a Third Letter Concerning Toleration.* Edited by I. T. Ramsey. Stanford, CA: Stanford University Press, 1958 (Originally published 1695).

Lührmann, Dieter. *Die Redaktion der Logienquelle* [*Editing the Sayings Source*]. WMANT 33. Neukirchen: Neukirchener Verlag, 1969.

Mack, Burton L. "The Kingdom Sayings in Mark." *Foundations and Facets Forum* 3/1 (1987): 3–47.

———. "The Kingdom That Didn't Come: A Social History of the Q Tradents." *SBL Seminar Papers* (1988): 608–35.

———. *A Myth of Innocence: Mark and Christian Origins.* Philadelphia: Fortress Press, 1988.

Meyer, Marvin. *The Gospel of Thomas.* San Francisco: Harper San Francisco, 1992.

Neusner, Jacob. *From Politics to Piety: The Emergence of Pharisaic Judaism.* Englewood Cliffs, NJ: Prentice-Hall, 1973.

Piper, Ronald A. *Wisdom in the Q Tradition: The Aphoristic Teaching of Jesus.* New York: Cambridge University Press, 1989.

Pistis Sophia. Text edited by Carl Schmidt. Translation and notes by Violet Macdermot. Nag Hammadi Studies. Vol. 9. Volume editor, R. McL. Wilson. Leiden: Brill, 1978.

Polag, Athanasius. *Fragmenta Q.* 2d ed. Neukirchen: Neukirchener Verlag, 1982.

Quintilian. *The Instituto Oratoria of Quintilian.* 4 vols. English translation by H. E. Butler. The Loeb Classical Library. Cambridge, MA: Harvard University Press; London: William Heinemann, 1920–1922.

Robinson, James M. " 'Logoi Sophon': On the Gattung of Q." In James M. Robinson and Helmut Koester (Eds.), *Trajectories through Early Christianity.* Philadelphia: Fortress Press, 1971. Pp. 71–113.

Sato, Migaku. *Q und Prophetie: Studien zur Gattungs und Traditionsgeschichte der Quelle Q* [*Q and Prophecy: Studies on the Genre and History of the Source Q*]. WUNT 2/29. Tübingen: J. C. B. Mohr, 1988.

Schenk, Wolfgang. *Synopse zur Redenquelle der Evangelien: Q—Synopse und Rekonstruktion in deutscher Übersetzung mit kurzen Erläuterungen* [*A Synopsis of* the Sayings Source of the Gospels: Q—A Synopsis and Reconstruction in German Translation with Brief Explanations]. Düsseldorf: Patmos Verlag, 1981.

Schmidt, Karl Ludwig. Der Rahmen der Geschichte Jesu. Literarkritische Untersuchungen zur ältesten Jesusüberlieferung [The Framework of the Jesus Story: Literary-Critical Investigations of the Oldest Jesus Traditions]. Berlin: Trowitzsch und Sohn, 1919.

Schulz, Siegfried. Q: Die Spruchquelle der Evangelisten [Q: The Sayings Source of the Gospels]. Zürich: Theologischer Verlag, 1972.

Schweitzer, Albert. Von Reimarus zu Wrede [From Reimarus to Wrede]. Tübingen: J. C. B. Mohr, 1906. English translation by W. Montgomery, The Quest for the Historical Jesus. London: A. & C. Black, 1910.

Sellew, Philip E. Early Collections of Jesus' Words: The Development of Dominical Discourses. Theological doctoral dissertation, Harvard Divinity School, Cambridge, MA.

Seneca. Letters. 3 vols. English translation by Richard M. Gummere. The Loeb Classical Library. Cambridge, MA: Harvard University Press; London: William Heinemann, 1925–43.

Strauss, David Friedrich. Das Leben Jesu, kritisch bearbeitet [The Life of Jesus Critically Examined]. 2 vols. Tübingen: C. F. Osiander, 1835–36. English translation of fourth edition (1840) by George Eliot, 3 vols. London: Chapman Brothers, 1846.

Streeter, Burnett Hillman. The Four Gospels: A Study of Origins. Rev. ed. London: Macmillan, 1930. (Originally published 1924)

Taylor, Vincent. The Formation of the Gospel Tradition. London: Macmillan, 1933.

Theissen, Gerd. Soziologie der Jesusbewegung: Ein Beitrag zur Entstehungsgeschichte des Urchristentums [A Sociology of the Jesus Movement: A Contribution to the Origins of Early Christianity]. München: Kaiser Verlag, 1977.

———. "Wanderrakikalismus: Literatursoziologische Aspekte der Überlieferung von Worten Jesu im Urchristentum" ["Itinerant Radicalism: Aspects of the Transmission of the Words of Jesus in Early Christianity in Light of the Sociology of Literature"]. Zeitschrift für Theologie und Kirche 70 (1973): 245–71.

Vaage, Leif. "The Kingdom of God in Q." Paper presented to the Jesus Seminar, Notre Dame, IN, 1987a.

———. Q: The Ethos and Ethic of an Itinerant Intelligence. Doctoral dissertation, Claremont Graduate School, Claremont, CA, 1987b.

Weiss, Bernard. *Die Quellen des Lukasevangeliums* [*The Sources of the Gospel of Luke*]. Stuttgart and Berlin: J. G. Cotta, 1907.

Weiss, Johannes. *Die Predigt Jesu vom Reiche Gottes* [*Jesus' Proclamation of the Kingdom of God*]. Göttingen: Vandenhoeck & Ruprecht, 1892. English translation by R. H. Hiers and D. L. Holland. Philadelphia: Fortress Press, 1971.

Weisse, Christian Hermann. *Die evangelische Geschichte kritisch und philosophisch bearbeitet* [*A Critical and Philosophical Study of the History of the Gospel*]. 2 vols. Leipzig: Breitkopf & Härtel, 1838.

"Who Was Jesus? The Debate Among Scholars Is as Heated as the One in Hollywood." *Time* (August 15, 1988): 37–42.

Wilke, Christian G., *Der Urevangelist oder exegetisch kritische Untersuchung über das Verwandtschaftsverhältniss der drei ersten Evangelien* [*The First Evangelist, or A Critical Exegetical Study on the Relationships Among the First Three Gospels*]. Dresden/Leipzig: Fleischer, 1838.

Zeller, Dieter. *Kommentar zur Logienquelle* [*A Commentary on the Sayings Source*]. Stuttgart: Katholisches Bibelwerk, 1984.

———. *Die weisheitlichen Mahnsprüche bei den Synoptikern* [*Admonitions in the Genre of Wisdom Contained in the Synoptic Gospels*]. Würzburg: Echter Verlag, 1977.